S/NVQ

vel 3

The teaching assistant's handbook

Secondary schools edition

Louise Burnham
Kate Carpenter

www.heinemann.co.uk
✓ Free online support
✓ Useful weblinks
✓ 24 hour online ordering

01865 888058

Heinemann

Inspiring generations

Heinemann Educational Publishers
Halley Court, Jordan Hill, Oxford OX2 8EJ
Part of Harcourt Education

Heinemann is the registered trademark of
Harcourt Education Limited

Text © Louise Burnham and Kate Carpenter, 2004

First published 2004

09 08 07 06 05
10 9 8 7 6 5 4 3 2

British Library Cataloguing in Publication Data is available from the
British Library on request.

10-digit ISBN 0 435463 71 3
13-digit ISBN 978 0 435463 71 7

Copyright notice

Websites
Please note that the examples of websites suggested in this book were
up to date at the time of writing. It is essential for tutors to preview
each site before using it to ensure that the URL is still accurate and the
content is appropriate. We suggest that tutors bookmark useful sites
and consider enabling students to access them through the school or
college intranet.

Typeset and illustrated by ⋆ Tek-Art, Croydon, Surrey
Printed in the UK by Bath Press Ltd
Cover photo: © OSF

Acknowledgements
Every effort has been made to contact copyright holders of material
reproduced in this book. Any omissions will be rectified in subsequent
printings if notice is given to the publishers.

Contents

Acknowledgements

We would like to thank all the students on the Lewisham College teaching assistants courses 2003 to 2004, in particular Christobel Volume, Jackie Braham, Nicholas Bent, Joanne Baker, Carol Wasilewski and Tracie Moran. Thanks to Melissa Lancashire and Jane Jordan at Larkmead school, Abingdon for an example of a medium term plan, and Nadeem Qureshi for information on secondary transfer.

Louise would like to thank Tom and Lucy for tea and sympathy during the writing of this book, especially as they have been in the middle of their GCSEs.

Kate would like to thank Simon, William and Eleanor for patience, forbearance, support and the odd idea.

Also thanks to Mary James, Julia Sandford and Humphrey Gudgeon for all their support.

Photo acknowledgements

Alamy page 147

Gareth Boden pages 184 and 273

Bubbles page 260

Corbis page 103

Peter Evans page 257

Getty Images page 123

Sally and Richard Greenhill pages 192 and 200

John Walmsley pages 79, 208, 219 and 232

Introduction

Welcome to this handbook for the National Vocational Qualification (NVQ) or Scottish Vocational Qualification (SVQ) for Teaching Assistants. If you are using this handbook, you will be setting out or have already begun to train for work as a Teaching Assistant. This handbook has been specifically written for assistants in secondary schools.

You may find yourself referred to under the general title of 'Teaching Assistant' within your school, although you may also be called a 'Classroom Assistant', 'School Assistant', 'Individual Support Assistant', 'Special Needs Assistant' or 'Learning Support Assistant'. These different titles have come about due to different types of work which assistants are required to do within the classroom. For the purpose of this book we will refer to all those who assist within the classroom as 'Teaching Assistants'.

As an assistant, you will be required to carry out many different jobs within the classroom. At the time of writing, assistants are being increasingly required to take on a more leading role alongside teachers and are being given more responsibilities. These have moved away from the traditional role of the teaching assistant to a more specialist role and may include working alongside pupils who speak English as an additional language and supporting literacy and numeracy intervention programmes.

Some background information about the NVQ

The structure of the NVQ requires you to achieve **ten** units of competence from the national occupational standards. You will need to complete each of the four **mandatory units** and six of the **optional units**. The mandatory units are longer than the optional units as they contain more information. The optional units are divided into sets A, B, C and D, and you must choose one from each section plus any two others. This book will provide you with the knowledge you need for each unit of the award.

Each unit within this book is given a separate chapter, apart from Units 3–13 to 3–16 which have been written as one chapter. For each unit, we have identified what you will need to know and understand, and then given information and activities related to these items of learning. At the end of each unit, there is a unit test which you can use to check through your understanding. As each unit stands alone, this will also mean that you will be able to use them in any order. There are places in which information overlaps, and you will find cross-references within the book for these. Throughout each chapter, there are a number of features to help you with your studies:

Knowledge into action

These are activities which ask you to check or try out ideas within your own workplace. They will help you to link your ideas with what happens in practice.

Find out about...

These activities help you to think more deeply about key issues and encourage you to carry out your own research.

Keys to good practice

These are checklists of the most important aspects of what you have just learned.

Think about it

These activities encourage you to apply theory in a practical way.

Case studies

These are examples within real settings where you can apply what you have learned to particular situations.

Evidence collection

These activities are to help you to collect evidence for each unit. They may be particularly helpful for those units in which you may need to use simulation.

Throughout the book, you will need to think about how the theory fits in with your experiences in the classroom. As you gain experience and expertise in your work with pupils, you may also find it a useful reference, particularly when thinking about specific issues such as supporting pupils who speak a second language, or working in different subject areas.

Values and principles underpinning the National Occupational Standards for teaching assistants

The National Occupational Standards for teaching assistants are built upon the following set of agreed values and principles of good practice:

▷ Working in partnership with the teacher
▷ Working within statutory and organisational frameworks
▷ Supporting inclusion
▷ Equality of opportunity
▷ Anti-discrimination
▷ Celebrating diversity
▷ Promoting independence
▷ Confidentiality
▷ Continuing professional development.

You will need to consider these in relation to all the work you undertake within a school. For a fuller description of each of these, see the National Occupational Standards for teaching assistants, produced by the Local Government National Training Organisation (LGNTO). You can find these on the LGNTO website: **www.lg-employers.gov.uk**. Under the A-Z listings, you will find a section called 'teaching and classroom assistants' standards'.

Mandatory units

Unit 3-1 Contribute to the management of pupil behaviour

There are two elements to this unit. These are:

3-1.1 Promote school policies with regard to pupil behaviour
3-1.2 Support the implementation of strategies to manage pupil behaviour.

As a teaching assistant, you will be working alongside the class or subject teacher, supporting them with the introduction of new activities and helping pupils, either individually or in groups, to work happily and productively. Your role is very important. Groups of young people can quickly and easily become distracted and start to become lively and noisy. By helping to manage pupils' behaviour, through understanding their needs, anticipating any problems and smoothing them over, you will play a significant part in creating a peaceful and productive learning environment in which they can really progress.

This unit outlines your role when dealing with pupil behaviour. It will show how you need to work alongside the teacher to support pupils and give you strategies for managing behaviour, through support which is available in school and also through other agencies. You will need to have an understanding of the behaviour which is expected of different ages and be able to recognise those pupils whose behaviour is more challenging. As an assistant, you should also be aware of how to promote good behaviour in schools and the ways in which you can do this.

Element 3-1.1 Promote school policies with regard to pupil behaviour

For this element you will need to know and understand the following:

▶ the stages of social, emotional and physical development of the pupils you work with

▶ factors which may affect pupils' behaviour

▶ how to identify behaviour patterns which may indicate problems

▶ school policies for rewarding positive behaviour and managing unwanted behaviour

▶ how to work in line with local and national guidelines and policies.

Stages of social, emotional and physical development

It is important for all staff who have contact with pupils in secondary school settings to be aware of the different stages of pupils' development. Assistants will need to understand the way in which pupils learn and develop socially, emotionally and physically. In this way they will be able to support and enhance the learning process through a wider understanding of pupils' needs. It is also important to recognise how the behaviour of those pupils who are not developing in these areas at the same rate as their peers may be affected.

Physical development

As an assistant, you will be working with pupils who are developing and refining skills through a wide range of physical activities. These may be gross motor skills such as running or other athletic activities, or fine motor skills such as handwriting or sewing. You will need to know the order in which pupils develop these skills, although the age at which they achieve them may differ from one pupil to another.

Pupils will undergo health checks at some of these stages to check that they are developing normally and to draw attention to any potential problems. If a pupil is not reaching the milestones which are expected, these can then be investigated straight away and any action taken.

▷ **Gross motor skills** – these are skills which involve large movements through the use of arms and legs and may include running, hopping and skipping, and using large apparatus such as athletic or gymnastic equipment.

▷ **Fine motor skills** – these are manipulative skills which involve finer hand control. They are vital for activities such as writing or mouse control, and for creative activities such as art and DT.

Basic stages of physical development

Age	Stage of development
0–3 months	Infant will start to have control of head.
3–6 months	Babies will start to roll from side to side and push themselves up with their arms when on their front.
6–9 months	Babies start to grasp objects and sit unsupported. They may start to move by trying to crawl or shuffle.
9–12 months	Babies will have started to crawl or even walk. Starting to reach for objects.
1–2 years	Starting to build using blocks, make marks with a crayon, turn pages in picture books. Gaining confidence. Enjoying repetitive play and games and songs with a known outcome, for example 'Pat-a-cake', or 'Round and round the garden'.
2–3 years	Uses a spoon, puts on shoes, begins to use a preferred hand. Walks up and down stairs with confidence.
3–4 years	Turns pages in a book, puts on coat and shoes, throws and kicks a ball, washes and dries hands with help.

Age	Stage of development
4–5 years	Draws a person, cuts out simple shapes, completes simple puzzles, starting to hop.
5–6 years	Forms letters, writes name, dresses and undresses, runs quickly, uses large apparatus.
6–7 years	Handwriting evenly spaced, ties laces, can complete more complex puzzles, chases and plays with others.
7–11 years	Refining physical skills such as running, jumping and skipping.
12–14 years	Early adolescence; rapid physical change although great developmental variety among peers. Some children will have reached puberty before starting secondary school. Others will not reach puberty until 14 years old. As a result there may be great variance in height and other aspects of development.
15-18 years	Physical changes slower and accepted although boys will still be growing at a fast pace. Good time to perfect skills and talents, competition or performances.

Physical needs of pupils

When pupils arrive in secondary school, the majority will already have developed a large number of physical skills. These will have been developed through practising and refining different physical activities, which they will have experienced from an early age. Pupils may also start to learn a new range of skills at secondary school through increased opportunities and a larger variety of tools, apparatus and equipment, for example using tools in DT. As they develop and change physically, they need to be able to gain greater control of these two types of movements. They will need to have opportunities to develop these skills within the learning environment, through a variety of indoor and outdoor activities.

The kinds of activities which may be used in secondary schools to promote physical development
Gross motor skills: running, jumping, games (tennis, football, rugby, volleyball etc.), athletics and track events, swimming, gymnastics.
Fine motor skills: writing, painting, drawing and other forms of artwork, sewing, design technology activities, playing musical instruments, keyboard and mouse activities.

Social and emotional development

The social and emotional development of pupils is directly linked to the way in which they relate to others. Pupils need to interact with others so that they have opportunities to gain confidence. This confidence will in turn influence their self-esteem or how they feel about themselves.

If there are physical difficulties, for example a hearing problem, these may affect the way in which pupils relate to others and cause a delay in their overall development. For example, they may withdraw socially, find communicating difficult or suffer a language delay. All of these could have a negative effect on their developing self-esteem.

Stages of social and emotional development

Age	Stage of development
0–12 months	Babies start to communicate through smiling and making eye contact with their families. They will enjoy being cuddled and played with.
1–2 years	Children start to gain a sense of their own identities. They will respond to their own names and start to explore independently. They will start to show anger if their needs are not met and they do not yet recognise the needs of others. Children start to play with others.
2–3 years	Children will start to show concern for others but will still have strong feelings about their own needs being met. They will be starting to come to terms with their own independence.
3–4 years	This is a more settled year and children will be growing in confidence and social skills. They may still have tantrums as they will still feel strong emotions, but will be starting to play independently for longer periods.
4–6 years	Children will generally feel much more confident in themselves and start to be proud of their own achievements. Close friendships are increasingly more important to them.
6–8 years	Children start to develop a sense of fairness and are more able to share items and equipment. They have a greater self-awareness and can be critical of themselves. They may start to compare themselves to their peers. Friendship groups can start to be problematic if children fall out with one another. Children will also make some gender friendships in this age group.
8–11 years	Children will be settled in their friendships and may form more stable 'groups'. They will continue to compare themselves with others and will need to 'belong'.
12–14 years	Seek peer recognition, uncomfortable but interested in the opposite sex. There may be periods of emotional swings, and a tendency to be self-conscious.
15–18 years	Capable of understanding others' feelings. Acceptance by opposite sex is now of high importance. Learning to co-operate with others on an adult level.

Pupils who are entering secondary school will be at an age where they are beginning to become more independent. Staff need to give them as many opportunities as possible to allow them to feel independent and to praise them as much as they can for good behaviour. In this way, pupils will continue to develop a positive self-esteem. The development of self-esteem may be high or low, positive or negative. Self-esteem is how we feel about ourselves and leads to our self-image, that is how we think about or perceive ourselves. Young people develop a positive self-esteem when they feel good about themselves and when they feel valued. Adolescence can be a particularly difficult stage for them and they may pass through phases of quite low self-esteem and have a strong need to feel accepted and worthwhile. The way in which we treat pupils has a direct effect on this so it is important that we encourage and praise them, value each one as an individual, and celebrate differences and similarities.

Knowledge into action

Identify two different pupils in your class. How does each of them behave? Is this 'normal' for their age and stage of development?

Case study

Pierce is a Year 7 pupil who is very quiet and easily upset. He seems very disorganised with his belongings and is often late to classes. He has one or two close friends and seems to rely on them for help in lessons.

Vijay is settled into Year 7 and does not have any difficulties with organisation and behaviour. He has several friends and is able to settle to tasks quickly.

1 Compare the two case studies above. How does the behaviour of these two children fit in with their age and stage of social and emotional development?

2 Are either, or both, 'normal'?

How might physical, social and emotional needs of pupils impact on their behaviour?

Pupils of secondary age will be going through a great deal of physical changes. This not only relates to their rapid growth but also to the onset of puberty and hormonal changes. When working with pupils of this age, assistants should remember that they may be particularly sensitive to any signs of rejection. They may feel uncomfortable about themselves and unclear about how they fit in. You may need to help and encourage them through taking time to talk to them about any issues which concern them.

✔ Keys to good practice
Working with adolescents

✔ Set them up in situations that require responsibility.

✔ Give them situations in which the leader provides reassurance and support rather than dictating directions.

✔ Allow them to develop independent and decision-making skills.

✔ Remember to treat each pupil as an individual.

✔ Compare present and past performances rather than one child against another.

Other factors which may affect children's behaviour

Background

Pupils will enter secondary schools with a variety of backgrounds and experiences, all of which will have affected the way in which their individual personalities react to others. Some pupils may come from a secure and loving family background while others may have had very unsettled experiences or a series of different homes and

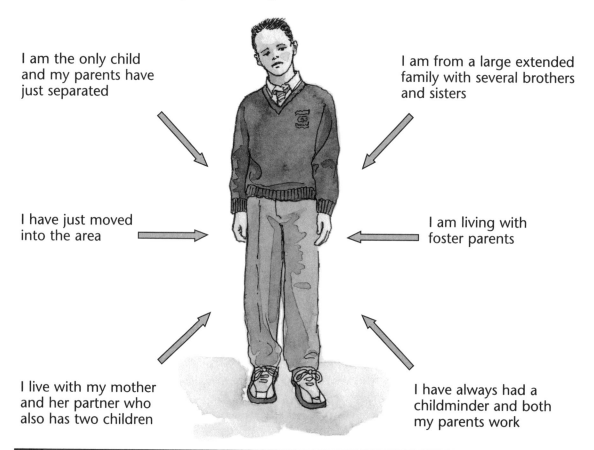

I am the only child and my parents have just separated

I am from a large extended family with several brothers and sisters

I have just moved into the area

I am living with foster parents

I live with my mother and her partner who also has two children

I have always had a childminder and both my parents work

carers. Some may have experienced many social situations while others' experience may be limited to family members or friends. These experiences will affect the pupil's ability and confidence when socialising with others.

There are also other factors which will have an effect on the way in which pupils behave.

Gender

It may be that a pupil enters secondary school with limited experiences due to gender, for example parents who only encourage 'male' or 'female' roles. As a result of this, the pupil may be reluctant to participate in some tasks.

Medical

Some pupils who have medical intervention for specific problems such as poor hearing may be less confident about becoming involved with tasks within the classroom. They may need encouragement and support to do this and you may need to seek advice from your school's SENCo.

Disability

It is now a statutory requirement to encourage the inclusion of pupils with disabilities into mainstream schools. According to the Disability Discrimination Act (1995), a person has a disability if 'he or she has a physical or mental impairment that has a substantial and long-term adverse effect on his or her ability to carry out normal day to day activities'. The inclusion of disabled pupils is to encourage more positive integration of disabled people into society, and to give all pupils a greater understanding of the needs of others. The impact of inclusion will mean that there are more pupils in mainstream schools who may have disabilities.

Culture

Pupils will enter schools from a variety of cultures. Some of these may encourage particular behaviours from men and women which differ from those in school. For example, some cultures may not encourage women to go out to work.

Case study

Richard has been in secondary school for a year. He is very able orally but has trouble with recording his ideas, as his written work is not of the same level as that of his peers. He often starts writing things down and quickly becomes frustrated, saying that his work is no good and wanting to tear it up and start again.

1 Why might Richard say that his work is no good?

2 Can you think of a way of helping Richard?

Stereotyping

Staff need to be aware of their own assumptions and opinions about pupils' behaviour, for example stereotyping pupils when giving them tasks within the school. 'I need some sensible girls to take this message for me' may sound to the boys that only girls can be sensible. Care should also be taken in other situations: it should not be assumed that a pupil with a disability should necessarily be excluded from activities, he or she should be included wherever possible.

Learning difficulties or inappropriate task given

If a pupil feels unable to complete a task, poor behaviour may result as the pupil will not be able to focus attention on the activity. This may be due to the teacher giving the pupil an inappropriate task for his or her ability, but could also be due to an undiagnosed learning difficulty.

How to identify behaviour patterns which may indicate problems

Learning how to behave is an important part of a pupil's development. This is because it is a learned skill which affects the way in which pupils will interact with others. Pupils must learn to be able to listen to others, take turns, share and show good manners. Some pupils may enter schools with less experience than others and need to have more guidance from staff.

Pupils may start to show signs of behaviour which are significantly different from those of other pupils immediately, or it may not be apparent until later.

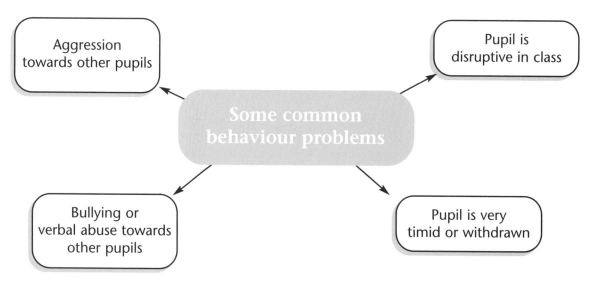

Aggression towards other pupils

Pupil is disruptive in class

Some common behaviour problems

Bullying or verbal abuse towards other pupils

Pupil is very timid or withdrawn

▲ Behaviour problems can take different forms

▷ **Pupil is timid or withdrawn** – this kind of behaviour may be due to shyness, and some pupils may take some time to settle into new surroundings, especially if they have had an unsettled home life. However, pupils will usually start to make friends and join in with activities fairly quickly, even if they remain shy with members of staff. If a pupil is very timid with parents but not within the setting, staff should be aware that this could be an indication of problems at home or even of child abuse.

▷ **Pupil is very disruptive in the class** – this could take the form of calling out or disturbing others. It can be caused by the pupil seeking attention from staff within the setting. This may be because the pupil receives a lot of attention at home and has become used to it. Pupils who do not receive much attention from adults at home may also resort to being disruptive, even though the attention they will receive is negative.

▷ **Pupil bullies or is aggressive towards other pupils** – this may be another attention-seeking device and may be caused by a number of factors. The bully or aggressor may feel a need to have control over others, perhaps because of their own insecurities. The pupil may physically or verbally abuse others, including racist, sexist, religious comments, personal abuse or bad language. Some pupils may have heard or seen abuse at home or on television and use it on others, copying poor role models. It is important that such behaviour is challenged and that positive role modelling occurs within schools.

Pupils who have been abused

Pupils may display behaviour to indicate that they have been abused in some way. Abuse can be physical, emotional, sexual or caused by neglect. A pupil could also be the victim of more than one of these.

Examples of behaviour which may give cause for concern including the following:

▷ Pupil is reluctant to change for PE or remove clothing. While this is perfectly normal for some pupils it may also be a sign that the pupil has been the victim of physical abuse and is aware that the abuse will be visible. Look for marks, bruises or burns which may not be caused by accident.

▷ Pupil displays uncharacteristic behaviour patterns from those normally shown. If a pupil suddenly starts to behave very differently and is particularly 'clingy' with adults or is reluctant to go home, this should be reported to the adult in charge of the class. This may indicate physical, emotional or sexual abuse.

▷ Pupil is unusually tearful or attention seeking. Where parents or carers emotionally abuse a child, the child may become insecure and need more attention.

You may also find yourself in the position of suspecting that a pupil has been subjected or exposed to some form of substance abuse. This could be through parents or older brothers and sisters. The main indicators would be health and emotional problems, or the pupil may not relate to others, either pupils or staff, as before.

Where staff have any suspicion of child abuse or neglect, they should immediately inform the teacher or supervisor with whom they are working. In this way steps can be taken to monitor the pupil and keep a record of any signs of abuse. When recording incidents, note should be taken of the pupil's name, any other pupil involved, the date and the exact behaviour shown. It is also important to reassure and listen to pupils if they are able to talk about what has happened to them, while taking care not to make promises to not tell anyone else or keep secrets. (There is more on this in Unit 9 on page 155.)

Case study

Melissa has always behaved well at school, although she is extremely quiet and is not naturally outgoing. She has recently started to become more interested in the group and mix more freely with the others, although she is still reluctant to talk to members of staff. When it is time to leave school one day, she says that she does not want to go home.

1 Why might Melissa have initially been so shy to join the class?

2 What would you do if this happened in your school?

3 What might be the problem in Melissa's case?

School policies for rewarding positive behaviour and managing unwanted behaviour

Theories about behaviour

There are three main theories about behaviour and how pupils learn.

▷ **Social learning theory**, developed by Albert Bandura in the 1960s, suggests that pupils will learn by copying the behaviour of those around them. They will tend to copy adults, and later their peers. This means that it is important that pupils have good role models for behaviour so that they learn appropriate behaviour themselves.

What this means for members of staff: staff should remember that they will be teaching pupils not only by what they say, but also by what they do. Where pupils see a member of staff being courteous and kind to others, it will encourage them to behave in the same way. Similarly, if pupils usually witness loud or aggressive behaviour, they will learn that this is the way to behave. Staff should therefore remember that they need to be good *role models* for pupils.

▷ **Behaviourist theory**, developed by B.F. Skinner in the 1940s, suggests that children will respond to praise and so will repeat behaviour which gives them recognition or praise for what they do. This kind of praise may take the form of rewards such as house points, charts, or staff attention. Pupils who receive praise or attention for positive behaviour, such as kindness towards others, are more likely to repeat this behaviour.

What this means for members of staff: staff need to remember to praise positive behaviour wherever possible, as pupils will also try to get their attention through undesirable behaviour. Where we can, we should ignore this kind of behaviour and instead give attention to those pupils who are behaving well.

▷ Another view widely held in psychology is the **self-fulfilling prophecy theory** – which states that children will be influenced by the way in which adults think about them. Children want to be noticed by adults and approved of. In this way, when adults believe a child is 'good', their opinion will encourage and influence the behaviour of that child. If adults think that a child is 'naughty', the child will live up to this expectation.

What this means for members of staff: when speaking to pupils about their behaviour, we should always label the behaviour rather than the individual: for example, 'That was a silly thing to do,' rather than 'What a silly girl you are'.

? *Think about it*

On the first day of term, you are helping the new pupils into a Year 7 class. One of the mothers says to you, in front of her child, 'This is Natalie – you will need to keep an eye on her!'
How do you think this will make Natalie feel?
What sort of behaviour might Natalie display?

Using strategies to manage behaviour

In any school, staff will need a series of agreed strategies to use both for managing unwanted behaviour and rewarding positive behaviour. They may even have their own classroom rules for behaviour, which the pupils can devise themselves with a little help. In this way, pupils will be able to take responsibility for their own behaviour and understand the results of their actions. Where pupils are showing unwanted behaviour, it is important for staff to know when to intervene, especially where children are a danger to themselves or others.

Strategies for promoting positive behaviour

In order that learning can take place in an effective environment, it is important to manage pupils' behaviour well. All members of staff within the setting should have high expectations so that a pattern of positive behaviour is established. Pupils need to be aware of what these expectations are, and there should be a behaviour management policy in the school with consistent staff expectations.

It is imperative in any school environment for pupils to be aware of a set of rules or guidelines so that they have a clear understanding of how to behave. Pupils need to be aware of the boundaries within which to behave so that they understand what is expected of them.

At secondary school it is likely that pupils will have guidelines to follow in different areas, such as behaviour, dress code, lateness and attendance, mobile phones and so on. They should be aware of the behaviour policy and the rewards and sanctions which the school has in place.

The school's expectations should be discussed frequently with the pupils, both in class and during assembly times, so that they understand and remember them. They should also be displayed around the school. Pupils should also be encouraged to behave in a positive way through watching the behaviour of staff. Pupils will soon notice if a member of staff is not acting in a way that they would expect, or there are not consistent expectations between members of staff. When a pupil is behaving particularly well, staff should remember to praise this behaviour so that it is recognised.

Case study

You are working with a large group of pupils on a history activity when you notice that some of them are not listening and are talking amongst themselves. How could you show the rest of the group that you are valuing their good behaviour while preventing the pupils who are talking from continuing?

Staff must remember that all pupils need to be praised for work and behaviour genuinely and frequently for effort and achievement. This will reinforce good behaviour and build self-esteem.

Where there are cases of unwanted behaviour, staff will need to be familiar with the school's behaviour policy so that their responses and strategies tie in with whole school policy.

Opposite is the first page of a school's behaviour policy.

Mountfield Secondary School
Behaviour Management Policy

At Mountfield School we believe that all pupils should be guided by a positive and professional approach to behaviour. This should be fairly and consistently applied by all members of staff (teachers, assistants, students, midday supervisors) who may have cause to discipline a pupil. It should establish the hierarchy for dealing with problems within school.

To work well, this policy must have the support of all members of the community, including the pupils, and should therefore be developed by them as a whole and be based on professional agreement. We have endeavoured to do this. This document therefore needs to be read and understood by all governors, teaching and support staff and midday supervisors.

Aims
The main aim of this policy is to help us to create an environment in which effective learning takes place. It should make us aware of the part our responses play in establishing a pattern of positive behaviour based on high expectations and mutual respect.

It aims to inform pupils, parents, governors and all teaching and support staff of our high standards and expresses our shared understanding of how we expect pupils to behave. It aims to inform all concerned of effective strategies that can be used to encourage positive behaviour and advise as to the consequences of misbehaviour. We will expect all pupils to know, understand and adhere to our school rules.

Objectives
The staff at our school will be encouraged to:
- ▶ Have a professional approach at all times
- ▶ Provide well structured environments to avoid disputes
- ▶ Create a working environment where pupils are able to achieve and where their work is seen to be valued
- ▶ Have high but realistic expectations of work and behaviour
- ▶ Praise work and behaviour frequently to reinforce good behaviour
- ▶ Be polite at all times to pupils and other adults to increase mutual respect and trust
- ▶ See parents as active partners and build positive relationships
- ▶ Make our expectations of work clear and consistent, ensuring our instructions are understood
- ▶ Intervene early so that misbehaviour does not escalate
- ▶ Be seen to be fair – try to establish all the facts

Your school's behaviour policy.

▶ What are the school's strategies for managing unwanted behaviour?

▶ How does the school ensure that all staff are aware of these strategies?

Where behaviour is undesirable despite modelling and encouraging good behaviour, you will need to have a scale of sanctions.

Keys to good practice
Managing unwanted behaviour

✔ Intervene early so that the problem does not escalate. If a situation arises where an assistant is the first to be aware of unacceptable behaviour, such as pupils misbehaving in the playground, it would be appropriate to draw the teacher's attention to it, or if this is not possible, to intervene.

✔ Give eye contact to the pupil who is misbehaving. Sometimes all that is needed is a stern look at a pupil so that they see a member of staff is aware of what they are doing.

✔ Make sure you have read the school or borough guidelines on the use of physical restraint.

✔ Proximity – move closer to a pupil who is misbehaving so that they are aware of your presence. This will usually prevent the behaviour from continuing.

✔ Time out – this is sometimes used when older pupils are consistently misbehaving and need to be given some time to calm down before returning to a situation. It can be applied within the classroom or on the playground.

✔ Use a scale of sanctions which the pupils are aware of, for example:

   a time out

   b miss one minute or longer of break

   c send to deputy head

   d send to headteacher/speak to parents.

Your role and responsibilities and those of others when managing behaviour in school

As a teaching assistant, you will need to be aware of your role within the school for managing pupils' behaviour. If you have any worries or concerns about how to deal with pupils' behaviour you must always refer to the class teacher or supervisor.

Teachers have the ultimate responsibility for managing behaviour of pupils within the class, and the headteacher has responsibility for all the pupils within the school. The school's behaviour policy will offer guidelines and school strategies for dealing with behaviour. (See also Unit 3-9, 'School policies and practices for pupils with emotional and behavioural needs', page 153.)

Some of the responsibilities of staff should include the following:

▷ Having high but realistic expectations of work and behaviour. Pupils will be aware of how they should behave and praised when they do. Staff need to give praise such as 'I know how sensibly you can sit' rather than, 'This class never sits quietly'.

▷ Creating a working environment where pupils can achieve and where their work and efforts are seen to be valued, thus developing their self-esteem.
This can be done not only verbally but through displays of pupils' work and sharing with other pupils and staff in the school.

▷ Making expectations of behaviour and work clear and consistent, ensuring instructions have been understood. If pupils are unsure of what they need to do, it is very difficult for them to automatically behave in a way which staff expect.

▷ Working consistently as a staff so that the same expectations apply throughout the school. This is vital so that the pupils understand that all staff are working together throughout the school.

▷ Being aware of your own values and opinions. You should ensure that you do not make assumptions about people on the grounds of gender, race or disability.

Working in line with local and national guidelines and policies

It will be useful to be aware of how your school's policies fit in with local guidelines and policies. You may need to ask other members of staff when the behaviour policy was devised and whether they used a borough model or local guidelines.

On a national level, the DFES training for behaviour management outlines some core principles to help those who are working with young people. Some of these are to:

▷ plan for good behaviour
▷ work within the 4 R's (Rules, Routines, Responsibilites and Rights) framework
▷ separate the (inappropriate) behaviour from the pupil
▷ use the language of choice
▷ actively build trust and rapport
▷ model the behaviour that you want to see.

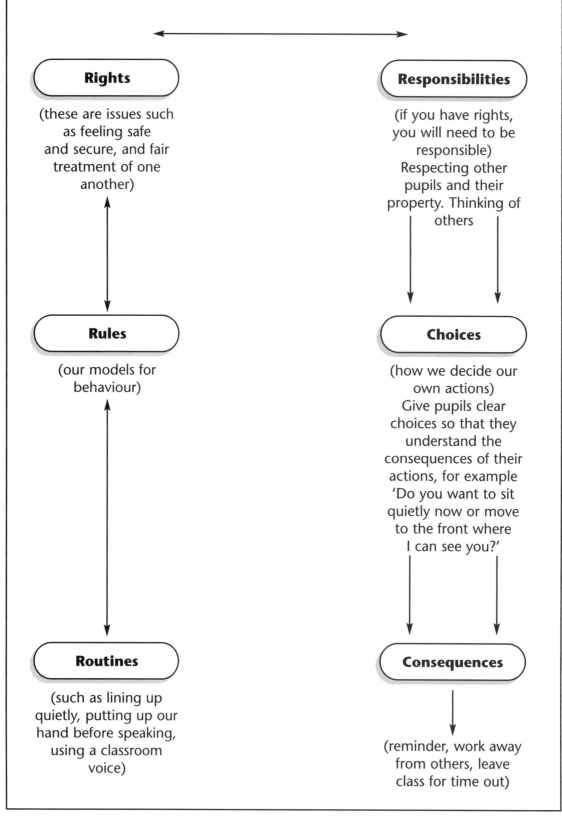

Rights

(these are issues such as feeling safe and secure, and fair treatment of one another)

Responsibilities

(if you have rights, you will need to be responsible) Respecting other pupils and their property. Thinking of others

Rules

(our models for behaviour)

Choices

(how we decide our own actions) Give pupils clear choices so that they understand the consequences of their actions, for example 'Do you want to sit quietly now or move to the front where I can see you?'

Routines

(such as lining up quietly, putting up our hand before speaking, using a classroom voice)

Consequences

(reminder, work away from others, leave class for time out)

▲ The 4 R's framework

As can be seen, these fit in with the types of ground rules which are expected of pupils in most schools. Pupils will need to be aware of others' expectations of them and how they fit into the school as a whole. These guidelines give the choice to the individual as well as an awareness of the consequences of their actions.

Evidence collection

Do you think that your school's behaviour policy draws on any of these principles? Make a list of phrases you could use to define behaviour using words from this model.

Element 3-1.2 Support the implementation of strategies to manage pupil behaviour

For this element you will need to know and understand the following:

▶ managing behaviour and the implications of the Children Act and child protection

▶ reporting behaviour or discipline problems to the teacher

▶ specialist advice for dealing with unwanted behaviour

▶ implementing behaviour support plans.

Managing behaviour and the implication of the Children Act 1989 and child protection

When looking at behaviour which is acceptable, staff should be aware that we all have different ideas and expectations. We should recognise that our ideas about what is acceptable or unacceptable will come from our own experiences and cultures. Pupils may therefore come to school with a variety of accepted 'normal' behaviour.

Think about it

Read and think about the following statements:
▶ Children should always write thank you letters at Christmas and birthdays.
▶ Children should never leave the table until everyone has finished eating.
▶ Children should be required to fast during Ramadan.
▶ Children should always stand up when an adult enters the room.
▶ Children should not be allowed to address an adult by their first name.

Work in a group and consider which of these statements you agree with.

Do others in the room give the same answers as you?

We may therefore have conflicting ideas about the kind of behaviour we view as 'normal' and what we expect from pupils. For this reason, many schools will have their own guidelines for behaviour. Parents should be informed of these so that they are aware of what is acceptable and not acceptable in school. Where parents and schools have conflicting ideas about acceptable behaviour, pupils will find it difficult to know how to conform.

As already mentioned, pupils should be aware and reminded of the school's expectations for behaviour so that they know how to conform in the classroom, playground and in other parts of the school. Where children are not conforming to the rules, they should know what the consequences are.

 Find out about...

The different 'normal' behaviours which may be expected of pupils at various ages.

Examples of behaviour and consequences

Action	Consequence
Running in the school corridor	Going back and walking
Disruptive behaviour in class	Time out – working alone
Verbally abusing other children/adults	Apology/letter of apology
Aggressive behaviour in the playground	One minute by the wall

The school's policies on behaviour and equal opportunities should set out guidelines for managing the way in which pupils interact with one another. Where assistants are unsure of the kinds of sanctions or consequences that they are able to use, they should always clarify this with their class teacher or supervisor.

The Children Act (1989)

This Act was passed in 1989 and has had far-reaching effects on the care and protection of children. It aims to put children first and to make professionals and local authorities dealing with families and children think about their individual needs. The Children Act covers a wide range of issues including the registration and inspection of childcare services for children under eight. It also provides guidance for child protection issues and should therefore be considered when selecting and using behaviour management strategies.

▲ It is important to encourage good behaviour but sanctions may still be necessary

The main area in which the Children Act relates to behaviour in school is through its section on the care and protection of children. All children who are placed in situations of care should be protected and the Act outlines the responsibilities of the local authority in ensuring that these needs are met. Where schools are looking after children it is important for all staff to know and understand the rights of pupils and how they should be protected – for example, that staff are not allowed to give corporal punishment. It is through the school's policies and guidelines for behaviour management that inspectors can see that all staff are aware of and adhere to these guidelines. Behaviour management strategies will need to take into consideration how we can encourage good behaviour and remain fair when applying sanctions for bad behaviour.

Reporting behaviour or discipline problems to the teacher

Working alongside the teacher to promote an effective learning environment

When working in partnership with the class teacher, assistants should be clear about their roles and responsibilities with regard to pupil behaviour. This is as important for staff in the school to know and understand as it is for pupils, since they are responsible for ensuring that school policies and rules for behaviour are maintained.

Structure of the way in which rules are defined

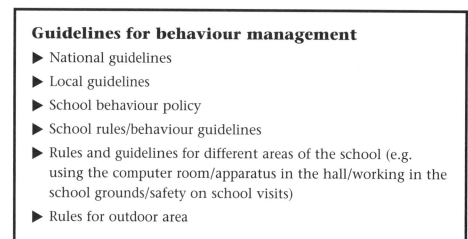

Guidelines for behaviour management
- ▶ National guidelines
- ▶ Local guidelines
- ▶ School behaviour policy
- ▶ School rules/behaviour guidelines
- ▶ Rules and guidelines for different areas of the school (e.g. using the computer room/apparatus in the hall/working in the school grounds/safety on school visits)
- ▶ Rules for outdoor area

Assistants may find it difficult to know when and how they should intervene when they are faced with issues of behaviour. It is important to be clear exactly what 'normal' behaviour is and to make allowances for pupils in different circumstances. Some examples of these circumstances might include the following:

▷ On the first day of Year 7, there may be several pupils who are upset and do not want to come to school. However, if this behaviour carried on over a long period of time, the teacher may find it necessary to impose some kind of strategy for managing the pupil or pupils.

▷ It is getting towards the end of term and the normal routines of school are slightly different due to end of term activities. The pupils in the class are excitable and restless. In this situation, which is not normal, some pupils may find it difficult to conform to the rules.

Teachers and assistants should also be informed if any individual pupils in the class have had any kinds of upheaval or distress at home. The teacher should inform any assistants as soon as a problem comes to his or her attention. Examples of these might be a parents' divorce, or a death in the family. Sometimes it may be the death of a pet or a parent going away on business which can make a pupil behave differently. The school should make it clear to parents that staff need to be informed of anything which may be distressing the pupil. If assistants notice a pupil behaving differently or out of character, this is worth mentioning to the teacher so that parents can be asked if there is any reason for it. When pupils are settled in school and are used to the rules and routines, they will know and understand what is expected of them. Where pupils display unwanted behaviours in a normal school situation, sanctions should be applied to control the behaviour.

Applying sanctions

As a teaching assistant, you should be aware of the types of sanctions or rewards which are available to you when managing behaviour. Usually if the teacher is present, your main strategies will be verbal or involve eye contact. If you are alone with the class for any reason, you should, as the responsible member of staff, be able to use any of those which the teacher would normally use. However, you should always clarify this with the teacher first. If you have any problems in implementing sanctions, or if the pupils do not respond to you as the responsible member of staff, you should also inform the teacher.

Case study

You have been left with the class for ten minutes as the teacher has had to speak to the headteacher urgently. You are reading the class a story but two or three girls at the back are not listening and are disturbing the others. You tell them to behave sensibly and listen to the story but one of them says that you are not the teacher and they don't have to do what you say.

1 What would you do in this situation?

2 What could the teacher say to the class before leaving to make sure that they behaved appropriately?

3 How could the teacher support you?

If sanctions are applied and the pupil is still consistently not responding, there may be a deep-rooted problem which should be investigated (see page 24 for specialist advice on behaviour management).

Think about it

You are working apart from the class teacher with a group of pupils who are undertaking some DT work using hot glue guns. One of the pupils has not behaved sensibly while using the glue gun and for health and safety reasons you have taken the gun away and asked the pupil to go back to the teacher. The class teacher has not seen what has happened and when the pupil goes back to her does not support you over your reaction. You feel that this is because she does not want the pupil back in the classroom. In groups discuss how you would deal with this situation.

Safety issues

Other situations in which you may need to apply sanctions or strategies are those when you find yourself or others at risk. It is important to be able to respond calmly and quickly in emergencies and other potentially dangerous situations. This may occur either within the school and grounds, or on a school trip.

Examples of this could be:

 ▷ a pupil or parent who becomes violent
 ▷ a pupil who unwittingly puts others in danger
 ▷ a pupil who displays severe behavioural problems and needs full staff attention
 ▷ a group of pupils who are misbehaving and putting others in danger.

If you find yourself in a situation where there is no other member of staff present and you are faced with a risk, you will be responsible for managing the situation. You must always remain calm, as young people will quickly panic if they sense panic in an adult. If it is a single pupil who is misbehaving or violent and they do not respond to your authority, you must make sure that other pupils are kept away from them and send a responsible pupil for another member of staff. Similarly, when faced with an adult who is aggressive or violent, remain calm and reassure them that you will need to ask for assistance from another member of staff. It is important that you seek further help as soon as possible.

Specialist advice for dealing with unwanted behaviour

In some situations, where a teacher or supervisor has used all the ideas and strategies already available, it may be necessary to ask for extra help and support. If you are in a mainstream school, you should have a SENCo, or Special Needs Co-ordinator, on the staff. There may be different situations which require the help of outside agencies, and as an assistant you will not be asked to contact them, but you should have an awareness of the support that is available.

 ▷ **SENCo or supervisor** – this should be the first point of contact for behaviour support and devising additional strategies for use within the classroom. They will also contact other professionals outside the school.

 ▷ **Behaviour Unit** – this unit is usually run by the local authority and will offer support and suggestions for dealing with pupils who have behaviour problems. They may also come into schools to observe or work with specific pupils.

 ▷ **Educational psychologists** – these professionals visit all schools regularly to support pupils and the staff who work with them. They offer help and advice on a variety of Special Needs problems, and may assess pupils and devise individual programmes. They are also involved with assessing those pupils who may need a statement of Special Educational Needs.

Implementing behaviour support plans

The SENCo will be the first point of contact for teachers and with their help, teachers may devise an Individual Education Plan for pupils with learning difficulties, or a Behaviour Support Plan for those who need it. This should set realistic targets for work or behaviour, which should be Specific, Measurable, Achievable, Realistic and Time bound (SMART). It is vital that pupils have achievable targets, so that they are able to experience success and start to build positive behaviour. If you are an individual support assistant and responsible for supporting a specific pupil in the class, it is likely that you are familiar with setting targets for the pupil with whom you are working.

(?) Think about it

Have you been involved with the development of a Behaviour Support Plan, or a behaviour target on an Individual Education Plan? Were you also involved in the review of the plan? What kinds of targets have you set for pupils with whom you have been working? You may be able to use this as evidence for your portfolio.

Below is an example of a Behaviour Support Plan. There should not be more than three or four targets on any one plan.

Behaviour Support Plan

Name: James Fraser
Class: 8SW
Date set: March 2004

Date for review: May 2004

Targets:

1. To sit close to the teacher to encourage him to listen carefully and prevent calling out.

2. To encourage good behaviour on the playground through the use of a 'buddy' system.

Review:

James has stopped calling out although still finds it difficult to listen. Ongoing target.

This has worked well – target achieved.

Reviewed by: L. Clark

No more than 3 targets – easier to achieve

At the review, you and the class teacher should discuss the success of any strategies used

The review column should contain comments and include next steps

▲ A Behaviour Support Plan

Working with your supervisor or mentor, look at the targets set for one individual pupil in your school. Discuss the strategies you might use to support the implementation of these targets. Write an account of your actions and keep a record for evidence.

End of unit test

1 What are the main areas of social and emotional development for adolescents?

2 List some common behaviour problems and how you might deal with them.

3 How could you reward positive behaviour?

4 True or false – a pupil who witnesses staff swearing and being aggressive will copy this behaviour.

5 How would you define your role as an assistant when managing behaviour in school?

6 What kind of specialist advice is available in schools to help support behaviour problems?

7 When would you provide feedback to the teacher about any pupils who have a Behaviour Support Plan?

8 How might you plan for good behaviour when taking a group of pupils to work in the school grounds?

9 What would you do if a pupil in your class showed uncharacteristically aggressive behaviour towards another pupil?

10 What are the main aims of the Children Act 1989?

References

Index for Inclusion (CSIE, 2000)

Websites

CSIE: http://inclusion.uwe.ac.uk

www.qca.org.uk

www.nc.uk.net/

Unit 3-2 Establish and maintain relationships with individual pupils and groups

There are two elements to this unit. These are:

3-2.1 Establish and maintain relationships with individual pupils

3-2.2 Establish and maintain relationships with groups of pupils

Element 3-2.1 Establish and maintain relationships with individual pupils

In your role as a teaching assistant, you will need to be able to establish and maintain relationships with individual pupils on both a short and long term basis. You will need to know about the pupils with whom you are working so that you are able to communicate effectively with them and support them during learning activities. This will involve knowing about them as individuals and being able to relate well to them. You will also need to know the type and level of individual support needed to enable the pupil to achieve the learning targets set by the teacher. In the short term, you will need to know how to establish relationships with others so that they feel comfortable working with you and able to ask for support if they need it.

For this element, you will need to know and understand the following:

▶ the principles underlying inter-personal skills and how to communicate effectively with pupils

▶ learning styles, needs and preferences of individuals and how this will affect your role

▶ problems which may arise when building and maintaining relationships with individuals.

Principles underlying inter-personal skills and how to communicate effectively with pupils

Effective inter-personal skills will be dependent on a variety of factors. Teaching assistants will need to have an understanding of these not only for developing their relationships with pupils but also for their relationships with others in the school environment. The main principles underlying inter-personal skills are:

▷ being interested in and valuing the other individual

▷ communicating effectively with others

▷ being sensitive to the needs and feelings of others.

Being interested in and valuing the other individual

As a teaching assistant, you may have more opportunities than teachers for getting to know individual pupils, particularly if you are working as an individual support assistant, as you may have more time to talk to and develop relationships with them. This means that you will be able to gain an insight into what motivates individuals, their interests and abilities, and how to keep them focused on learning activities. As you get to know pupils, you will be able to recognise when they are achieving or not achieving for their own ability.

You will need to be careful when giving pupils attention for bad behaviour as this can cause it to be repeated – although it is not always possible to ignore. Montgomery (1990) emphasises 'catching them being good' as an effective strategy for behaviour management. This is particularly helpful when building relationships with pupils as they will respond well to positive attention, however small. It can include the use of positive eye contact, smiles and quiet praise.

Knowledge into action

In small groups, discuss situations you have experienced where you have given pupils positive attention to help and keep them motivated on a task. What kinds of reactions have you had from pupils? What other reinforcement do you think helps pupils to raise self-esteem and motivate them in their learning?

When listening to pupils, staff should also be aware that they need to show they are interested in what pupils are saying: it is very frustrating when we are talking to another individual to find that they are not listening and we need to repeat what we have said. We can also show that we are listening through the use of body language and the amount of interest we display, including how we respond. If we only appear half-interested this will also give the pupil the message that we do not value what they are saying. It is important for children to gain the approval of adults and most pupils will respond better to a member of staff who is taking the time to listen to them. This also means that pupils will be more likely to talk to staff and let them know if there is anything troubling them, as these kinds of factors will influence their learning.

Being aware of differences

Assistants should remember that individuals should be treated as such and there may be gender, social or cultural based influences on how they respond to us. For example, in some cultures it is not appropriate to give eye contact when speaking to others, whereas in Western cultures this may be misinterpreted as a sign of rudeness or insecurity. It is important for all pupils to feel accepted and an awareness of differences can affect how we relate to others. Your school will have policies, for example equal opportunities, and procedures for ensuring that within the school there is no discriminatory behaviour and that all cultures are valued.

Communicating effectively with others

We need to interact with others, and we use communication as a key factor when we are doing this. Young children will use their communication skills, whatever these are, to express their needs, desires and questions about the world around them. As they develop their language skills, they will increasingly use language to do this, and effective language skills are vital when they are learning. Children who have difficulties in communicating will become increasingly isolated and frustrated in any environment, so it is important for us to be able to support their language and communication development. In order to think about how we communicate effectively with pupils, we need to look at the difference between communication and language and how we can use both effectively.

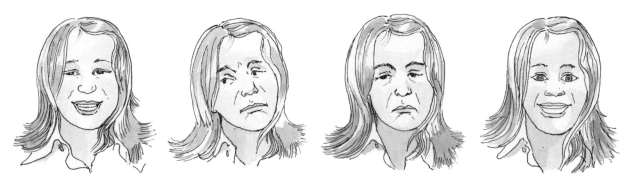

▲ Non-verbal communication can give us a lot of information

Forms of communication

Communication involves the passing, receiving, interpreting and understanding of information. Communicating with others enables us to relate to them, explore the environment, understand concepts, formulate ideas and express feelings. People use a variety of ways to communicate – these are essential to be able to relate effectively and be involved in a wide range of social interactions. This communication may be verbal or non-verbal.

Non-verbal communication can be a very powerful tool. We can give messages to others using a variety of methods including body language, expressions and gestures. Using non-verbal communication, we can also interpret messages which others send to us. In schools, non-verbal communication is often used by staff to demonstrate a variety of statements.

You may also find that you or others also use touch as a way of gaining the attention of pupils or comforting those in distress. However, care should be taken with this and it should generally be avoided as it may be inappropriate or misinterpreted. Your school or local authority may have a policy or guidelines on the use of touch or physical restraint of pupils and it would be worth finding out about this.

➔ ## Knowledge into action

In small groups take turns in demonstrating non-verbal communication. Role-play the following statements.

1 What on earth are you doing?
2 That looks really good.
3 Hello!
4 Are you sure that's a good idea?
5 Look out!
6 Come here!
7 I'm very tired.
8 This is boring.
9 We did it!

Verbal communication includes listening, speaking, reading and writing. Each mode of language involves a variety of skills that are inter-related, for example the use of sign language or Makaton. Some are required in more than one mode, such as reading and writing which both involve the processing of oral language in a written form. Verbal communication is the form which we use most often in schools although it is important to consider the different areas. (See also Unit 3-18, page 227, Help pupils to develop their literacy skills.)

▷ **Speaking and listening** – individuals will need to be able to initiate language and also to actively listen to others. When communicating with pupils, you will need to be particularly aware of active listening (see also page 38). You should also make sure that any questions you ask pupils are open-ended, which means that they will need to react more fully. An example of this might be, rather than asking a group of Year 8 pupils whether they have heard of Shakespeare, which will only elicit 'yes' or 'no' as an answer, asking what they can tell you about him will make them think in context and act as a better basis for a discussion.

Sign language is a form of communication which may also be used in schools with children who have special educational needs. You may find that you have the opportunity to go on courses to teach you methods of signing such as Makaton or British Sign Language.

? *Think about it*

In pairs, speak to one another for five minutes about a hobby or interest that you have. Then share the information your partner has just given you with the rest of the group to see how much you have actively listened and retained information.

▷ **Reading and writing** – both of these methods of communication involve the processing of verbal language in a written form. In order to communicate effectively in this way, individuals will need to be competent in these skills. If you are working with pupils who need to have support when communicating using these methods, you will need to make sure that you enable them to put their ideas across whilst encouraging them to try for themselves as much as possible.

Being sensitive to the needs and feelings of others

An important part of communicating with others is being able to empathise and understand why they may react in a certain way. For example, if you are working with a pupil who you know is having difficulties or upheavals in their home life it may be understandable if they are finding it difficult to concentrate whilst at school. If a pupil displays very different behaviour from normal, you will usually find that there is an underlying reason, although there can be problems if the pupil is unwilling to share this

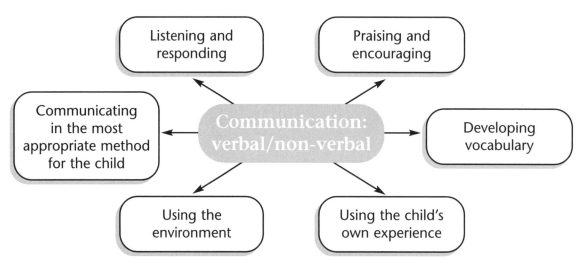

▲ Communicating with children effectively

with a member of staff. If you suspect that a pupil is having to cope with difficult issues but is not talking about them you may need to mention this to other members of staff.

Learning styles, needs and preferences of individuals and how this will affect your role

Another way in which assistants will develop their relationships with pupils will be through their understanding of different learning styles (see also Unit 3-3, page 64, Support pupils during learning activities, for definitions of these). It will be helpful if you are able to find out the learning styles of different pupils you support simply because you may be more likely to be able to explain things to them. Pupils of secondary age may also be interested in finding out what kind of a learner they are as it will also benefit them in the long term.

➡ Knowledge into action

In order to find out about what kind of learners you are supporting, there is a learning styles quiz on the Internet which gives an immediate score and states what kind of learner individuals are. Find this at **www.chaminade.org/inspire/learnstl.htm**. (If this quiz is no longer at this address, there are others to be found on the Internet.)

When supporting individual pupils you will also need to be clear about the learning objectives and targets which have been set by the teacher so that you can make sure you keep these in mind. Make sure that you are clear about exactly what you are required to do. You will need to monitor pupils' responses so that you are able to feed these back to the teacher.

Similarly, if you are working with a pupil who has special educational needs, you will need to find out about what these needs are and attend training if necessary so that you are able to support them fully. Pupils who have special needs may become frustrated or anxious about what they are doing if they are not working at the appropriate level for their understanding or ability.

These pupils should also have their own individual education plan (IEP) and you will need to be aware of what their targets are. These may relate to the pupil's learning, or specific social or emotional needs (see page 203 for an example of an IEP).

Case study

Jimmy is in Year 8 and has a speech and language impairment, which makes it difficult for him to pronounce some words clearly. He is also behind others of his age academically. As you get to know Jimmy you find that he has quite low self-esteem and lacks confidence when putting his ideas across as others can become impatient with him. You have carried out a learning styles questionnaire with Jimmy and found out that he is quite an auditory learner.

1 What kinds of strategies do you think you could use as you get to know Jimmy and his individual needs?

2 Where could you go for more ideas to help Jimmy?

As you get to know the way in which individuals learn, it will be easier for you to find ways to support them during learning activities. It is important however that you are able to recognise the amount of support you should give pupils – if you give them too little they may become frustrated if they are unable to carry out learning activities, whereas too much help will make them more reliant and dependent on you and less likely to be able to try things out for themselves. Assistants will also need to remember that pupils of any age will respond well to praise – different forms of encouragement can make an enormous difference to a pupil and be a great motivator.

Case study

You are working with Matt who has Duchenne Muscular Dystrophy and consequently has limited mobility in the classroom. Although he has severe physical difficulties, Matt is able to work at the same intellectual level as others in the class although he has difficulty recording and relies heavily on the computer. As you have got to know Matt, you have noticed that he is able but that he very quickly becomes disheartened when carrying out activities and when he has got to this point it is difficult to motivate him.

1 What would you need to do to support Matt in this situation?

2 How do you think you could help Matt to regain his motivation?

Long and short term relationships

Your relationships with individual pupils may be as different as the pupils themselves, particularly if the time allocated with them also varies. If you are only working with a pupil once a week for example, you will need to make sure that you remember what you were doing last time so that they immediately have a sense that you remember them and this will raise their self-esteem. However, if you work with a pupil every day you may find that this can also be a disadvantage depending on personalities and the needs of the pupil, even though support will be more constant.

> ✓ **Keys to good practice**
> **Supporting the needs of individuals**
>
> ✔ Give the appropriate amount of intervention – not too little or too much.
> ✔ Make sure you are up-to-date on the needs of individuals.
> ✔ Find out about any special educational needs of pupils.
> ✔ Monitor individual pupils' responses to learning activities.
> ✔ Praise and encourage them for their own achievements.

Problems which may arise when building and maintaining relationships with individuals

When you are working in a secondary classroom there may be factors which hinder your ability to develop relationships with individual pupils. These may vary from problems which are school-based to problems surrounding the pupil. Where you find that there are difficulties which you are unable to resolve, you should always report these to the teacher with whom you are working as soon as possible. (See also Unit 3-2.2, page 42, How to deal with difficulties within the group.)

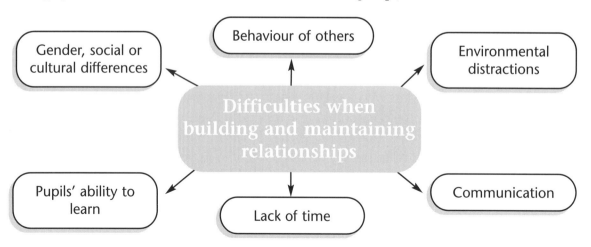

▲ There can be different factors which create barriers to relationships

▲ Alternative locations may not always be comfortable when working with pupils

Environmental distractions

Depending on where you are working with individuals, you may find that there are distractions which make it difficult for you to work effectively with them. For example, if you always work alongside the pupil in a classroom you may find that other pupils are a distraction and that you are unable to focus the pupil on what you are doing. Similarly, if you are working in an alternative location with a pupil there may be other distractions which make it difficult to work or which are uncomfortable due to temperature or noise.

Often schools do not have many alternative locations in which to work if the classroom is not practical for the task you are carrying out, and those which are available may be problematic, or double-booked. Also if you are working with a pupil who has mobility problems, the location may be difficult to access. If you are working with pupils in different locations you need to be prepared if possible so that you can check that the environment is suitable. If teachers do not give you advance warning or have not checked that the location is available this may be difficult for you.

Lack of time

Owing to timetabling or other constraints you may find that you do not have sufficient time to form effective relationships with pupils during learning activities which have been set. It is also important for pupils that you give as much time as is needed to tasks so that they do not feel that you do not have time for them. If you do not have time to finish an activity, make sure that you set a time to return to it with the pupil, to show that you are valuing what they do.

The pupil's ability to learn

You may be working with a pupil who finds a task or concept particularly difficult and is struggling to complete it. In this case you will need to attempt to modify the task so that it is possible for them to achieve it. Similarly, you may need to add an extension activity if a pupil completes it too quickly and still has some time within the lesson. If you have used either of these methods with pupils you will need to tell the teacher at the end of the lesson in order to inform their planning for next time.

Gender, social or cultural differences

You may perceive that it will be more difficult to form relationships with pupils who are of a different gender, social or cultural group from yourself, or you may be working with a pupil who has similar reservations. Some pupils may find it easier to work with a member of staff who is the same sex, or who is from the same social or cultural group.

Communication

Difficulties surrounding communication may be varied but will usually occur when pupils themselves have communication disorders or difficulties. In this situation, you will need to find out as much as you can about the nature of the disorder and the pupil's individual targets so that you can support them fully. They may need to have specialist equipment or materials in order to help them communicate and it is possible that you may need to be trained in order to support their use.

You may also find that issues occur around misunderstandings with pupils where they have not understood the requirements of tasks or are unwilling to communicate any problems they are having. If you suspect that a pupil is anxious about a task you should ask them whether they need any help in order to give them the opportunity to tell you.

Behaviour of others

If you are working with an individual pupil you may find that others are a distraction and that you need to speak to them about their behaviour or the level of noise which they are making. You may also find that you have been asked to work with a group although you support an individual pupil, and others in the group are making it difficult to do this effectively. You should make sure that you speak to the other pupils straight away and do not allow the disruption to continue. If you have any problems in gaining control over the group you will need to inform another member of staff so that this can be resolved.

Evidence collection

You are working on a literacy activity with Maria who has learning difficulties. You have a limited amount of time to complete the activity, as you need to pick up a group of pupils for the next lesson and take them to the other end of the school. Maria is finding the activity challenging and you are aware that you have already asked her to work quickly to make sure that she completes the task.

▶ What can you do to make sure that Maria does not feel rushed in this situation?

▶ Are there any other ways in which you could demonstrate to Maria that her work is valued?

Element 3-2.2 Establish and maintain relationships with groups of pupils

This part of the unit is concerned with your work with groups of pupils in a variety of situations. As a teaching assistant, you will often be working with groups of pupils who may have special educational needs and for whatever reason find it difficult to keep up with others in the class. Alternatively, you may be working with pupils who are more able than others and need to have extra tasks to extend and motivate them further. When working with groups of pupils you will need to keep in mind the learning outcomes of the task and monitor how pupils are progressing.

For this element you will need to know and understand the following:

▶ how to work effectively with a group of pupils

▶ how to monitor the behaviour and learning of the group

▶ how to deal with difficulties within the group.

How to work effectively with a group of pupils

Often, separate groups within the classroom have to work on different tasks and towards different learning outcomes. This is because pupils are of different abilities and will need to have work that is set at an appropriate level for them. This is called **differentiation**. If you are working with a group of pupils, they will generally be of the same ability but you will sometimes be asked to work with groups whose abilities are mixed. This is often beneficial as it encourages interactions with others and gives pupils opportunities to help one another through discussion in a supportive and safe environment.

Before starting to work with a new group you will need to think about some of the same issues and principles which apply to working with individuals.

Many of the interpersonal skills which teaching assistants will use in their work with individuals (Unit 3-21) will also be applicable when dealing with pairs and groups of pupils. For example, you will still need to:

▷ **Find out what you can about individuals within the group** – This is important in order to support them effectively, but be careful not to have any preconceived ideas which may negatively influence your interactions with a pupil.

▷ **Ensure that there is effective communication between individuals within the group** – In order to do this, individuals within the group must feel comfortable with the others so that they are not anxious about putting their point of view across.

▷ **Actively listen to pupils** – As before, you must show that you are interested in what pupils are saying. You need to be able to engage with each member of the group in order to support them fully.

▷ **Make sure that those within the group are able to be sensitive to the needs and feelings of others** – This involves managing the group so that you deal with any problems in this area straight away. You may need to speak to individuals after the session if there have been any issues (see also 'How to monitor the behaviour and learning of the group', page 40).

You should also encourage positive behaviour between pupils which is non-discriminatory. Pupils will have their own values and beliefs which should be respected by others: your school will also have policies to encourage non-discriminatory behaviour and to value cultural diversity. These will usually be discussed periodically in school through assemblies, PSHE and Citizenship sessions, but if issues come up in your work with groups you may need to remind pupils about them.

You may be asked to work with groups either in the long or short term. **Short-term groups** are those which come together to complete a single task or work on a one-off activity. This may be within the classroom but could also be out of school on a trip or in situations where you may be asked to cover other assistants who are absent.

Long-term groups will generally be those with whom you will work on a regular basis to support a particular subject area. This kind of group may work together on a project or have specific needs and need regular support, such as pupils who need to work together on activities to support literacy and numeracy.

There are advantages to being in both short and long term groups, as pupils will sometimes gain a great deal in one-off situations, but long term groups will offer a greater range of experiences through its stages of development.

Stages in the development of groups

When working with groups long term, you should be aware of the different stages which groups tend to pass through, as these will affect group dynamics. They have been identified by Tuckman and Jensen as **forming**, **storming**, **norming** and **performing**. (See also Unit 3-21, page 271, Support the effectiveness of work teams, for a fuller definition of these.)

The different stages of groups
Stage 1: Introductory stage where individuals are polite and get to know each other. (Best behaviour away from home!)
Stage 2: Known as the conflict stage, where individuals start to fall out with each other. Getting to know each other and not liking all that is seen or heard.
Stage 3: This is the negotiation stage, where the group forms unwritten rules of procedure.
Stage 4: This is the working stage, where the group starts to work together after sorting out individual differences.

? *Think about it*

Think about your own experiences of being in different groups. Do you think that the groups have passed through these stages?

Groups in schools will be required to work together in different ways. It has been suggested that there are four main types of groups in the classroom.

Different groups in the classroom
▶ Seating groups: pupils sit together but are engaged in separate tasks and produce separate outcomes, e.g. pupils who are working on the same maths activity may be working at their own pace, and will therefore achieve differently.
▶ Working groups: where pupils tackle similar tasks, which result in similar outcomes, but their work is independent, e.g. using reference books and the Internet to find out about a subject.
▶ Co-operative groups: where pupils have separate but related tasks which result in a joint outcome, e.g. a book of poetry on a particular subject containing poems by individual children.
▶ Collaborative groups: pupils have the same task and work together towards a joint outcome, e.g. a large Roman display for a parents' Cheese and Wine Party.

The way in which your group is expected to work and its stage of development may also affect the way in which it is managed. For example, a group of pupils who have been working together for some weeks at the same time will have established boundaries and be comfortable working together, whereas a newly-formed group will still need to work out rules for working and its members may take longer to settle at the beginning of a session.

Keys to good practice
Working with groups

✔ Be aware of individuals' learning needs.

✔ Remember to give praise and encouragement.

✔ Make sure you are aware of the learning objectives.

✔ Involve all pupils in the activity.

How to monitor the behaviour and learning of the group

As with individuals, you will need to be able to monitor how effectively pupils are working towards the learning outcomes. Clearly this will be more difficult where there are disruptive pupils within the group (see 'How to deal with difficulties within the group', page 42) and all groups will have their own dynamics.

You will also need to make sure that the behaviour of pupils within the group is such that it encourages them to work together and that they do not distract one another.

Monitoring behaviour

Before starting to work with a new group it is always useful to establish a few ground rules. This may be through going through with the group the school or class rules and expectations, so that all members of the group are clear on what is expected of them and why. You will also need to have some strategies for re-focusing pupils who are struggling to complete the task. These could be verbal, such as praising what they have already achieved, but may also be non-verbal through your body language, positive gestures and facial expressions. Remember that the most important aspect of this is to be positive.

It is unlikely that you will be able to decide on the size of the group, but monitoring smaller groups may be easier, as pupils who may be behaving inappropriately will have a smaller 'audience'. They will also have less opportunity to disturb others as you will have closer contact with them. In a smaller group, pupils are more likely to feel comfortable, and less confident pupils more likely to put their ideas forward.

When monitoring behaviour, you may find that you may have to make exceptions if pupils have special needs which mean that their behaviour is affected. This will always impact on the dynamics of the group and pupils will usually be aware of this. It may manifest itself in aggressive behaviour or outbursts if pupils become frustrated – if you are an individual support assistant for this child you may have specific strategies in place for these occasions and they may have individual targets (see also Unit 3-1 on behaviour).

▲ It is easier to control the behaviour of a small group

Monitoring learning

The main difference between working with individuals and working with groups is that you will need to have more information from the teacher at the outset to enable you to support them as a group whilst bearing in mind the needs of individuals. There also needs to be a balance between individual and group demands on your attention so that all members of the group are involved. The way in which you manage this should be to ensure you interact with all members of the group, whether you or they initiate this. For example, if a pupil is being very quiet and is not involved, you may need to ask them directly what they think or pose a question about the activity. In this way you will ensure that you manage the learning of the group and also maintain each pupil's interest.

Another way of sustaining pupils' attention should include noticing when they are making particular progress and giving plenty of praise and encouragement. They will need this to stay motivated.

Case study

You are working with a group of pupils in Geography to discover their feelings about litter in their local area. Three members of the group are taking over the discussion and you notice that one pupil at the end of the table is not involved at all.

1 What would you do to try to involve the quiet pupil?

2 Why do you think it is important for all members of the group that everyone is involved?

You may also be asked by the teacher to assess and feed back about each pupil following the learning activity, so you and the group need to be clear about exactly what the learning objectives are so that you are able to do this. Some aspects of the task may need to be clarified to different members of the group, either because they have not listened carefully to the requirements of the task or because they are having difficulties understanding what they need to do.

How to deal with difficulties within the group

Difficulties will inevitably occur when you are working with groups of pupils, and it is vital that as the responsible member of staff you deal with these immediately. Several of these have also been discussed in 3-1.1 and will also apply when working with groups of pupils. You will need to think about both short and long-term factors which can cause difficulties.

Look at the diagram below, on short-term factors which can cause difficulties in groups. For each of the 'short term' situations listed, discuss in small groups:

▶ how a pupil might be affected

▶ what type of behaviour may manifest itself

▶ how you could deal with the behaviour.

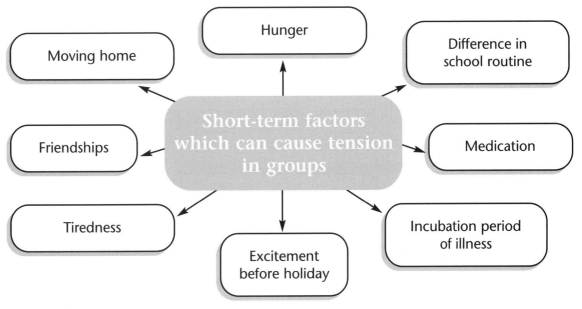

▲ What causes difficulties in groups?

Long-term situations may also affect the behaviour of pupils with whom you are working. These could be issues such as:

▷ moving or relocation of families

▷ divorce, separation or remarriage of parents

▷ severe illness of family members

▷ bullying and other social issues

▷ changes in carer/foster parents.

You may or may not be aware if pupils in your group are facing any of these issues – however, if you find out that they are, you will need to speak to other members of staff in the school as pupils' learning may be affected (see also Unit 3-2.1).

The way in which you deal with any issues which occur is important as you have authority and control over the group and the pupils need to see this. If you allow situations to escalate so that the pupils appear to be in control, this will be very difficult to regain.

Keys to good practice
Dealing with difficulties

✔ Anticipate any potential causes of conflict.

✔ Deal with any issues immediately.

✔ Remember school policies when dealing with behaviour or conflict.

✔ Always remain calm when dealing with difficulties.

✔ Report any problems which you are unable to overcome to a teacher.

Pupils can 'gel' together well but there may also be children within the group who aggravate one another. If you are aware of difficulties either due to your own experiences of the pupils or through being warned by the teacher, you should make sure that you are prepared for them as they arise.

Evidence collection

Next time you are working with a group of pupils in either the short or long term, think about and record the following:

▶ the background to the group

▶ how relationships are established and maintained during the session(s)

▶ any difficulties which occur and how you deal with them.

End of unit test

1 What are some of the principles underlying effective interpersonal skills?

2 How can eye contact be an effective form of communication in a classroom?

3 How are the terms 'language' and 'communication' different?

4 What do you need to know about individuals in order to support them fully in the learning environment?

5 Why do you need to give feedback to the class teacher about individual pupils?

6 How can you make sure you give the right amount of support to individuals?

7 What different types of groups may be found in classrooms?

8 What are the different stages which groups pass through?

9 Why is it important to show sensitivity to the feelings and needs of all individuals within the group?

10 What kinds of difficulties might an assistant have when supporting individuals or groups of pupils?

References

Montgomery, D., *Managing Behaviour Problems*, (Hodder and Stoughton Educational, 1990)

Tuckman, B and Jensen, M. A., 'Stages of small group development revisited' in *Group and Organisational Studies*, 2, 419-427 (1977)

Support pupils during learning activities

There are two elements to this unit. These are:

3-3.1 Provide support for learning activities
3-3.2 Promote independent learning

Element 3-3.1 Provide support for learning activities

This element examines how you can best support pupils when undertaking learning activities in school. You will need to understand how young people learn and develop in order to implement a range of strategies for supporting them. As a teaching assistant you will also need to be able to manage problems within the classroom when supporting learning activities. This element will give you some idea of the types of problems you may encounter and how to deal with them. It is also important to be familiar with the National Curriculum at Key Stages 3 and 4 and how different subjects and activities are planned within this framework.

When you are supporting the delivery of learning activities, you will need to carry out the work with the pupils as agreed, using the appropriate materials and support. You will need to make sure that you monitor the learning activities and if necessary break down or extend the pupils' work. You should then evaluate the learning activities and report back to the teacher.

For this element you will need to know and understand the following:

▶ basic principles and influences on how young people learn and develop
▶ understanding curriculum plans
▶ how pupils may be supported in learning activities
▶ the school's policies and practices for equal opportunities and inclusion, including supporting pupils with Special Educational Needs
▶ managing problems when supporting learning activities.

How young people learn and develop

Theories of learning

There have been several theories put forward by educationalists and psychologists about how children learn and are influenced as they develop and mature. There are other, inbuilt influences on children's learning which will be discussed on page 50, as they will also have a direct effect on how children learn. The two main ideas about how children's learning takes place are behaviourist theory and cognitive theory. By looking at these we are able to focus on different aspects of children's learning and consider how best to support them in school.

Behaviourist theory

This theory was first put forward by Burrhus Frank Skinner (1904–94). It states that as individuals we will repeat experiences which are enjoyable and avoid those which are not. This is as relevant for learning experiences as for behaviour itself. For example, a pupil who learns that it is enjoyable to work creatively will want to repeat the experience and do this again. If children are praised for working at a particular task, this may also reinforce their desire to repeat the experience. Skinner stated that good experiences are *positive reinforcement*. Many educationalists use the strategy of positive reinforcement when working with young people – for example, by praising and encouraging them and by giving them tasks which they can carry out successfully.

We can ensure that pupils are gaining positive experiences when working by giving them:

▷ praise and encouragement
▷ enjoyable tasks
▷ manageable tasks.

▲ Staff will need to be aware when pupils are not able to focus on a task

Assistants will need to be aware of pupils' reactions to tasks as sometimes pupils may find it difficult to become motivated and lose enthusiasm quickly. It is important to recognise when pupils are not enjoying tasks and find out what may be the cause, so that we may encourage and motivate them. As assistants get to know pupils, it will be more apparent when they are not 'themselves', or are unable to focus on what they are doing. Where pupils are not responding to a task, assistants should address them individually and try to find out the cause.

There may be a variety of reasons why the pupil is not motivated:

▷ Pupil does not understand the requirements of the task.

▷ Pupil is unable to complete the task as it is too difficult.

▷ Pupil finds the task too easy.

▷ Individual reasons why the pupil is not able to focus on the task, such as illness or anxiety.

Once the cause has been established, assistants may need to work closely with the pupil or speak to the teacher about the problem to decide the best way forward. Where the task is too easy or too difficult, it may be possible to put the pupil with another group and restructure their work for later. Pupils whose work is not enjoyable or manageable will be unlikely to want to repeat the experience.

Cognitive development theory

The second theory of learning is that which was put forward by Jean Piaget, (1896-1980) and is based on the cognitive model. This states that a child will need to pass through different stages of a learning process. He stated that children pass through stages of learning which are broadly related to their age, and that they cannot move from one stage to another until they are ready.

This theory has been criticised as all children learn and develop at a different pace and it is hard to say at exactly what age particular skills will develop. It is however accepted that children have individual learning needs and requirements.

Piaget's stages of learning

Age	Stage of learning	Characteristics
0–2 years	Sensory Motor	Babies are starting to find out about world around them and are discovering what things around them can do.
3–7 years	Pre-operational	Children are starting to develop thought processes, and are using symbolic play. They find it easier to learn when they can see and use practical examples.

Age	Stage of learning	Characteristics
8–11 years	Concrete Operational	Children are able to think on a more logical level. They can use more abstract concepts, for example a box can represent a car.
12–15 years	Formal Operational	Thought becomes more abstract and less tied to concrete reality. Greater ability to formulate abstract hypotheses and their outcomes.

As an assistant, it is important to recognise that pupils' learning will be based on their own individual experiences, and that they will pass through learning stages, but that the age at which they reach them is not fixed.

Factors which influence children's learning

Children's learning is not only influenced by their stage of development. There are also a number of individual factors which will affect each child when it comes to their learning. These are based on their own experiences and personality so will be different for each pupil. An assistant will need to consider these factors when supporting pupils in order to understand each pupil's needs.

▷ **Intelligence and creativity** – each pupil will have their own talents and aptitudes, so will be more or less able at different tasks within the classroom. They may also perceive themselves to be better or worse than other pupils, and this may affect their motivation. For example, if they notice that another pupil is particularly good at a creative task such as art, they may think that their own work is not as good

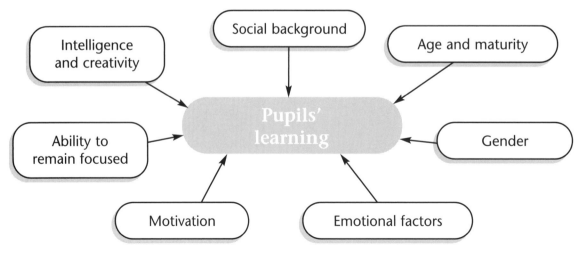

▲ Individual factors will affect each pupil's learning

and feel inadequate. The member of staff will need to speak to and encourage the pupil so that they are able to continue. As pupils will always have strengths and weaknesses in different areas, the role of members of staff will be to encourage pupils and instil an awareness that all of us are different and that this is a positive thing.

▷ **Social background** – pupils' background will have an influence on their learning as they may come to school with a variety of experiences. Some pupils may have had a wide range of social interactions, while others may have had very little. Where pupils' experiences are limited, they may lack confidence with others, find the school difficult to adjust to or take longer to relate to other adults. This may affect their learning as they will take longer to adjust to the school and to others before they are able to focus on tasks. They will need encouragement and praise to develop their confidence and skills when dealing with others.

▷ **Age and maturity** – as we have already seen, children will develop at an individual pace and so in any group of pupils there will be some who are more mature than others. Also, due to the way in which some schools have their intakes, there may be pupils in the same class or group who are almost a year apart in age. This may make a big difference to the range of abilities which exist in the class. Staff should therefore be aware of this factor when monitoring pupils' learning.

▷ **Motivation** – this will directly affect the pupil's learning as it is the pupil's desire to learn and the interest which they have in a task. Where a pupil is not interested, does not see the purpose, or is unable to do a task, they may quickly become de-motivated. Staff should therefore be aware of this and make sure that the task is at the right level, is enjoyable, and makes sense to the pupil.

▷ **Emotional factors** – naturally, pupils will be affected by whether their home life is happy and settled. Some may have been living with parents who are going though a divorce, or they may have been bereaved. Others may be experiencing some form of abuse, or be unsettled by a home life which does not give them stability: for example, irregular meals, parents not often at home. In addition, adolescent children will often have their own agenda and become very involved with groups of friends, experiencing emotional highs and lows which will have a impact on their ability to learn at any given time.

▷ **Gender** – the sex of a pupil may affect their learning, particularly if they have been given greater or fewer opportunities owing to their gender. It is important that we do not favour boys or girls in school when directing questioning and do not have expectations of one sex over another. For example, research shows that girls are generally quicker to read, but this could be due to the expectations of adults.

▷ **Ability to concentrate** – pupils will vary in their ability to concentrate on tasks and to sit and listen when required. Teachers should be aware of the length of time the pupils in their class are able to focus on a task, so that the work given or the amount of time they are required to sit still is not too demanding for them. Where one pupil's ability to concentrate is markedly different from that of their classmates, this may affect the learning of both the individual and of the rest of the class.

Length of concentration expected of children at different stages of development

Very young children will be unable to concentrate for long on one activity and will copy adults and other children, seeking reassurance about what they are doing. As they become older, the length of time children are able to focus on activities will increase although they may be easily distracted and find waiting difficult. By the time children reach secondary school, most of them will be able to concentrate on a task for a given time without distractions, even though some of them may enjoy distracting others!

How to recognise when a pupil is losing concentration

A pupil who is not focused on the teacher or the task may:

▷ start to disturb other pupils
▷ be distracted and fidgety
▷ misbehave and try to gain attention
▷ start daydreaming.

Where pupils are not concentrating on a given task, the teacher or assistant must ensure that they try to engage them again as soon as possible. This can be done through re-involving them in the task. You can do this by:

▷ removing any distractions. This will refocus the pupil's attention on what they are doing.

▷ giving praise where possible for good work which pupils have completed, to give them encouragement.

▷ noticing the good behaviour or work of others so that you are giving positive attention to those pupils who are focusing on their work.

▷ making yourself available and approachable so that pupils are able to ask you for help if they are finding an activity challenging. You will need to develop a good relationship with the pupils so that they will respect and respond to you.

▷ being able to manage spontaneous opportunities which may arise when pupils are working, and remembering to make learning fun!

▷ varying the pace of learning if pupils are finding a task too easy or too difficult. You may need to backtrack, to ensure pupils understand the task, or find ways of extending the task if they complete it quickly.

Think about it

You are working with a group of Year 9 pupils on a geography activity. They have been asked to locate a series of countries on an atlas and to fill in some of the corresponding countries on a sheet. One of the pupils working with you has completed some of the activity but has started to become distracted and is disturbing the dynamics of the group.

▶ What could you do to try to re-involve the pupil in the task?

▶ Are there any other strategies that you could use to make sure that the pupil completes the activity?

Understanding curriculum plans

During Years 7, 8 and 9, pupils will be working from Key Stage 3 of the National Curriculum. In years 10 and 11, when they are working through their GCSE options, they will be in Key Stage 4. It is useful to see how these stages fit in to the education system as a whole:

Curriculum stage	School year
Foundation	Children will be working to the Foundation stage from nursery to the end of the Reception year (ages 3–5)
Key Stage 1	Years 1 and 2 (ages 5–7)
Key Stage 2	Years 3, 4, 5 and 6 (ages 7–11)
Key Stage 3	Years 7, 8 and 9 (ages 11–14)
Key Stage 4	Years 10 and 11 (ages 14–16)
Pupils will take SATs (Standardised Assessment Tasks) at the end of Key Stages 1, 2 and 3, and GCSE at the end of Key Stage 4.	

For the purpose of this unit, you will need to understand that during each of these stages, schools and subject teachers will be working to curriculum plans. These will need to incorporate all areas and subjects that are to be covered under the National Curriculum. Your role as an assistant is to be able to support teachers in the planning and delivery of these plans.

Knowledge into action

Find a copy of the National Curriculum in your school or visit **www.nc.uk.net/** for details of different subject areas.

Planning will usually take place in subject areas and will be broken down into different units of work at the medium term stage and then into short term plans. Each subject should have a member of staff responsible for making sure that they are monitored throughout the school, to attend curriculum courses to remain up to date, and to offer curriculum support to other members of staff. These subject leaders will usually be called subject co-ordinators, or subject managers, for example 'Geography Manager' or 'Head of Modern Languages'. They will also need to devise school curriculum policies for each subject which should outline the school's approach to planning and delivering the subject, and will tie in with National Curriculum guidelines. They may also observe other staff teaching their subject. In this way, each subject is thoroughly monitored.

Find out about...

Curriculum areas in your school.
▶ Who is responsible for English, Maths and Science?
▶ How do they monitor the curriculum within your school?

Long-, medium- and short-term planning

Where teaching staff devise plans for use over a term or half term, these will then be broken down into medium-term plans and short-term plans, which will give greater detail. Lesson plans give precise detail as to the lesson structure, including the length of time to be spent on each activity, the resources needed, the groups to be formed and the role of the teaching assistant. Lesson objectives will be explicitly stated, as will the procedures for differentiation and any homework tasks to be set.

The headteacher may wish to see all copies of plans and staff may discuss them at the long-term planning stage so that everyone's suggestions and expertise are included. When teachers' plans are at the medium-term and short-term stages, there should be consultation with assistants so that they are aware of their role, and have copies of plans so that they can refer to them. This should take place so that assistants can be involved in planning and make their own suggestions as to how they can best support pupils, based on their own experiences. It will also ensure that the assistant is aware of any changes to the normal routine that are to take place during the following week.

Year 7: Non-Fiction Writing	
Teaching Sequence	***assessment pieces**
Week 1	Writing to persuade. Holiday brochure Pre-reading, how texts persuade, words linked with different languages, tenses
Week 2	Writing to argue. Computer games Pre-reading, exploring different views, articles on computers, link words and phrases, using quotes, presenting an argument
Week 3	Writing to advise. 'If' by Kipling Pre-reading, 'If', rhyme and apostrophe, using punctuation, advice phone in
Week 4	Writing to analyse Pre-reading, balancing different views. Supermouse to superman, the meaning of words, topic sentences, discussing a situation, writing to analyse
Week 5	Writing to review Pre-reading, inferring meanings, Jurassic Park, vocabulary, complex sentences, contributing to a discussion, writing a review
Week 6	Writing to comment Pre-reading, human cloning, exploring different views, informal language, expanding sentences, role play and evaluation
Week 7	Review of writing to persuade, argue and advise, reading log, snakes and ladders game. Review of writing to analyse, review and comment, spelling log, word games, crossword

▲ Example of a medium-term plan for English. Such a plan would also contain clear learning objectives for the unit (Larkmead School English Faculty)

▲ Assistants should be aware of the teacher's plans

How pupils may be supported during learning activities

When supporting pupils for different activities, assistants may find themselves in a variety of situations. An individual support assistant, for example, will be assisting and supporting a particular pupil and will usually work alongside or close to that pupil. As that child may have a Statement of Special Educational Needs, they will need that adult support to ensure that they have full access to the curriculum.

Sometimes, teaching assistants will be asked to work with a group of pupils. In this situation, it is vital that all pupils are given the same opportunities to give their thoughts and opinions.

You may also find in the course of your work with pupils that, while working on a particular idea, other learning opportunities become available. You should always use these wherever possible so that the interest of the pupils is maintained and you capitalise on any ideas that they put forward. Assistants will need to use a range of strategies to support the planned learning activities.

▼ Strategies to support learning activities

Skills and strategies used	What to do
1 Instructing pupils	
Teacher may give you methods to teach specific concepts	Ensure that you are clear about the concept and understand the method
You may have the freedom to work on your own ideas	Give pupils a starting point so that they are able to focus
2 Questioning pupils	
Use open-ended questions	Who/what/why, rather than yes/no
Find out what they know first	Make sure pupils understand topic/are focused
Question all in group	Address pupils by name – ensure both quiet and enthusiastic are included

Skills and strategies used	What to do
3 Monitoring pupils Monitor pupils' response to learning activities	Ensure that the pupil is able to achieve Adapt the work so that the pupils maintain their interest
4 Explaining to pupils Make sure all pupils understand the task Make sure all pupils understand the concept they are required to learn	Before you start the activity ask the pupils what they have to do Talk to pupils to check their understanding – rephrase any difficult vocabulary

Effective use of praise during learning activities

As you will be working with pupils who are learning all the time, it is vital that you use praise and encouragement to keep them on task and motivate them in their learning. This kind of reward is very effective, although it must be clear to pupils why they are being praised. It is important as you get to know pupils to praise their efforts as well as their achievements. They will need to have recognition for what they do, and this could take several forms, although you will need to find out the school's policy on the use of rewards, for example:

▷ verbal praise – this could be simple praise as the pupils are working, by saying 'well done, that is a very good sketch,' or by asking the pupil to go and show the teacher at a convenient moment and so gaining another adult's attention

▷ house points and charts – there should be a school policy on how these are used, and you should be aware of this and how much you are able to use them as an assistant.

▷ a school recognition of a good effort, such as the pupil showing the headteacher, or gaining a school certificate, will offer motivation at all ages.

Keys to good practice
Supporting pupils during learning activities

✔ Ensure both you and the pupils understand what you are required to do.

✔ Use a range of questioning strategies.

✔ Make sure you listen to all the pupils.

✔ Reassure pupils who are less confident about their ideas.

✔ Give positive praise wherever possible.

✔ Adapt work where necessary.

✔ Inform the teacher of any problems which have taken place.

✔ Provide a level of assistance which allows pupils to achieve without helping them too much.

Equal opportunities and inclusion, including supporting pupils with Special Educational Needs

As a teaching assistant, you will need to be aware of the way in which pupils with special needs are supported in school and how the process works. Some assistants are also employed specifically to support individual pupils and may need training to be fully aware of that pupil's needs. There is a range of reasons why a pupil may have special needs, for example pupils with:

▷ communication and interaction difficulties

▷ cognition and learning difficulties

▷ physical and/or sensory needs

▷ social or behavioural needs.

The Education Act (1996) states that a pupil has Special Educational Needs if they have a learning difficulty which calls for special educational provision to be made for them. This may be a difficulty in learning which prevents the pupil from working at the same level as the majority of pupils the same age. The pupil may also have a disability which prevents or hinders them from making use of facilities available to others the same age. However, this should not mean that the pupil is excluded from mainstream school, and wherever possible these pupils should be included. (See also pages 98, 99 and 211 for more on the Disability Discrimination Act.)

Pupils who speak English or Welsh as an additional language may also have special educational provision, although they should not be regarded as having a learning difficulty. This support may come from an outside agency that specialises in working with pupils whose first language is not English. They should not need to be put on the school's Special Educational Needs register while they are having support for their language skills. For more on supporting pupils who speak English or Welsh as an additional language, see Unit 3-12.

Statementing

You may encounter pupils who have been given a Statement of Special Educational Needs, or you may have been employed as an individual support assistant to help one of these pupils in the classroom. They will have been through a process to determine whether they need to have support in school, which will result in the pupil being given a Statement and this means they will have an individual support assistant for an agreed number of hours per week. At a classroom level, this will mean that the assistant will work with the pupil's teacher, taking into account the individual pupil's needs. There is more about pupils with special needs in Units 3-13 to 3-16.

Schools need to provide a range of strategies and support while pupils are at different stages on the Special Needs Register, but at Stage S, or when they have a Statement, these will be specified by the Local Education Authority and written down on the pupil's Statement. The pupil's case will need to be formally reviewed annually, which means that everyone who plays a part in supporting the pupil in school will need to attend a review meeting. Where an assistant is specifically employed to work with a pupil who has a Statement, the assistant will be expected to take part in the annual review. This will involve writing a short report about the pupil and attending the review meeting with the Special Needs Co-ordinator, teacher, parents and other representatives. (There will be more on special needs and individual support assistants in Units 3-13 to 3-16.)

Knowledge into action

Find out about any assistants in your school who are employed specifically to work with individual pupils. How might their role be different from that of other assistants?

Promoting equal opportunities and inclusion

At the time of writing, there is much work going into the promotion of inclusion in mainstream schools. This means that more pupils with special needs and disabilities are to be educated alongside their peers wherever possible. The reasons for this are as follows:

1 Human rights

▷ All pupils have a right to learn and play together.

▷ Pupils should not be discriminated against due to learning difficulties or disabilities.

▷ Inclusion is concerned with improving schools for staff as well as for pupils.

2 Equal opportunities in education

▷ Pupils do better in inclusive settings, both academically and socially.

▷ Pupils should not need to be separated to achieve adequate educational provision.

▷ Inclusive education is a more efficient use of educational resources.

3 Social opportunities

▷ Inclusion in education is one aspect of inclusion in society.

▷ Young people need to be involved with all of their peers.

As a result of this, schools may be in the process of writing or reviewing their codes of practice concerning equal opportunities and inclusion. There may also be more assistants in schools supporting pupils with Statements. You should be familiar with your school's policies on inclusion and equal opportunities. There will be more information on inclusion in the learning environment in Unit 3-5.

Case study

Hannah is a Year 8 pupil with a hearing impairment who attends a mainstream school. She has two hearing aids and has a Statement of Special Educational Needs for five hours a week. As Hannah's support assistant, you receive advice from the local sensory support service who have said that she needs to build her confidence when working with others as she feels isolated by her hearing impairment.

1 How could you help Hannah and involve her with other pupils so that she can gain confidence?

2 What could other pupils do to help Hannah?

Managing problems when supporting learning activities

It may be that assistants who are supporting individuals, groups or the whole class encounter problems when supporting learning activities. These could take different forms but could relate to learning resources, the learning environment or the pupils' ability to learn.

▼ Strategies for resolving difficulties

Potential difficulties	How to resolve them
1 Learning resources	The task will usually require a certain amount of resources, for example pencils, paper, worksheets or textbooks, maths apparatus, paint-pots, science equipment and so on. If you have been asked to set up for the pupils you are working with, make sure that you have enough equipment and that it is accessible to the pupils. Also, where you have equipment which needs to be in working order, check that you know how to use it, it is functioning and that the pupils will be able to use it. If the teacher or another member of staff has set up for your task, it is still worth doing a check to ensure that you have everything you will need. In this way you will have avoided potential problems before they arise.
2 Learning environment Problems may arise if there is:	This relates to the suitability of the area where the pupils are working.
a insufficient space to work	If the pupils are working on weighing, for example, and there is no room for them all to have access to the scales, they may quickly lose their focus on the task. There may not be space around the table or work area for the number of pupils that you have been asked to work with. You should always ensure that you have sufficient space for people and equipment before you start.
b too much noise	The pupils may be working with you in a corner of the classroom but any other kind of noise will be a distraction, whether it is from other pupils in the room or from some kind of outside disturbance, such as grass cutting, or noise from a nearby road. It may be possible in this situation for you to investigate another area within the school which is free from this kind of noise, or inform the teacher that the noise level within the classroom is preventing the pupils from benefiting from the activity.
c disturbances from other pupils	This can often be a problem if you are working within the classroom as tasks with close staff supervision can often seem exciting to other pupils. They may be naturally curious to find out what the group or individual is doing, and if there is a continual problem, the teacher should be informed.

Potential difficulties	How to resolve them
3 The pupils' ability to learn Here, again, there may be a variety of reasons why pupils are not able to achieve:	
a pupils' behaviour	If any pupils are not focused on the task due to poor behaviour, you will need to intervene straight away. If they can continue interrupting, they will do so and you will be unable to continue with the task. If there is a particular pupil who is misbehaving and disturbing others, a last resort will be to remove them from the group and work with them later.
b pupils' self-esteem	Sometimes a pupil with low self-esteem may not think that they are able to complete the task which has been set. Some pupils are quite difficult to motivate and you will need to offer reassurance and praise wherever you can to improve their self-esteem. However it is very important to remember that your role is one of a facilitator and that you are not there to complete the task for the pupil. Some pupils may just need a little gentle reassurance and coaxing to 'have a go', while others may be more difficult to work with, and require you to use your questioning skills.
c pupils' lack of concentration	There may be a few reasons for pupils finding it hard to concentrate on the task set. These could include an inability to complete the work – the teacher has made the task too difficult – or the pupil completes the task quickly and needs more stimulation. Some pupils have a very short concentration span, and the task may be taking too long to complete. If this is the case, you will need to stop the pupil and continue with the task later.
d pupils' range of ability	You may find that you are working with a class or group of pupils whose wide range of ability means that some of them are finished before others. If you are faced with a situation where one pupil has finished while others are still working, you may need to have something else ready for them to move on to.

You have been asked to work with a group of Year 7 pupils within the classroom on a task which involves the use of Newton Meters and other equipment. Although you have sufficient space to carry out the task, you quickly find that due to the interest generated, pupils from other groups are repeatedly disturbing your activities, as they are interested in finding out what is happening.

▶ How could you ensure that other pupils do not continue to disturb you?

▶ What could you say to the pupils with whom you are working?

Where you are faced with difficulties in supporting pupils and are unable to get them to achieve the learning outcomes which have been set, you must always make sure that the teacher is aware of the problems. This is because each pupil needs to be monitored with regard to their learning, and this will need to be recorded.

Evidence collection

You are working with a group of pupils to support a language activity in German, as this is one of your areas of strength. Although you are only working with a group of five, two of them are clearly not focused on the activity and will not achieve the learning objective of the session.

▶ What would you say to the pupils who are not focused on the task?

▶ How could you encourage them to work with the others on what they should be doing?

▶ What would you do if the pupils continued to behave in this way?

Element 3-3.2 Promote independent learning

Pupils will always need to be encouraged to think and act for themselves as much as possible. As an assistant, you will need to learn skills and strategies for developing these abilities in pupils. You will also need to be aware of different learning styles and how to adapt your support strategies to accommodate them. Remember that pupils develop at very different rates – some will be able to pick things up quickly and concentrate for long periods, while others will seem 'younger' and need to have more support. As a result, the teacher will need to differentiate tasks, or give pupils work that is appropriate to their own ability.

For this element you will need to know and understand the following:

▶ supporting different learning styles

▶ strategies to encourage pupils to learn independently

▶ helping pupils to review their own learning.

Supporting different learning styles

Pupils will have a variety of learning styles, owing to the fact that we will all absorb information and learn differently. Howard Gardner (*Multiple Intelligences*, 1993) describes a view of seven intelligences. These have been formulated using biological as well as cultural research, and vary from traditional views of how we learn. This has implications for how we teach children, as Gardner's theory states that all seven intelligences are needed to productively function in society. Traditionally, our education systems have placed a strong emphasis on verbal and mathematical intelligences. We must therefore teach pupils a broader range of talents and skills.

The seven intelligences are:

▷ **Logical mathematical intelligence** – this consists of the ability to think logically and sequentially and reason deductively. It is most often associated with scientific and mathematical thinking. Those who learn best in this way tend to be very organised in their learning.

▷ **Linguistic intelligence** – these people will have the ability to manipulate language, both in order to express themselves and as a means of remembering information.

▷ **Spatial intelligence** – those who have spatial intelligence will find it easy to manipulate images or pictures in order to solve problems, for example when following instructions such as furniture assembly.

▷ **Musical intelligence** – this means that these individuals will respond to musical pitches, tones and rhythms. They may find it easier to retain information if they learn it while listening to music or through rhythms.

▷ **Bodily-Kinaesthetic intelligence** – those who learn in this way are more likely to need to learn things in a physical way, for example through practical tasks.

▷ **Personal intelligences** – these include **interpersonal** feelings or how people relate to others, and **intrapersonal** – the ability to understand one's own feelings and motivations. These two intelligences are separate from each other.

▷ **Naturalist** – those who can distinguish among, classify and use features of objects in the environment, for example, a pupil who is able to talk about the features of different makes of car.

Although everyone is born possessing the seven intelligences, pupils will come into the classroom with their own unique set which have been developed to a greater or lesser extent. This will determine how easy or difficult it is for them to learn information

▲ Different methods of teaching will accommodate the different learning styles of pupils

when it is presented in a particular way. Pupils will need to be given different methods of learning within the framework of lessons to accommodate these different learning styles, and you will need to be aware of this in order to support their learning activities.

Case study

Jack is in Year 9 and finds it hard to remember and retain information. He has approached you as he is worried about his SATs and knows that he will have to revise, which he finds difficult.

How do you think you could help, knowing about different learning styles?

Different methods of learning

▷ **Repetition** – the pupil is given a task which involves going over something which the teacher has done in class, for example working on a point of grammar in a foreign language. The pupils may then be asked to complete some work which involves writing and repeating several times, but is set out in such a way as to challenge the pupils and also to ensure that they achieve the objectives. When working on a repetitive task, pupils will need support which involves reminding them about what the teacher has said and provoking them to think about what they are doing, but without giving them the answers. Sometimes it is a good idea to ask the pupil what they have been asked to do, as it is a starting point to finding out how much they have taken in.

▷ **Instruction** – pupils may be set a task which involves following a series of steps. This will lead them to arriving at a set outcome, for example when they are learning to make an item for design technology or a new art technique. It could also include learning to carry out simple number operations. In this situation, assistants will find that they are leading pupils to a particular outcome, so the types of questions they should be asking would be, 'Why do you think we do it this way rather than another way?' or 'Do you think that this is the best way of doing this? Can you find another way?'. Questions like this will encourage pupils to think about what they are doing and why they are doing it in that way, which may help them to remember what they have learned.

▷ **Facilitating** – this method involves giving pupils the tools to carry out a task and then allowing them the freedom to devise their own outcome. An example of this may be showing them how to mix colours and then allowing them to experiment to find different shades, or giving them construction equipment and letting them discover how to use it and what they are able to do. Similar questioning styles could be used for this method as for learning by instruction, although assistants could ask pupils first to talk them through what they are doing and why.

▷ **Collaboration** – this method involves groups of pupils working together to discuss or discover ideas. In doing this, they will also learn how to work as part of a team and to listen to others' views. Some pupils find this easy although others will need more guidance, which is where an assistant is needed to help. An example of this could be deciding on the best way to carry out a simple maths investigation or working on an argument for a debate. This is one of the more challenging activities to support, as there will always be pupils who wish to dominate the flow of ideas and similarly pupils who do not mind taking a less active role. The important thing to remember is to allow everyone to give their opinion and then work out a way within the group of tackling the task.

▷ **Problem solving** – pupils should be given regular opportunities to solve problems and to think about different, open-ended ways of approaching tasks which may not have a set outcome. In this way they will be encouraged to think for themselves rather than relying on a particular way of working.

In a classroom, there should be a balanced mix of methods of learning. However, it is important for pupils to have as many opportunities as possible to be responsible for their own decision-making (see opposite 'Strategies to encourage pupils to learn independently'). This will encourage their own independence and creativity, and will also help them to gain confidence in their abilities.

Resources

These learning methods, along with the resources used, should also be agreed with the teacher before tasks are carried out. The kinds of resources you may be required to use with pupils will vary from books and other paper-based materials to use of the Internet and CD-ROMs. The teacher should usually give you an indication of the resources required but you should be aware of where different curriculum areas store their resources in case you need to find them.

▲ Some pupils enjoy the challenge of making their own decisions but others need more guidance

Strategies to encourage pupils to learn independently

Where you are working with pupils on any task, you must remember that in order to learn they should carry out the task independently as far as possible. Depending on the way that the task has been set, you should offer as much encouragement as is needed while allowing pupils to develop their own self-help skills.

What you can do:

▷ Find out about pupils' different learning styles, if possible, so that you can encourage the pupils in a way which makes sense to them.

▷ Give positive encouragement and praise – this will give pupils a feeling of achievement and desire to sustain their interest in learning activities. Pupils will be visibly boosted by praise when they are doing well.

▷ Listen carefully to pupils – they will be aware if a member of staff is only partially interested or paying attention to what they are saying. It is important to take notice of their contributions so that they feel that they are being valued. In this way they will feel confident in their own abilities.

▷ Motivate pupils through positive experiences which are interesting and can be made real to them. Pupils will particularly enjoy and benefit from having artefacts and real objects to handle when learning. For example, pupils learning about a religion will remember more if they have seen examples of different items which may be used.

▷ Provide a level of assistance which allows pupils to achieve without helping them too much. This could be simply giving them a list of things which they may need to consider when carrying out a task, or remembering not to give them help as soon as they ask for it. Try saying, ' Have you thought about another way of doing this?' or 'Are there any other things you need to remember?'

▷ Ensure that pupils have sufficient resources to complete the task so that they do not need to seek staff help. If you know that pupils are going to need particular items to carry out a task, ensure that they are accessible – or that pupils know where to find them within the classroom.

Think about it

You have been asked to work with a group of pupils on individually designing and making a puzzle. What method of learning would you use with the pupils? How could you manage their independent learning without giving them too much help?

Knowledge into action

Ask the teacher if you can observe a group of pupils working alongside him or her. In what ways are they being encouraged to work independently?

Helping pupils to review their own learning

When pupils have completed a task, staff may review it with a group, or with individual pupils, or as a whole class. This means that they should discuss what they were asked to do and how they went about it. They may then talk about whether they think that the task went well and what they felt was successful or unsuccessful and why. This encourages the pupils to think about strategies and ideas they used, and also to compare their method with that of others. It is important for pupils to look at different ways of doing tasks so that they are aware that there may not be a right or wrong way; some pupils are lacking in confidence and worried about 'getting it wrong'.

Knowledge into action

Think of an example of a strategy which you have used in class to help pupils to review their learning achievements. How did this help them to plan for future learning activities?

Case study

Max has designed and made a lunchbox using recycled materials. He has included a handle to pick up the box. Max has found that the first handle he made was not strong enough to pick up the lunchbox, so in his review he discussed the problems that he had and how he found a better material. He then thought about and discussed with the class whether he thought any other materials may have produced even better results. Through working on different ideas and looking at other materials, Max was able to improve his design so that the lunchbox had a stronger handle.

Evidence collection

The next time you are asked to carry out an activity with a group, think about how it will appeal to pupils who are more developed in the areas of linguistic and logical intelligence. How can you make it more appealing to those in the group who may be less developed in these areas? What other support can you give the pupils to encourage them to learn independently? Write a report on this to use as evidence.

End of unit test

1 What are the two main theories of how children learn?
2 How can you keep pupils motivated when they are working?
3 What are some of the factors which affect the way in which children learn?
4 How could you help a pupil who is losing concentration on a task?
5 Name the three different types of planning found in a secondary school.
6 What kinds of praise can you give to pupils to motivate them?
7 What are the seven different learning styles?
8 What are the main principles of inclusion?
9 How can you promote independent learning in pupils?

References

Children Act 1989 (HMSO)

Education Act 1996 (HMSO)

Index for Inclusion (CSIE, 2000)

Gardner, Howard, *Multiple Intelligences: The Theory in Practice* (Basic Books, 1993)

Unit 3-4 Review and develop your own professional practice

There are two elements to this unit. These are:

3-4.1 Review your own professional practice
3-4.2 Develop your professional practice

Element 3-4.1 Review your own professional practice

As a professional member of staff within a school, you will be expected to undergo regular staff training and courses to keep you up to date with developments in secondary education. You should also expect to have an annual appraisal after being in post for 12 months, or completing your probationary year. This element looks at how the appraisal or Performance Management system works within schools, and what you should expect from it. It will also explore your role and responsibilities within the school and how these fit in with the roles and responsibilities of others. For the purpose of the NVQ, you will need to collect evidence to demonstrate how you make contributions to support the teacher, the pupil, the curriculum and the school.

For this element you will need to know and understand the following:

▶ procedures and principles of self-appraisal and how to apply these to working practices
▶ school expectations and requirements about the role of a teaching assistant
▶ how to measure your own practice against the expectations of your role
▶ the main roles and responsibilities of others within the school: working with others.

Procedures and principles of self-appraisal

The appraisal system is designed to help members of staff to consider their own professional performance on a regular basis. This should ensure that they think about their career and highlight areas for development.

The main consideration is that the appraisal process is a positive and non-threatening one. Each member of staff, including headteachers, will be appraised by the person who has responsibility for managing them. In the case of the headteacher, this will usually be done by governors. With teaching staff, the process is an ongoing cycle which takes place annually. As an assistant, you may be appraised by your line manager or member of staff responsible for teaching assistants. In the case of individual support assistants, this may be done by the school's Special Needs Co-ordinator (SENCo).

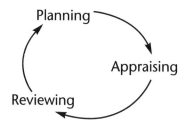

Planning

Appraising

Reviewing

▲ The planning cycle

Assistants should find that the appraisal process is a good opportunity to discuss issues which may not otherwise be approached. It is also useful for discussing with your line manager anything you have done which you feel has been more or less successful than you had anticipated.

How the appraisal system works

The general appraisal form opposite gives some idea of how the initial discussion with your line manager might be structured. However, this is a basic outline and further ideas such as whether you would like a more formal observation of your work may be recorded. If this is the case, the focus and timing of the observation should be decided at the initial meeting. An observation may take place if you or your manager feel that you would benefit from some feedback concerning your work: for example, if you are not sure that your methods for giving pupils praise are as effective as you would like. You will then agree on any action to be taken and new targets for the coming year. Following the meeting, copies of the appraisal form will be given to you and to the headteacher for record keeping, but will be confidential.

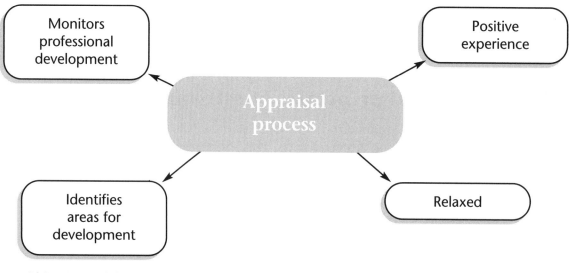

▲ Objectives of the appraisal process

Keys to good practice
Individual appraisal

✔ Check through your job description before the meeting.

✔ Be prepared by having some ideas of strengths and successes.

✔ Think about areas you may wish to develop before going to the meeting.

? Think about it

To help you to think about your appraisal, try completing the questions on the appraisal form below.

General self-appraisal

It would be useful if you could bring this information with you to your initial meeting, to help you to identify your needs as part of the appraisal process.

1 Do you feel that your job description is still appropriate? Do you feel that there are any changes which need to be made?

2 What targets were set at the last appraisal/when you started your job? Have you achieved your targets?

3 What are the reasons for not having achieved your targets?

4 What aspect of your job satisfies you the most?

5 What aspect of your job has not been as successful as you had anticipated?

6 Are there any areas of your work that you would like to improve?

7 What training have you received? Has it been successful?

8 What are your current training needs?

▲ The first page of an appraisal form

School expectations and requirements about the role of the teaching assistant

When starting at a new school, the duties and individual requirements of each teaching assistant's job will be outlined in their job description. It is important to keep a copy of this, as it will be useful to read it from time to time to check that it is a realistic reflection of expectations.

Assistants may take on a number of different roles depending on these criteria (see also the introduction for a description of these). Broadly speaking, their role is to encourage, guide, assist and support – both practically and on a curricular level.

The types of responsibilities which may be required of teaching assistants

Assistants are likely to have a number of responsibilities within the school, both in and outside the classroom. The responsibilities of a teaching assistant and individual support assistant will be slightly different, although there may be areas in which they overlap – for example helping to prepare resources in the classroom as all assistants should be prepared to give this type of help.

How the responsibilities of classroom assistants and individual support assistants may differ

Classroom assistant	Individual support assistant
Duties may include:	**Duties may include:**
Assisting teacher with classroom organisation	Developing an understanding of the specific needs of the pupil
Attending planning meetings	To assist the class teacher with the development of an individual programme of support
Preparing resources	
Supervising individual pupils or groups	To help the pupil to learn effectively

You will need to be aware of the many different tasks which an assistant may be asked to carry out. Although schools will usually have outlined these at interview or in a job description, you do not want to be surprised by any requests on the first day! Make sure that you are aware of the possible tasks which you may be required to do. You may require training or help if you have not done some of these before.

How would you feel about being asked to:

▷ mount and put up wall displays
▷ give extra support to a pupil who was new to the school
▷ get a computer suite ready for a class to use
▷ help pupils who speak English as a second language
▷ do playground duty
▷ tidy a resource cupboard.

? Think about it

What types of tasks have you been asked to do in the classroom? Are any of them different to those listed above?

The list above is not exhaustive and there will be a much broader range of activities which an assistant may be asked to perform. In many cases, simply having another member of staff in the classroom will take the pressure off the teacher when calming pupils or managing practical tasks. It would be useful to have some time with teachers on a weekly basis or access to timetable or plans so that work may be fully supported and there is some prior knowledge of the kind of work that will be required during the week. The teacher should also give more detailed guidance when the assistant is required to work with a group of pupils.

If there are any administrative difficulties, with details such as contracts or hours worked, they will usually be addressed by the school office in consultation with the headteacher.

It should be remembered that the role of a teaching assistant is one of support. The assistant may need to be able to take responsibility for the class on some occasions but this will always have been indicated by the class teacher. It may be difficult on occasions to 'read' a situation and the advice of the teacher should always be sought if there is any problem or doubt as to how to proceed.

Case study

Sarah has been employed as an individual support assistant in a secondary school. She has been working there for three weeks when she is asked to accompany the pupil she supports on a school trip. Although she is only employed to work mornings, she is expected to be on the trip for the whole day.

1 What should Sarah do if she is concerned about the hours she is expected to work?

2 Would Sarah be justified in saying that she was unable to go on the trip?

Oakhurst Secondary School

Job Description

Teaching Assistant

Responsibilites

Responsible under the direction of the headteacher or another designated teacher to assist in the classroom.

Duties

Main duties will include:

▷ Assisting in classroom organisation, preparing materials and resources where appropriate.

▷ Supervising activities organised by the classroom teacher.

▷ Supervising pupils usually in the presence of a teacher.

▷ Providing general care and welfare.

▷ Any other duties as required commensurate with the level of responsibility of the post.

▲ An example of a job description for a teaching assistant

There may also be a 'Person Specification', which should set out personal qualities which are relevant to the particular post. It may include some of the strengths listed below.

Be a good communicator/enjoy working with others

It is vital that an assistant is able to share thoughts and ideas with others, and is comfortable doing this.

Use initiative

Assistants will need to be able to decide for themselves how to use their time if the teacher is not always available to ask. There will always be jobs which need doing in a classroom, even if this just means sharpening pencils or making sure that books are tidy and in the right place.

Respect confidentiality

It should be remembered that in a position of responsibility, it is essential to maintain confidentiality. Assistants may sometimes find that they are placed in a position where they are made aware of personal details concerning a pupil or family. Although background and school records are available to those within the school, it is not appropriate to discuss them with outsiders.

Be sensitive to pupils' needs

Whether an individual or teaching assistant, it is important to be able to judge how much support to give while still encouraging pupils' independence. Pupils need to be sure about what they have been asked to do and may need help organising their thoughts or strategies, but it is the pupil who must do the work and not the assistant.

Have good listening skills

A teaching assistant needs to be able to listen to others and have a sympathetic nature. This is an important quality for your interactions, both with pupils and other members of staff.

Be willing to undertake training for personal development

In any school there will always be occasions on which assistants are invited or required to undergo training and these opportunities should be taken wherever possible. You may also find that your role changes within the school due to movement between classes or changing year groups. You will need to be flexible and willing to adapt to different expectations.

Be firm but fair with the pupils

Pupils will always quickly realise if a member of staff is not able to set fair boundaries of behaviour. Staff should always make sure that when they start working with pupils they make these boundaries clear.

Enjoy working with pupils and have a sense of humour

Assistants will need to be able to see the funny side of working with pupils and it is often a very useful asset!

▲ It is important to be a communicator to build a relationship with pupils

How to measure your own practice against expectations of your role

As part of your NVQ, you will be expected to be able to show how you contribute to your working environment by the support you give to others. You should work closely with your line manager or supervisor, who should be able to advise you on the most effective ways of turning your experiences into evidence for your portfolio. Think carefully about your job description and how it relates to the following:

How you support the teacher within the school

This will include the type of support you give to the teacher, which may be in the form of many different tasks. It may be helpful for your line manager to discuss with you some of the ways in which your work and that of the teacher complement one another. This could be through planning, practical tasks or support you give with often minor activities, which can build up when dealing with a class or group.

How you support the class or individual pupil

You will also be required to provide evidence of ways in which you support and raise pupil achievement within the school. It can be easier for individual support assistants than for teaching assistants to find this evidence. This is because they are working with one pupil and are focusing on individual targets and areas for that pupil, through working on Individual Education Plans (IEPs). They will also have the input of other professionals, as well as the class teacher, to give them ideas and support when implementing IEP targets. They will therefore be able to see how that pupil is developing and have more evidence of how their work has had an effect.

Teaching assistants may need to keep records of achievement of specific pupils with whom they work within classes in order to demonstrate that they are raising pupil achievement. You will need to ask the teachers of these classes what kinds of work you may be able to use for evaluation purposes. You may also be able to photograph pieces of work the pupils have done with you, or any displays for which you have been responsible. These will all be valuable sources of evidence.

How you support the curriculum

You will need to think about ways in which you help the class to gain access to the curriculum. Consider especially the support you give during Literacy and Numeracy and any additional training which you have undertaken.

▲ You can help the class to gain access to the curriculum in a variety of ways

How you support the school

This will be through your attitude to others, your reliability and sense of responsibility, the way in which you react to situations which may sometimes be unexpected, and how you encourage the pupils in their own development of these qualities. You might also support school activities, for example a school fair, or be part of school community events.

? Think about it

You are an assistant working in a classroom, which is located in two mobiles away from the rest of the school. You have arrived early one day to prepare the classroom and notice two pupils from Year 8 who are damaging some plants in the school's wildlife area.

▶ What would be your first reaction?

▶ Why shouldn't you ignore what is happening?

Working with others

Assistants should be aware of how their role fits into the school as a whole, in order to gain an overall view of how systems will fit together.

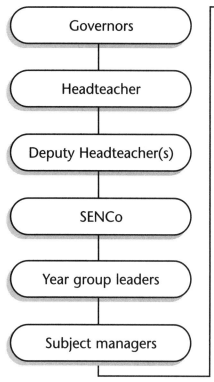

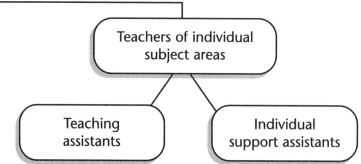

It may be that within this system responsibilities overlap, for example a year group leader may also be a subject manager, or a deputy headteacher may also be a SENCo but without a heavy teaching commitment. There will also be a Senior Management Team who work with the headteacher to discuss priorities as they occur and then disseminate these to other staff. As will be seen later, the most important thing to remember is that the lines of communication between members of staff are kept open and that all staff are valued.

▲ Example of the management system within a secondary school

The role of the school governors

Every school will have a governing body. This body is responsible, along with the headteacher, for making decisions about the school. It is made up of different groups, or committees, each of which should meet on a regular basis. These groups should then report back to the full governing body. The groups below are examples of the kinds of committees that may be found within a school governing body.

Finance Committee – this is responsible for making sure that the school's finances are managed efficiently.
Personnel Committee – this will be responsible for staffing and personnel management.
Facilities Committee – this committee has responsibility for the buildings and site management of the school.
Curriculum Committee – this will make decisions on issues involving the curriculum and whether to adopt new policies.

The governors will be representatives from the local community along with teacher and parent representatives from the school who may bring different areas of expertise. There may be a governor who has particular knowledge about legal issues. Another may be more knowledgeable in the area of finance. Together these volunteers will have a wide area of knowledge which may be useful when discussing issues relating to the school.

Find out about...

Your school's governing body.
▶ How often do they meet together?
▶ Are staff in the school aware of the role of the school governors?
▶ Is there a teacher or staff governor?

The role of the headteacher

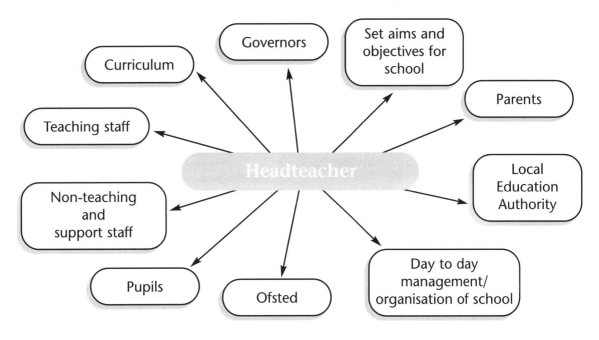

▲ The role of the headteacher is to manage all aspects of the school

The headteacher is responsible for managing the school and all those within it, as well as making sure that the curriculum is being effectively taught and managed. He or she is answerable to parents, the local authority and Ofsted for the smooth running and efficiency of the school, and whether it represents good value for money. The headteacher will be a member of all the committees in the school's governing body and will need to attend all meetings.

The role of the deputy

The deputy headteacher usually still acts in a teaching role, although in some larger schools this may not be the case. The deputy may be responsible for managing day-to-day arrangements such as organising supply staff and setting up training courses, arranging visits by student teachers and so on. The deputy needs to liaise with the headteacher on a daily basis concerning the day's priorities. The deputy works alongside the headteacher to manage the school, and can advise staff. When the headteacher is absent from the school, the deputy is responsible for its management. In larger schools, there may be two deputy headteachers.

→ Knowledge into action

What role does the deputy headteacher play in your school? If the deputy has a teaching commitment, does he or she have time out of the classroom for any managerial duties?

Year group or subject leaders

Year group or subject leaders will have responsibility for a subject or for managing a group of teachers within their year. This may be the case in both primary and secondary schools. These teachers may be members of the school's senior management team and, along with the headteacher and deputy, be involved in decisions about practical and day-to-day issues, such as:

▷ organisation of staff

▷ planning extra curricular activities

▷ fundraising events

▷ arranging the school calendar

▷ initial discussion of areas for development (School Improvement or Development Plan).

Special Educational Needs Co-ordinator (SENCo)

The SENCo is responsible for managing pupils with special needs throughout the school. They will need to keep up-to-date records on all these pupils as well as being responsible for the management of individual support assistants in the school. The SENCo will be the line of contact for any outside agencies who need to come into the school to look at individual pupils with special needs.

These may include the following:

▷ **Speech and Language Unit** – offers therapy and advice for pupils with speech and communication difficulties. Parents will usually take pupils for therapy. May also come into school to give advice for targets.

- ▷ **Behaviour Management Unit** – SENCo may refer pupils to this unit. They will then come into school to observe and give individual or group sessions.
- ▷ **Educational psychologist** – based at the local authority, the EP will come into school to assess pupils who are in need of extra support.
- ▷ **Learning Support Service** – offers advice for staff and comes into school to offer support. It may be able to provide additional help in areas such as literacy. Usually a limited number of hours per term.
- ▷ **English as an Additional Language Unit** – takes EAL pupils for assessment and small group work during school hours.
- ▷ **Sensory Support Service** – offers advice and support for pupils with sensory impairment, e.g. visual or aural.
- ▷ **Occupational therapist/physiotherapist** – may be referred by school but usually takes place elsewhere. There may be a waiting list.

→ *Knowledge into action*

If you are an individual support assistant, what contact have you had with any of these agencies? How do they help the pupil you are supporting?

Form tutors

The class teacher is responsible for delivering the National Curriculum in their subject as well as the pastoral care of their class. In both primary and secondary schools they may also be responsible for managing a subject area. They may also advise any support staff within their class as to what they are required to do on a daily basis.

How information is passed through the school

Clear communication within any establishment is important. Within each school there will be procedures through which information reaches each member of staff. This is to ensure that everyone is aware of their responsibilities and knows what is happening in the school.

Information can be passed on through:

- ▷ meetings (governors, teaching staff, senior management, year groups, assistants, midday supervisors may all have their own meetings)
- ▷ noticeboards and newsletters
- ▷ informal discussions
- ▷ staff bulletins
- ▷ Parent Teacher Association.

Support staff may report to individual subject teachers on a daily basis and be guided by them as to their activities with pupils. However, classroom and support assistants may also have their own manager, or teacher who is responsible for passing on any information to them. In a larger school there may be regular meetings specifically for assistants. In a smaller school, or if there is no such meeting, it is important that there are opportunities for them to discuss their role with a named member of staff. This will ensure that assistants are aware of important issues within the school as a whole. It is also a good way of getting to chat to others who are doing the same job, and to share ideas and experiences. While classroom assistants and individual support assistants report to the class teacher on a daily basis and are guided by them as to their day-to-day activities with the pupils, it is usually the case that another member of staff will be their overall manager.

Case study

Alex has just started as a support assistant in a secondary school. She is to support Jack, who is autistic, for three hours each day, but is also responsible for a small group of EMAS* pupils during the afternoons.

1 What might be the advantages and disadvantages of working in two separate roles?

2 What opportunities should Alex have to speak to someone about her roles?

* EMAS groups are set up to support pupils who are speakers of other languages.

Evidence collection

How often do you have meetings with your line manager? What sorts of topics are discussed? Keep a record of these so that you are able to report on them if you need to. You will be able to use these records as evidence for your portfolio.

Element 3-4.2 Develop your professional practice

This element shows how you can make use of development opportunities within your employment. It will give an idea of some of the ways in which you can access specific training opportunities to benefit your own needs and those of the pupils you support. It will also give you examples of how you may raise your own professional development through other opportunities which arise in your normal day-to-day practice. You will also need to know how to demonstrate and present evidence that you are raising pupils' achievement within the class. Finally, you need to be aware of national and local developments and how these will affect your role within the school.

For this element you will need to know and understand the following:

▶ development opportunities and support systems which are available to assistants

▶ models of performance which apply to teaching assistants

▶ the implementation of School Development Plans and local and national plans for development which may have an impact on your role within the school.

Development opportunities and support systems

Teaching assistants may find that, following the appraisal process, there are particular targets which they need to address concerning their own professional development. In order to develop professionally, it is important for assistants to be aware of the different opportunities which are available to them. The targets which are decided upon at appraisal need to be SMART, that is, Specific, Measurable, Achievable, Realistic and Time-bound.

▷ **Specific** – you must make sure your target says exactly what is required.

▷ **Measurable** – you should ensure that you will be able to measure whether the target has been achieved.

▷ **Achievable** – the target should not be inaccessible or too difficult.

▷ **Realistic** – you should ensure that you will have access to the training or resources which may be required.

▷ **Time-bound** – there should be a limit to the time you have to achieve your target.

Example of the types of targets decided upon at appraisal

Target	Action
To develop confidence using computer. To access training and qualifications	To take at least one basic computer course during the year
To develop understanding of dyspraxia during the year	To undertake training courses with qualifications where available

The individual support assistant who was the subject of this appraisal (see table above) felt that she did not have enough awareness of dyspraxia to support the pupil effectively. It was agreed that she should attend training courses as soon as possible in order to benefit both her and the pupil. She also felt that she did not have enough confidence when using the computer and that this was preventing her from helping both the pupil she was supporting and also other pupils in the class. It was agreed that she should attend further courses for this but in the meantime to use the computer in the classroom wherever possible so that she could increase her confidence. The class teacher would need to be aware of this target so that the assistant could be fully supported.

There may also be other targets which assistants feel they need to develop and which can be accessed through visiting other classes in the school or observing Literacy or Numeracy lessons. These targets should all be agreed within a set time scale so that they can be reviewed at a later date.

Finding out about courses which are available

Assistants will usually be able to find out through their school the different courses which may be available to them. You may find that the school invites people from various agencies to speak to staff about particular subject areas during staff meetings, and these may be optional for support staff. Your line manager or supervisor should be able to give you information about training and help you to decide on the best courses and meetings to attend. The SENCo may be able to give you details about specific special educational needs courses, such as those run by the Sensory Support Service, or Behaviour Management Unit. Where you are not in a school or have difficulty finding help, the Local Education Authority should publish details of courses which are run for teachers and support staff. You may also be able to contact the local borough for information about training for assistants as this is undergoing a period of national change. The borough's education department should have a member of staff responsible for training who will also be able to advise you.

Case study

Shona has been working in Year 7. She has just heard that a pupil with a hearing impairment is to start at the school in the following term. She would like to find out more about how she may be able to help the pupil when he starts.

1 Where could Shona get some more information about helping hearing-impaired pupils?

2 Is there anything else Shona could do to prepare for the pupil's entry into secondary school?

Other development opportunities which may exist in school

If you are employed by the school as a teaching assistant on a permanent contract, you may find that you are able to have some say in choosing to work in an area of particular interest. For example, if you have always supported one or two particular subject areas but have an interest in others or a skill which you would like to use, you may be able to request this through discussion with your supervisor or at appraisal. You may also find that this means you have always worked with the same teachers. It is always of benefit to see how different staff work and to pick up on ideas which may be useful to you in your role.

→ **Knowledge into action**

What particular areas of interest do you have in the curriculum? Do you know the member of staff responsible for this curriculum area? How could you develop your interest in this area?

✓ **Keys to good practice**
Areas for development

✔ Make sure you are aware of when and where courses are run for support staff.

✔ Look out for opportunities for development as they become available.

✔ Speak to your line manager or the curriculum manager about particular areas of interest.

✔ Keep up to date with national developments through reading educational publications.

Models of performance which apply to teaching assistants

Assistants should be aware of models of performance which will have an impact on their training needs for professional qualifications. The National Occupational Standards for Teaching Assistants offer guidance on the wider aspects of competent performance. They have been accredited by the Qualifications and Curriculum Authority (QCA), and are an important basis of practice. They form the basis for the NVQ and SNVQ Levels 2 and 3. Other models of performance which are accessible to assistants include local and national guidelines for codes of practice, provided by government bodies such as the DfES and Ofsted. These are often available in school or through the DfES and Ofsted websites.

Assistants should also be aware that they can access expert advice and working practices by looking at practitioners within both the school and local authority. You may need to ask your line manager if you can watch experienced assistants at work in the school, or whether you can speak to local support service staff about any particular needs which you may have.

The types of problems which may arise

You may find that while you are working towards your own professional development you come up against problems within your own school. These may, for example, be concerning other individuals with whom you work, or your own training needs.

You should make sure that you address any problems as soon as possible although this can often be difficult to do.

▷ Speak to your line manager if you feel that you are not being given enough direction by the class teacher. It may be that there is a limited amount of time to discuss plans or go through work that you are going to do with the pupils. It is vital that you are able to communicate and will save valuable time in the long run.

▷ If there is not enough management time or advice being given to you and other assistants, you should approach a member of staff that you feel is experienced and will offer practical advice. This may be a teacher or another person within the school who you can approach in confidence.

▷ If you feel that your training needs are not being met, or that you do not have access to training materials and information, you should discuss this with your line manager or, if this is not possible, another member of the senior management team. They will be able to advise you and give you ideas about career development.

▷ If there are any targets which have been set but which are not being addressed, again you should discuss these with your line manager.

Where there are difficulties with individual members of staff, for example your line manager is off sick long term, you may need to use your discretion and ask for advice from any member of staff in the school who you feel is approachable. Remember it is important for the school as well as your own personal development that you are properly trained and guided in your role.

Case study

You have been asked to work with a pupil with Down's Syndrome in a Year 8 class for two terms to cover another assistant's maternity leave. You feel that you should have some training in this area but there has been none offered. You do not like to rock the boat as you are happy in your school but feel that you need to know more about your role in order to carry out your duties effectively and to support the pupil to the best of your ability.

▶ What should you do?

The implementation of school development plans

School Improvement, or School Development Plans, are documents which are usually devised by the headteacher in consultation with the teaching staff. They give details of any curriculum or other areas within the school which are to be developed over the coming year. They may be broken down into sections which set out the aims and success criteria for each area of development. Support staff should be involved in areas for development as they may require training along with teaching staff. An example of this would be the introduction of new IT training within the school, or a set of new school rules. The School Development Plan may list around 8-10 areas for development over the year. There may also be a long-term Improvement Plan at the back which will give details of priorities over the next few years.

Below is an example of part of a School Development Plan in which support staff are involved.

Assessment	
Aims: To review short term planning to enable more precise assessment.	**Action Plan:** 1 Short term planning documents amended and trialled. ▶ Years 7–9 ▶ Years 10 and 11
To update the Assessment Policy to reflect new practice in the school.	2 Review and amend the Assessment Policy.
To develop the role of teaching and support assistants to enable them to be involved more effectively in assessment.	3 Staff have training to develop the assessment role of all assistants. 4 Staff have training on aspects of formative assessment.

Targets and success criteria:
1 Short-term plans will enable more precise assessment by March 2004.
2 Assessment Policy will have been amended by March 2004.
3 Teachers will use a wider range of formative assessment skills to improve teaching and learning by March 2004.
4 Teaching assistants will be used in assessment by March 2004.

Monitored by: Headteacher
Governor's Curriculum Committee

Evaluated by: Deputy Headteacher (Assessment Manager)

There may not be many areas for development in which support staff are specifically involved: there should, however, be school procedures in practice to ensure that they are aware of this involvement.

Any involvement which you are expected to have will have an impact on your contribution to the school's performance as a whole. It may therefore be worth considering including any involvement which you are to have as part of your own professional development targets when deciding on these at appraisal.

Are you aware of any involvement which support staff have in your current School Development Plan? What system does your school have in place to raise your awareness of any involvement you may have?

Local and national plans for development

As support staff, assistants will be involved with any local or national plans for development which come into effect. An example of this on a national level would be the new Code of Practice for Special Educational Needs, which came into effect in January 2002 and has implications for individual support assistants in their work with SEN pupils. All secondary schools will be expected to have a written SEN policy to provide an adequate level of support for pupils with special needs. Support staff need to understand the implications of all curriculum changes and how they will have an effect on everyday classroom practice.

On a local level, there may not be as many changes which take place, but the Local Education Authority will advise the school, which in turn should tell you, of any changes that occur. These may involve restructuring of management within the borough or a change in documentation requirements which schools are asked to provide. If you are involved in specific requirements, you should receive guidance from your line manager or class teacher.

Within your school environment, the changes which occur are likely to be in relation to those with whom you work or working practices. If your school has a new headteacher or SENCo, or you are asked to work with a different teacher, you may find that they have a slightly different approach. You may also be able to update your own development objectives as a result of these changes, as their areas of expertise will be different.

Evidence collection

Think about the different evidence you could present to demonstrate the work that you have done with children. How can you show that you are supporting:

a the teacher

b the pupils

c the curriculum

d the school?

End of unit test

1 Why should support staff have regular appraisal?

2 What is the role of a teaching assistant?

3 Which of the following would a teaching assistant be expected to do:

   a sharpening pencils

   b taking pupils on school trips

   c doing playground duty

   d attending meetings

   e administering first aid?

4 What are the main committees of a school governing body? What are they responsible for?

5 Name five areas for which the headteacher is responsible.

6 What does the SENCo do within the school?

7 List some of the outside agencies who may come into school and outline their role.

8 What are the main ways in which information is passed around a school?

9 How often should an assistant expect to have an appraisal?

10 What opportunities exist for assistants to develop professionally?

11 What is a School Development Plan?

12 What types of changes may come into effect which would have an impact on your role within the school?

References

Fox, G., *A Handbook for Special Needs Assistants* (David Fulton, 1999)

National Occupational Standards L3 (CSC Consortium)

DfES, *SEN Code Of Practice*

DfES, *Performance Management in Schools* (Model Policy)

Websites

www.ofsted.gov.uk

www.teachernet.gov.uk/teachingassistants

Optional units

Set A

Unit 3-5 Preparing and maintaining the learning environment

This unit looks at some of the different areas in which you will work within the school environment. It considers how you will need to familiarise yourself with different locations within the school and be able to work safely in them. You will need to know where to find equipment and learning materials for a variety of subjects as well as items in everyday use. You should also have an awareness of those members of staff responsible for maintaining stocks of materials and resources for different subjects.

Familiarisation with the learning environment

When working in a school, assistants should be aware of the different environments in which they may be expected to work. The activities within a class will not just be restricted to the classroom itself.

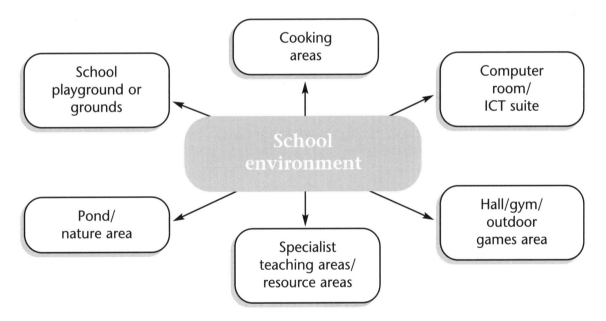

▲ The learning environment is more than just the classroom

As an assistant, you will need to be familiar with all these areas before working in them, so that you are able to plan effectively when working with pupils. If you are asked to work with a group or class of pupils and are not familiar with a particular area of the school or do not know where it is, you should always seek advice. It may not always be apparent that a particular area of the school is set aside for science activities, or where you should go to look for design and technology equipment. The school should have resource areas where members of staff will have access to equipment for each particular subject area, for example:

▷ science resources

▷ maths equipment

▷ D and T tools and equipment

▷ art resources

▷ musical instruments

▷ PE equipment

▷ geography/history resources

▷ CD-ROMs for computers

▷ RE resources

▷ citizenship and PSHE resources

▷ modern languages.

Some of these, such as PE equipment, may be immediately apparent. However, if there is a subject area which you are not often required to support, you may need to ask other members of staff. You should also make sure that you are familiar with how different items of equipment work before you come to use them.

→ Knowledge into action

Are you aware of where the following resource areas are in your school?

► Science

► Design and technology

► Art

For more information on setting out learning resources, see page 102.

The roles and responsibilities of others

All members of staff within the school will have responsibilities for maintaining the learning environment. There will, however, be certain members of staff whose responsibilities should be familiar to assistants.

▷ **Health and safety representative** – this designated member of staff has responsibility for making sure that there are systems and routines in place to maintain the safety of everyone within the school. You should be aware of the health and safety representative and the procedures for reporting any concerns to them. Health and safety will be discussed in more detail in Units 3-10 and 3-11.

▷ **School keeper or caretaker** – this member of staff works alongside the safety representative to maintain a safe environment. They will also be responsible for making sure that the general environment is kept in a safe condition, for example that minor repairs are undertaken as and when they happen, or that items such as light bulbs are replaced where necessary. The school may have a maintenance book so that members of staff can report any issues as they arise. Caretakers may also help with preparing larger items for use within the learning environment, for example using a video or overhead projector.

▷ **Facilities committee** – this part of the school's governing body is responsible for the school site and grounds. The committee will meet to discuss issues such as the repair and maintenance of the school. They will oversee contracts for people such as cleaners and gardeners who come to the school and will also make sure that health and safety guidelines are being met. Governors from this committee may include the teacher governor and will always include the headteacher.

▷ **Subject managers or co-ordinators** – these members of staff are responsible for making sure that their subject area has all the resources required. For example, the art co-ordinator will need to keep up to date on the amount of materials such as paint which are being used at any given time. They may have their own systems in place for doing this, and you will need to find out how to report shortages to them. The different subject co-ordinators will need to make sure that there are adequate resources if particular activities have been planned for a year group, such as working with clay.

▷ **Person responsible for maintaining stocks of materials** – this member of staff will need to be aware of the kinds of resources which are used on a daily basis and which may be quickly used up. These will be items such as paper for photocopying, sharpeners and rubbers, chalks or pens for whiteboards, exercise books, staples and so on. You should make sure that you know who this is so that you can report any shortages when you find them.

➔ *Knowledge into action*

Find out who you would report to if you found a piece of equipment was broken. What is the procedure for reporting breakages?

Considering pupils' individual needs within the learning environment

When preparing the learning environment it is important to remember that the focus of the activities is always the pupils. You may find that you have set up an activity to work on with a group and that materials are not accessible to all pupils. Assistants who support individual pupils with special needs will be aware that it is vital to be able to focus on the needs of everyone.

Principles of inclusive education

As has already been discussed in Unit 3-3.1, the main principle of inclusive education is that all young people have the right to be educated alongside their peers in a mainstream school wherever possible. This will include those who have Special Educational Needs or a disability which means that they have been educated in another setting, or away from 'mainstream' schools. The SEN and Disability Act 2001 makes significant changes to the educational opportunities which are available to prospective pupils with disabilities and those with Special Educational Needs. This means that it will be more likely for these pupils to be accepted into mainstream schools. There will always be some children for whom mainstream education is not possible, for example where highly specialised provision is needed, but the majority of children should not need to be separated from one another in order to be educated. The advantages of inclusive education, compared to separation, are shown below.

Separation	Inclusion
'Special' or different treatment	Equality – all pupils to receive the support they need to build on and achieve their potential
Learning helplessness	Learning assertiveness
Participation of some	Participation of all
Builds barriers in society	Involves all members of society

The table below shows the number of children in Special Schools in England and Wales from 1897 to 1999.

Year	Number of children
1897	4,739
1914	28,511
1929	49,487
1955	51,558*
1977	135,261*^
1999	106,000*^
*Hospital Schools not included ^Includes Severe Learning Difficulty	

(*Source:* Cole 1989, based on Chief Medical Officer, Ministry of Education, Dept of Education and Science Annual Reports (Disability Equality in Education 2001))

The Disability Discrimination Act 1995 was amended in September 2002, to include education and cover the following:

▷ to make it unlawful for schools to discriminate against disabled pupils and prospective pupils in admissions

▷ a requirement for schools and LEAs (Local Education Authorities) to develop a plan to make schools improve access to the environment, curriculum and written information for disabled pupils

▷ a duty for schools to ensure that they do not put disabled pupils at a disadvantage.

Find out about...

Pupils in your school who have needed to have the learning environment adapted to help them. (You may need to ask your school SENCo.)

Look at the factors the teacher has had to consider and how they have used this information to help the pupil. Find out about the pupil's progress before and after these changes were made and evaluate how the adaptations have made a difference to the pupil's learning.

The implications for learning environments of inclusion is that all staff should be aware of those pupils who have specific needs, wherever they are in the school. For the Special Needs Co-ordinator, this may mean speaking to staff as and when pupils with special needs come into the school, so that pupils are fully supported in all learning environments.

Case study

Ramona has recently joined Year 8. She has a hearing loss of which the class teacher and teaching assistant are both aware, and they have taken Ramona's needs into consideration during daily activities – for example, sitting her in the most beneficial place to hear effectively. However, one day the assistant is out on a course and the class teacher is off sick.

▶ What effect might this have on Ramona?

▶ How could the teacher and assistant have prepared for this eventuality so that others coming into the class can work to help Ramona?

Environmental factors

As far as possible, pupils should all be given equal opportunities and this should be remembered in the learning environment. All pupils, including those with special needs, should be considered when planning and setting out materials and resources. The environment may often need to be adapted for the needs of particular pupils within the class for different lessons.

Factors which need to be considered include the following:

▷ **Light** – where there is a visually impaired pupil, the light may need to be adjusted or teaching areas changed if the pupil's eyes are light sensitive.

▷ **Accessibility** – a pupil in a wheelchair needs to have as much access to classroom facilities as other pupils. Furniture and resources may need to be moved to allow for this.

▷ **Sound** – some pupils may be sensitive to sounds in the learning environment, for example an autistic pupil may be disturbed by loud or unusual noises. It is not always possible for these kinds of noises to be avoided, but assistants need to be aware of the effect that they can have on pupils.

? Think about it

Look at and evaluate a classroom in your school and assess whether its layout takes the following into account:

▶ accessibility for all pupils
▶ maximum use of space
▶ good use of storage areas
▶ safety issues
▶ accessibility of materials.

➡ Knowledge into action

Look at the layout of your classroom. How easy is it for pupils and staff to find their way around?

What adaptations do you think you would need to make for a pupil who was in a wheelchair?

Would the example on the next page be suitable?

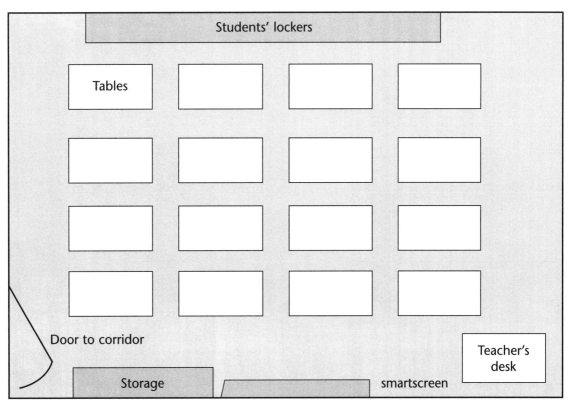

▲ Classroom layout

Understanding pupils' physical needs within the learning environment

In order to understand pupils's physical needs within the learning environment, assistants will need to have an awareness of their physical development. Stages of physical development are given in Unit 3-1 on page 4, which shows the approximate ages of different milestones. These may be divided into gross and fine motor skills.

▷ **Gross motor skills** include running, throwing a ball, racket skills.

▷ **Fine motor skills** include holding a pen, pencil or paintbrush, holding a knife and fork, using a computer mouse.

Where some pupils develop more quickly or slowly than their peers, they will reach these milestones at different ages. Assistants may notice that some pupils need more help than others within the learning environment when using some of these skills. If some individual pupils have difficulties, they may have been referred through the SENCo for help and advice from outside agencies. For example, a pupil who has immature fine motor skills may need to be referred to an occupational therapist. Different professionals will give the school ideas and guidelines to help the pupil develop their skills. These may be put onto the pupil's IEP (Individual Education Plan) as targets.

▲ Pupils need to be sitting properly in order to be able to write correctly

As an assistant, you will need to be aware of individual pupils' needs when considering how to position furniture, equipment and materials in the learning environment. For example, in order to write correctly, pupils need to be sitting properly at the desk with their feet touching the floor. While there will always be an 'average' size for pupils of a particular age, some may find the furniture too small or too big and need to have adaptations made within the classroom.

→ *Knowledge into action*

Look at three different areas of the learning environment in your school. How might you have to adapt these for pupils with the following special needs?

▶ visual impairment

▶ hearing impairment?

Preparing learning materials

All schools will have a variety of materials which will need to be prepared daily. Some of these will be easily accessible, such as basic classroom equipment and resources, but others may take longer to organise, for example where pupils are working on practical activities. Secondary schools usually have large numbers of pupils, and if year groups plan the same activities, subject managers will need to ensure that there are enough resources available.

▲ It is important to have time to set out materials before use

Subject teachers will have general responsibility for managing classrooms and other areas in the learning environment and making sure that there are sufficient resources for pupils. This will include subject specific items such as science or DT equipment. However, as an assistant you may be asked to prepare or set up equipment or resources. You should always make sure you are clear about where different equipment is to be found in the school and whether it is accessible – for example, is it kept in a locked cupboard? Teachers should ensure that the items which are needed will be available when required, and that there will not be other classes or groups needing to use it at the same time. Schools should have rotas or other procedures in place to ensure that all classes have equal access to resources and facilities. You may be asked to prepare and set out resources for planned activities within the classroom on a daily basis, according to what has been planned alongside the teacher.

Knowledge into action

Find out where resources for different subjects are kept in your school. Many of these will be obvious – for example, foreign language audiotapes or resources for ICT – but some may not. You should also know where to find general consumable items such as pencils, scissors, exercise books and so on and who is responsible in the school for ordering replacements. What is the system for informing this person when stocks are low?

Keys to good practice
Using learning materials

✔ Use the amount of materials required for the number of pupils.

✔ Remember safety when using tools and equipment.

✔ Keep waste of materials to a minimum.

✔ Return materials and store equipment correctly after use.

✔ Report shortages in materials to the appropriate person.

Safe use and care of learning equipment and materials

Assistants should always be aware of health and safety issues when working with pupils. It is a duty of all staff to keep pupils safe, and children should be able to explore their environment in safety and security. Assistants should know who the health and safety representative is, and how to report any accidents or hazards which they discover in the learning environment. Many schools will have systems in place for reporting safety issues, but in the case of any doubt it is best to report any concerns to the health and safety representative.

In urgent cases, such as broken equipment which is an immediate hazard to all, you will need to find out who you should contact – usually the school keeper. Your school may also have a 'Maintenance Book' or other method of reporting unsafe or faulty equipment which is less urgent. You should also make sure that you clearly label faulty equipment or materials so that others do not try to use them.

Example of a page of a maintenance book:

Date	Action required	Reported by
12/3/04	Broken table in room 12 – leg wobbly	H. Leonard
14/3/04	Faulty overhead projector – no light	M. Clarke
14/3/04	Dangerous goalpost on bottom field	C. Mangwiro
17/3/04	Smartscreen not working – room 4	B. Ward
22/3/04	Broken locker – sixth form room 7	M. Lees
23/3/04	Path next to mobile 2 – paving stone dangerous	J. Mutabeni

First aid

Assistants should also know the location of safety equipment in school and the identity of trained first aiders. It is strongly recommended that there are first aiders in all educational establishments. They need to have completed a training course approved by the Health and Safety Executive (HSE), which is valid for three years. Assistants should also be aware of the location of first aid boxes in the school. The school's trained first aider should be responsible for ensuring adequate supply and regular restocking of the first aid box. Supplies should be date stamped when they are received as they have a five-year shelf life. If assistants find that there is not sufficient equipment, this should be reported to the health and safety officer.

There is no mandatory requirement for the contents of first aid boxes but they should include certain items, as listed below.

First aid boxes should include:

- ▶ a leaflet giving general advice on first aid
- ▶ 20 individually wrapped sterile adhesive dressings (assorted sizes)
- ▶ two sterile eye pads
- ▶ four individually wrapped triangular bandages
- ▶ six safety pins
- ▶ six medium-sized individually wrapped unmedicated wound dressings
- ▶ disposable gloves

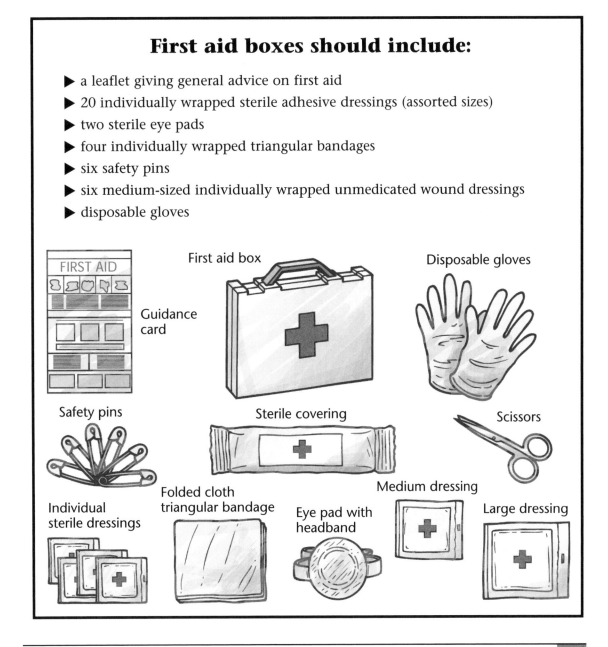

Guidance card

First aid box

Disposable gloves

Safety pins

Sterile covering

Scissors

Individual sterile dressings

Folded cloth triangular bandage

Eye pad with headband

Medium dressing

Large dressing

→ **Knowledge into action**

▶ Find out the identity of the trained first aider in your school.
▶ Find out the location of first aid boxes.

Health and safety policy

The school will have a health and safety policy which outlines responsibilities and requirements within the school regarding health and safety. This will also set out the school's guidance within the setting when dealing with health and safety issues. There should be information available on specific requirements in areas such as cooking, PE, first aid, fire procedures and reporting accidents.

→ **Knowledge into action**

▶ Locate a copy of your health and safety policy.
▶ Find out about procedures for reporting accidents in your school.

You will need to be vigilant and look out for situations in the learning environment which are potentially dangerous. Such situations may not always be obvious, but may be linked to a variety of factors.

▲ See how many potential dangers you can find in this classroom

Sometimes, materials and equipment which are being used within the learning environment may have related health and safety aspects to consider, for example when using electrical equipment. This should always be handled and used according to manufacturers' instructions. Assistants may require training and guidance when using some equipment, and should also be given guidelines on the disposal of any waste following their use.

It is also a good idea to draw pupils' attention to safety issues which they can control within their environment, for example pushing chairs under desks when they get up.

Health and safety will be covered in more detail in Unit 3.10.

Evidence collection

You are asked to prepare for a DT activity to make a nesting box. You will be working with a group of pupils at a time and will be using a variety of tools and equipment.

▶ How would you plan for the activity to ensure that you had enough materials?

▶ What would you do with any left over materials?

End of unit test

1 Name three learning environments.

2 Who is responsible for individual subject resources within a school?

3 What are the principles of inclusive education? Name two advantages.

4 What are the implications of inclusive education for setting out and maintaining learning environments?

5 What document should assistants have access to which will give them guidelines on the school's requirements for managing equipment and materials safely within the learning environment?

6 List some of the contents of a first aid box. How often should the contents be renewed?

7 Who else in the school is responsible for establishing and maintaining learning environments? To whom would you report any damaged equipment?

References and further reading

DfES, *Guidance on First Aid for Schools: A Good Practice Guide*

DfES, *SEN Code of Practice* (2001)

Paterson, G., *First Aid for Children Fast – Emergency procedures for all parents and carers* (Dorling Kindersley in association with the British Red Cross)

Index for Inclusion (CSIE, 2000)

Training for Inclusion and Disability Equality, *Disability Equality in Education* (2001)

Websites

Disability Equality in Education: www.diseed.org.uk

CSIE: http://inclusion.uwe.ac.uk

www.dfes.gov.uk/sen

www.network81.co.uk

Contribute to maintaining pupil records

This unit will give you an understanding about the different kinds of records which you may be expected to keep when working in schools. These records may take a variety of forms and be kept in different parts of the school. You may be required to work with teachers to update records and need to be aware of issues such as confidentiality and legal requirements. As an assistant, you will also need to make sure that your contribution to school records is thorough and complete. Where you find any problems or issues surrounding the information you are required to maintain, you must report these straight away to the person responsible.

The range of different records used in schools

There is a variety of different records with which assistants may come into contact when working in schools. These may be kept in different parts of the school, for example general pupil records may be in the school office, or located in classrooms. Very often, records are now kept on computer systems.

School records

All schools will keep these records, which are particularly important on a day-to-day basis. In the case of medical records, the school may also keep lists of pupils who have particular conditions such as asthma, and keep inhalers in school so that they are accessible in an emergency. It is vital to keep these records up to date, especially emergency telephone numbers, and schools should have systems in place to remind parents about this. If school staff are asked to administer daily medication, such as Ritalin, records need to be kept of the amount of tablets in school and the exact dosage given.

It is recommended that schools keep records of school attendance for 5 to 7 years. If pupils are persistently absent without parents and carers giving a written reason, these absences will be classified as unauthorised. Where pupils show a series of unauthorised absences, these may be noted by the educational welfare officer who should visit the school regularly.

Individual teachers' records of progress and assessment

These records will contain each subject teacher's individual comments and assessments when working with pupils. These are necessary as they will give a breakdown of each child's progress over a period of time, and may be used to help with planning.

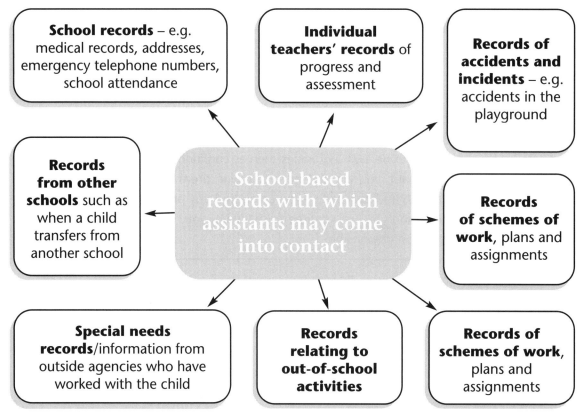

▲ Different types of school records

There are two kinds of assessment which are most regularly used in school. These are known as formative and summative assessment:

▷ **Formative assessment** – this is an ongoing form of assessment, which means that the teacher is constantly monitoring each pupil's progress as they work. For example, pupils working on maths activities will be assessed in this way to see whether they have understood new concepts. Teaching assistants will therefore be required to feed back to teachers following learning activities so that pupils' reactions can be monitored. In some schools this may take the form of a recording sheet, whereas in others the feedback may be verbal.

? Think about it

How do you give feedback to teachers with whom you work following sessions with individuals or groups of pupils? Are you given opportunities to speak to other staff either formally or informally following learning activities?

Look at the sheet opposite. This is a feedback sheet completed by teacher and assistant for each session. Why might this be a useful record?

Teacher input

Name of assistant _____

Subject _____

Activity _____

Resources needed _____

Vocabulary _____

Key learning points:

1)

2)

Assistant input

Pupils (names)	Achieved	Not achieved	Comments
1)			
2)			
3)			
4)			

▷ **Summative assessment** – this is the term used to describe assessments which take place in the form of a test or at the end of a school year. These may be national tests such as SATs (Standardised Assessment Tasks) at the end of Key Stage 3 in Year 9, CAT scores and other results.

Pupils will also be tracked throughout to make sure that they are meeting targets which have been set by teachers in line with individual expectations. For example, a pupil who has entered the school in Year 7 with high SATs results at Key Stage 2 would be expected to achieve at a similar high level as they progress through secondary school. Pupils may also be put in sets as a result of test results to make sure that they are working in the best possible environment for their ability.

Special needs records, information from other agencies

Pupils with special needs will often be the subject of a lot of paperwork. The SENCo will have their own systems for keeping this, so that information about the pupil is easily accessible when needed. The information which may be contained in these records will usually be reports from professionals such as speech and language therapists, who will record their findings and pass the information on to the school. Special Needs records will also contain information about what the school is doing to address an individual pupil's needs, and the pupil's Individual Education Plans (IEP's) or Behaviour Support Plans.

Records of schemes of work, plans and assignments

These records will give a breakdown of the work that is being covered with the pupils during the term. There may be schemes of work broken down into subject areas, and topic based activities to be carried out with the pupils. This will give a record of what each pupil in the class has been taught.

Records from other schools

When pupils transfer from other schools, the school will forward any records which they have about the pupil's achievement. This will be useful for the class teacher as it will give an indication of the level which the pupil has reached, and the results of any tests which have been completed.

Records of accidents or incidents in school

There are times when you may be required to record details of an incident in school such as a pupil banging their head, or one pupil acting aggressively towards another. The school will usually have an accident book, as there needs to be a record kept of any incidents, particularly if a pupil has been injured as a result. (See Unit 3-10, page 168 for an example of an accident record form.)

Records relating to out-of-school activities

These may include details of a variety of school trips, excursions or outings which pupils undertake whilst in school. Records will need to be kept of medical details and contact numbers, and schools will usually request these along with parental consent when they send information about the trip to ensure that they are up-to-date.

Schools will also need to keep information on work experience activities which pupils will usually undertake during Year 10 or 11. They will need to have lists of companies and organisations that are prepared to take on work experience students and details about insurance and other work-related issues. The school will then need to check that pupils have filled in information sheets regarding work experience.

You should only be asked to access records under the direction of a teacher or, sometimes in the case of individual support assistants, the SENCo. The teacher will need to be aware of the location of the records at all times due to some of the confidential material which they contain. Assistants should be aware that records should not be removed from the school for this reason.

→ **Knowledge into action**

Find out the location of the different types of records held within your school. How often do they need to be updated?

Roles and responsibilities within the school for maintaining pupil records

The different records which are held within the school will be the responsibility of different members of staff.

Members of staff who will need to maintain pupil records
Headteachers – to collect and collate school records including results of national tests and assessments
SENCos – to keep records of all pupils on the school's Special Needs Register
Subject managers – to keep and monitor records of achievement in their subject
Subject teachers – to keep records of individual pupils' progress
Office staff – to update and check medical and attendance records within the school

Headteachers, SENCos and subject managers will need to have a knowledge of pupils' records as it is part of their job responsibility to be able to report to others. This may include, in the case of the headteacher, reporting to governors and parents about the school's achievements. The subject managers will need to be able to report to the headteacher and staff about teaching and learning in their subject. They may also need to monitor and moderate work, as well as looking at achievements and areas for development. The SENCo will need to keep detailed records so that they have access to concerns about a specific pupil.

School policies for maintenance of pupil records

The school should have an Assessment, Recording and Reporting Policy, which will give information and guidelines about recording within the school. The system may be such that most of the school's records are kept on computer, so staff will need to be trained in how to use it. Assistants may have opportunities for training with other staff and this will be important if they are to help them to update records. Even if they are not expected to do this, it will be useful to see how they are used and how information is kept within the school.

Legal requirements concerning personal information

Assistants should be aware of the school's legal responsibilities when handling pupil records. This is because personal pupil information should not be used for any other purpose. According to the Data Protection Act 1998, information should:

▷ be obtained fairly

▷ only be kept for as long as is necessary

▷ be relevant to requirements

▷ not be used in any way which is not compatible to its purpose.

Schools should offer guidelines for the use of personal information and make sure that systems and documentation are secure and only restricted to appropriate staff. They may have a policy for the storage and security of pupil records within the school and assistants should be familiar with this if they are dealing with pupil records.

The Children Act 1989 requires that children's welfare must always be put first. It outlines some of the principles which need to be taken into account when children are being considered. Its main requirements are that children should always be consulted and informed about what will happen to them, particularly in cases of family mitigation. Where their personal information is concerned, schools should ensure that this is only accessible to the adults who need this information.

The Statementing Process is the way in which schools send information to the local authority to decide whether a pupil qualifies for extra support in school. This information will be detailed and confidential, and assistants who work with pupils with special needs will need to be aware of issues surrounding confidentiality.

Find out about...

Guidelines for data protection within your school.

Name some of the ways in which your school protects information.

Your role in helping to maintain records

Assistants will not have overall responsibility for maintaining records, but they may be asked to help teachers to keep them up to date and in order. Records which are medical or relating to special needs should be updated as and when changes occur since it is vital that the school has up-to-date information. Those assistants who support pupils with a Statement may be required to help with records for that pupil, although it is more likely that this will be done by the SENCo. Records which relate to the curriculum will be updated at least once a term or as planning takes place, and assistants should be aware of these but will not usually need to help with them. Most records should be updated on a regular basis since they are working documents. For this reason, it is important to be aware of the school procedures for this. Records relating to assessment are the most likely to be completed by assistants and this may consist of a number of tasks, including filing and transferring information. If a pupil has recently transferred from another school, information about them will need to be put onto the new school's records.

Knowledge into action

Find out what kinds of records you may be asked to contribute to in school.

Confidentiality

All staff who work in schools will need to be aware of issues concerning confidentiality. They will be building up the trust of parents, pupils and other staff with whom they work. It is important for assistants to ensure that any information which they are given is not passed onto other people. This is because the trust which has taken time to build up can be quickly damaged by a few careless words. There is also a legal requirement for schools to keep records of pupils and staff confidential.

Case study

Simone is working as an assistant at a secondary school for Saad, who is autistic. She has just found out from Saad's teacher that he has scored very highly in an assessment which has just been carried out in school. Simone tells another assistant and the news somehow reaches one of the parents.

1 Why should Simone have kept this information to herself?

2 What should she have done if she was unsure about repeating the information?

3 What damage will she have done to the school's relationship with the parent?

Guidelines for keeping information secure

▷ Computer systems should not be left unattended when personal information is accessible.

▷ Passwords should keep information secure.

▷ Passwords should not be displayed in office or classroom areas.

▷ Disks and files should be locked away when not in use.

▷ Review and dispose of any unwanted personal data.

Find out about...

Does your school have a confidentiality policy?

Keys to good practice
Maintaining pupil records

✔ Ensure you understand what you are asked to do.

✔ Make sure records are kept up to date and accurate.

✔ Ensure records are relevant.

✔ Maintain confidentiality.

✔ Report any problems or breaches of confidence to the appropriate person.

Problems when recording and storing information

When you are asked to update pupils' records, you may find that you come across problems. There may be a variety of reasons for this:

▷ **Instructions are unclear** – the teacher may not have fully explained the system, or what you have been asked to do may not make sense to you. Make sure that you clarify any queries as soon as they arise.

▷ **Record keeping system is difficult to access** – you may find that the system (either electronic or paper based) is complicated and you need more help to complete the task. If you have not had sufficient training, you must not be afraid to say so.

▷ **Information is not complete** – you may not have enough information to complete the task. Always point out any gaps in the records to the class teacher.

▷ **Information is not from a reliable or valid source** – you may be unsure about the information which you are dealing with, for example information which has been given verbally.

▷ **Record keeping system is not secure** – you may be concerned if you find that the system you are being asked to use is not secure. It could be that for example it is not accessed by passwords, or information can be seen by other adults who come into the school. You should speak to a teacher or to your line manager if you feel that the system is not secure.

▷ **Information which you find may indicate potential problems** – if the school has been sent information about a pupil who has just started.

Whenever you come across something which you feel is a potential problem, it is important that you report it straight away to the teacher so that it can be resolved.

End of unit test

1 What types of records exist in schools?

2 Where might different records be kept?

3 Which staff might be responsible for different types of records? Why do schools need to keep records of out-of-school activities?

4 Why might assistants need to access different records?

5 Outline four requirements of the Data Protection Act.

6 Why is confidentiality important?

7 What sorts of problems might assistants face when maintaining pupil records?

Websites

Data Protection Act 1998: www.legislation.hmso.gov.uk/acts/acts1998/19980029.htm

Children Act 1989: http://www.doh.gov.uk/busguide/childhtm/cpt6/htm

Unit 3.7 Observe and report on pupil performance

This unit looks at how assessment and observation of pupils takes place in schools. You will need to be aware of methods of observation and how the process may affect pupils. You will also need to know the purpose of any observations you undertake so that you can pass on the required information to the teacher. There are different methods of observation and ways of organising pupils, so this unit gives a breakdown of situations in which you may find yourself when carrying out observations. Assistants should also make sure that when they are observing pupils their presence is not a distraction to them, and that they are acting in a supporting role to both pupils and teachers. Finally, you will need to be able to record your observations so that you are able to report back to the teacher.

Why pupils need to be observed in school

When working as an assistant, you may be asked to undertake observations of pupils working in a variety of different situations. This is because teachers will need to build up profiles of each pupil. Assistants will need to be able to observe pupils and report back to the teacher on what they have seen. Before undertaking observations you should be given some guidance as to what the teacher is looking for and how it should be approached. As you become more experienced, you may need less support when observing pupils.

The types of learning you may be asked to observe will include the following skills:

▷ **social and emotional skills** – how pupils relate and respond to others
▷ **physical skills development** – using gross and fine motor skills
▷ **intellectual and cognitive development** – how pupils apply concepts and knowledge
▷ **language and communication skills** – how pupils communicate with others and use vocabulary.

Social and emotional skills

Assistants may be asked to observe specific pupils who are working or socialising with their peers. This may be for a variety of reasons, for example because the pupils are experiencing social difficulties and find it hard to make and retain friends, or because they have behaviour problems. When observing social or informal situations you may be asked to ensure that the pupil is unaware that you are watching, as this could have an influence on how they behave. Clearly in this situation you will need to observe the pupil's interaction with others and whether they are proactive in seeking out other pupils with whom to socialise. Those pupils who often spend lunchtimes on their own, or are not confident when socialising with others may need support in school to help them to develop these skills.

Physical skills and development

Assistants may be asked to observe pupils in situations where they are demonstrating their physical skills. One of the situations which you may be asked to observe is recording pupils' progress during PE lessons. This is because it is difficult to observe individual pupils when teaching a class. In this situation, the best way to record information about pupils' progress is by exception. For example, if the lesson is a gymnastics class and the objective is to learn about balance, the recording may be about a pupil or group of pupils who are finding the skill difficult. Sometimes a particular pupil may display difficulties with gross motor skills, which needs to be recorded as evidence so that the school can seek help for the pupil. Assistants may also be required to observe pupils who have difficulties with fine motor skills, such as using scissors or pen control.

There are also occasions in the classroom or other areas in the school where assistants may be asked to record how pupils with disabilities are organising themselves within the learning environment. This may be a pupil who has sensory loss, such as a visual impairment, or a pupil with cerebral palsy who relies on a wheelchair for mobility. These pupils will need careful monitoring at all times and if assistants see a particular problem they should report it straight away to the class teacher.

? Think about it

Have you worked with pupils in school who need extra help with developing fine or gross motor skills?

▶ What kind of support have they been given?

▶ Have you been asked to observe any pupils who have problems with motor skills?

Intellectual and cognitive development

Assistants will often be asked to work with groups and individuals to complete tasks. They may also be asked to sit back from a group and observe how they interact with each other when completing a task. It should be clear whether you are expected to join in with the task or whether your role is purely to observe the pupils. Teachers should give clear instructions as to why you are observing the pupil or pupils and exactly what you need to record.

You may need to look at how the pupil or pupils is approaching the task. For example, is the pupil methodical? You may be looking at whether the pupil has understood a new concept or one which should be familiar to them. It is also useful to observe whether the pupil approaches the task with confidence or will wait for assistance from other pupils or members of staff

Find out about...

The Individual Education Plan or IEP targets for a pupil in your class.

How do teachers plan to take account of these targets and made sure that the pupil is given the opportunity to work on them?

Language and communication skills

Language and communication skills are an important part of how pupils learn. Those who experience difficulties when communicating with others may need to be observed both in the classroom and in other environments, such as the playground or dining hall. Assistants should have a clear idea of what they are expected to observe and whether they should intervene. The school may have been given advice and targets from a speech and language therapist about how to maximise the pupil's speech development, so that the school and therapist can work together.

Where pupils have communication difficulties, such as autism, assistants may be asked to observe and monitor their behaviour and interaction with other pupils. Agencies such as those who support social and communication difficulties may be available to offer help and advice when working with these pupils. The school may also have been given advice and targets from a speech and language therapist about how to maximise

▲ It is important to be aware of individual pupils' targets

the pupil's speech development, so that the school and therapist can work together. Assistants should always be aware of individual pupils' targets, particularly if they are supporting children with special needs. These will be set out on the pupil's Individual Education Plan or IEP. If you are an individual support assistant and have not seen the targets of the pupil you are supporting, it is important to have these from SENCo.

Behaviour to be expected at various stages of development

As already seen in Unit 3-1 page 6, children will display a range of behaviours at different stages in their development. When working with a particular age or stage of pupil, assistants will quickly start to learn the kinds of behaviours which are 'normal' for that age. Pupils who display abnormal behaviours for their age will usually be showing a type of behaviour as shown in the diagram below.

Where pupils are not on task for reasons of behaviour, assistants will need to intervene, particularly if the group or individual is working away from the teacher. You will need to determine what is the cause of the behaviour so that you can encourage the pupil to return to the task. It is important to have clarified the boundaries of behaviour and how to deal with any problems with the class teacher. This is because if the behaviour continues, you will need to have agreed strategies for how to proceed (see Unit 3-1 on page 13 about the management of pupil behaviour). It is important for staff to be firm and for pupils to know what is expected of them. Your school should also have a behaviour policy which you can refer to if you are unsure of the kinds of sanctions which you should apply.

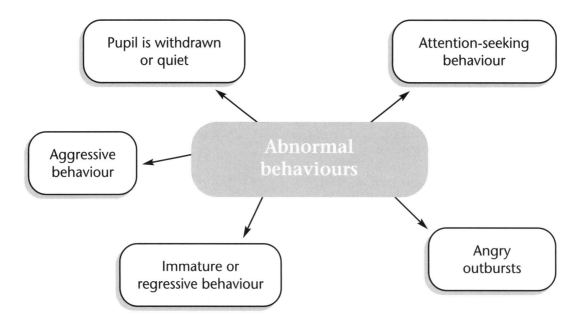

▲ There are different types of abnormal behaviour

▲ You must keep the objectives of the observation in mind

Your role when observing pupil performance

Although you will have been given guidance by the school and class teacher when carrying out pupil observation on exactly what is required, there will be other factors which you need to consider. It is important that you always keep the lesson objectives and required observation in mind, so that you can redirect the pupils to what they are doing if they start to go off task. You must also be aware of how you can maximise the pupils' interest and focus on the task, through questioning and directing their work.

Other factors to remember when carrying out observations

It is important to be aware of recording information which is relevant to the observation you have been asked to carry out (see page 126 on how to record information). This is the case unless you notice something which you feel needs to be reported to the class teacher. This could include one of the following:

▷ pupil is distracted/showing disruptive behaviour which is preventing them or others in the group from completing the task

▷ pupil is showing uncharacteristic behaviour – for example, is unusually quiet during the session

▷ pupil is playing up to being observed – the observation may not be a realistic interpretation of the pupil's abilities

▷ environmental factors and interruptions – these could be caused by physical factors, such as noise levels, and will prevent the task being carried out successfully.

If a pupil is disruptive or does not participate in the activity owing to others' disturbance, this information should be recorded as part of the observation because it will have an effect on whether the pupils are fulfilling the required learning objectives of the lesson.

You may be aware of potential causes of disruption and should always speak to the teacher if you anticipate any problems before starting the observation. It is also important to be aware of and to try to maintain the normal rules and routines of the school or classroom before undertaking any observations. This is so that the pupils will not be working in an artificial situation. If you set out the activity in a different environment, the pupils may find this too much of a distraction to focus on the activity.

Other potential sources of disruption include:

▷ pupils' behaviour

▷ task too difficult/too easy for pupils

▷ physical factors – noise or light levels

▷ interruptions by other pupils in the class

▷ insufficient space, materials or equipment to carry out the task

▷ faulty equipment.

Case study

You are carrying out an observation on a group of Year 9 pupils who are working on a science investigation on the properties of metals. You have been asked to observe the group to see how they work together and only to intervene if necessary. They have been carrying out the investigation independently but one of the pupils has started to display disruptive behaviour and this is beginning to prevent the others from staying on task.

1 What would you do in this case?

2 Following your intervention, what would you do if this behaviour continued?

3 How might this affect your observation of the session?

Influences on pupils when being observed

Assistants may also need to encourage pupils who find it difficult to demonstrate the extent of their knowledge or skills when being observed. It is important therefore to know the pupils with whom you are working before undertaking the observation. Some pupils will be able to work on the task without being distracted by the observer, while others may play up to the staff to seek attention. Assistants may also need to put the pupil or pupils at ease so that they are more likely to work constructively with one another. You may need to encourage some pupils to participate so that you are given a clearer idea of their understanding.

Groups of pupils will need to be chosen carefully so that there are not combinations who may disturb or influence the reactions of one another. This may be due to a number of reasons.

Cultural factors: in schools where there is a high percentage of mixed cultures, there may also be problems of language and understanding where pupils speak English as an additional language. Some bilingual assistants are employed by schools in areas where there are a high number of pupils who speak English as a second language. Assistants should be aware that there are currently developments to raise the achievements of ethnic minority pupils in schools, as many of these pupils are under-achieving. This also includes pupils from traveller families, who may not spend more than a few weeks at a time in school. Your school may have a strategy in place for helping these pupils to achieve their full potential, and local authorities may soon be offering staff training, so that all staff can help to raise attainment.

Social factors: some pupils may not be able to work with those who they feel are more able or more confident than themselves. This will have an influence on the observation as they will be less likely to put their ideas forward. If pupils have confidence in themselves, they will gain more from what they are doing.

Gender-based factors: i.e. pupils who are not comfortable with, or find it difficult working with, children of the opposite sex. This may be particularly true of adolescents. This may be because there is a group of pupils who are more confident, or because they have preconceived assumptions – for example, that boys are better at science or girls are better at art. This may make them less likely to volunteer information when working in a group.

Pupils who are being observed individually may be working on their own or as part of a group. Those who are working on their own may not react to the observation in the same way, mainly because they will not be interacting with others to complete the task. When you are observing an individual, you may find that you need to ask the pupil questions about what they are doing so that you have more understanding of their approach to the task. Questioning strategies will need to be consistent with the objectives of the task and the pupil's age and understanding.

How to record when undertaking pupil observations

Schools may have different guidelines when approaching observations and, as we have seen, there may be a number of reasons for asking assistants to observe pupils. The principal points to remember are as follows:

Make sure you understand exactly what you need to observe. You must only record information which is relevant to the observation, although see page 123 for awareness of other factors. One way of doing this is to record at set intervals, or only to write down relevant observations.

Use any methods of recording which are consistent with what you have been asked to do. For example, when observing pupils for a specific assessment, the school may have an observation form which will give guidelines for required information. You may be asked to make notes of your own, or simply use a checklist to make sure the pupil has achieved a set of criteria.

Below are examples of a blank observation form and also one that has been filled in, together with comments on the observations made.

Hazelwood Secondary School
Pupil Observation Form

Name of pupil(s) .... **Class:**...

Date:.. **Lesson:**...

Teacher .... **Assistant:**..

Lesson objectives:

Group/class activity:

Focus of observation:

▲ An example of an observation form

St Peter's Secondary School

Pupil Observation Form

Name of pupil(s) ..Keith Crewe...   **Class:** ....10 JA...........................

Date: ..22 February 2004..............   **Lesson:** ....History.....................

Teacher ...Sara Shorter.................   **Assistant:**..........Jackie Brown..........

> What pupil should know by the end of the lesson.

Lesson objectives:

To be able to give 2 reasons why Abyssinia was invaded by Italy in 1935.

> This shows what the pupil or the group they are in is expected to do.

Group/class activity:

Investigate using texts and internet.

Focus of observation:

How much the child relies on others in the group and how much he works on his own.

> This gives clear indication of what the observer is expected to record.

Further comments:

Keith was not able to work independently for a sustained period. If working on his own he may have been able to do this. He could not stay focused on his work or away from others during the observation.

> The comment about if he had worked on his own is subjective and therefore should not have been included.

Did pupil meet learning objectives?

Difficult to say as Keith did not complete enough of the work on his own.

> This commentary does not give an indication of how much time was spent doing the activity, so does not demonstrate how long the pupil worked during the session.

? Think about it

What sort of observations have you been asked to carry out in school? Have you been encouraged to report back formally to the teacher with written evidence, or verbally?

Keep your recording as simple as possible. You will need to report your findings to the teacher and it is important that you are able to remember what you observed, so you will need to record clearly and legibly. You may need to summarise the information you have gathered, or simply explain to the teacher what you have observed. Whatever you report will need to have evidence to support it, so you should be careful to back up your findings.

Remember to keep your written observations confidential. If you need to use them for any reason apart from classroom records, for example for training purposes, you should always change the names of any pupils you have observed.

If you are carrying out an observation which requires you to record information in any other way, for example using a video or still camera, you should always ask permission beforehand from those concerned. This is so that they are aware of what you are doing and why.

Remember that all observations are subjective. You should report what you see but do not need to give an opinion about it. Pupil observations are to give the teacher an idea about the pupil's progress or how the pupil copes in particular situations. Do not be tempted to give any more information than is needed.

✔ Keys to good practice
Observing pupils

✔ Record clearly.

✔ Keep information relevant.

✔ Remember confidentiality.

✔ Follow school guidelines.

Case study

You have been asked to carry out an observation during an outdoor games lesson on Joseph, who has been demonstrating 'clumsy' behaviour and giving his teacher cause for concern. He has shown some physical behaviours which the class teacher feels are not in the normal spectrum.

1 How would you go about recording your observations?

2 How would you know whether his physical behaviour was age appropriate?

End of unit test

1 Why might pupils be observed in school?

2 What types of skills will assistants be asked to observe?

3 What sort of 'abnormal' behaviour might you see in a classroom?

4 What should you do before starting an observation in order to minimise disruption?

5 Why might a pupil from another culture find it difficult to participate in a group activity?

6 What should you remember when recording observations?

References

Teaching Assistant's File (DfES)

Managing Support for the Attainment of Pupils from Minority Ethnic Groups (Ofsted 2001) or on the website www.ofsted.gov.uk

Unit 3-8 Contribute to the planning and evaluation of learning activities

This unit looks at the way in which assistants work with subject teachers to plan and evaluate learning activities. It is important for assistants to be able to work collaboratively with others and to judge the effectiveness of the learning activities with which they are involved. This unit looks at the way in which you plan, manage and evaluate teaching activities through the support of national, local and school-based documentation. You will need to be aware of the types of documents which are available and should know where to find them in your school. You will also need to manage any difficulties as they arise and be able to report back constructively to the teacher about them.

Your role and that of others in planning, implementing and evaluating learning activities

Planning activities

In your role as a teaching assistant, you may be asked to help with the planning of learning activities in the learning environment. Although the subject teacher will have completed long-term plans for the class, you may be asked to work with the teacher to discuss and plan activities for the week so that you are aware in advance of what you are required to do. You will need to work with the teacher to ensure that the work you are covering fits in with activities and lessons which have been planned for the term.

Example of part of a weekly Literacy Hour plan for Year 7

Year: 7	Objectives		School priorities
	Word		❏ Writing
Term: 3	• W2 Pluralisation		❏ Spelling
	Reading		❏ Inference
Week: 1	• R6 Active reading		
	• R8 Infer and deduce		
Teacher:	*Writing*		
JH	• Wr3 Exploratory writing		
	Speaking and Listening		
	• S&L12 Exploratory talk		

	Word/sentence activity (10 minutes)	Introduction (20 minutes)	Development (20 minutes)	Plenary (10 minutes)	Homework
Lesson 1 1 hour	es plurals • Word sort activity • Work out which endings need es • Listening game (for extra syllable)	Shared reading chapter 1 What questions and expectations does the text pose? Text marking on OHT	In groups: Read to end of chapter Collect impressions of the world he lives in. Underline words or phrases that give that impression * Work with group A	Collect key phrases Draw out differences between explicit information and implied meanings	Read chapters 2 and 3 Identify how first impressions are confirmed, changed or developed
Lesson 2 1 hour	ies plurals • Brainstorm y words • Sort ys/ies • Work out rule • Plural race	Recap chapters 2 and 3 Reread discovery of Skellig Pick out words and phrases Speculate about his origins	Individuality: In journals, sketch the man from given information Jot down possible ideas about who he is and why he is there. Cite evidence from text * Work with group B	Share sketches and ideas Identify common features inspired by text	Read chapters 4 and 5 Predict how the story will unfold, and point to clues in text
Lesson 3 1 hour	• Test plurals	Share predictions Read to the end of chapter 6, picking out examples of sound effects, e.g. onomatopoeia, repetition, short sentences, alliteration. Note examples on paper	In groups, each looking at one technique: Go over chapters 4–6 and note examples on post-it notes Stick on posters * Work with group C	Draw out common techniques and their effects Generalise about the writer's style	
Lesson 4 30 mins	In groups: Read chapters 7–8. Discuss presentation of Skellig. Note plot as a flow chart in journal (20 minutes) * 10 minutes with groups D, E and F * Mrs Jones: guided reading with group A				Homework: read up to end of chapter 9 Use journal to note impressions of Mina

Each subject teacher's weekly plan should show which individuals or groups of pupils are to work on tasks at a particular time, and give an indication of whether they are to be supported by a member of staff.

Principles underlying effective communication, planning and collaboration

Schools should have positive opportunities for teaching assistants to share information
about the school and about pupils. It is important to make these times available, as
many teaching assistants work part time, or work in one class with one pupil.
Assistants need to have opportunities to share ideas and experiences with others so
that they do not feel isolated. These could include:

▷ regular meetings for teaching assistants

▷ sharing information about the school

▷ assistants working together to support classes or individuals

▷ notice-boards and year group meetings.

These meetings and opportunities for discussion do not need to be long, but are an
important part of an assistant's role. They are part of a communication process which
should take place within the school for passing information between all staff. If these
kinds of opportunities are not given to staff for communicating with one another, they
will find it much more difficult to work with one another and use time effectively.

When meeting with the teacher, the main areas for discussion should be the planning
and evaluation of learning activities. Your role and the role of the teacher should be
one of a partnership, where there are clear roles and responsibilities for working
together to support the pupils. You may also be involved in planning a series of
activities to be carried out over several sessions. This could be with the same group, if
the pupils need to work on a particular idea, or with different pupils on a similar,
perhaps differentiated, task. As you become more experienced, or if you are working
with a pupil who has special needs, you may add some of your own ideas during the
sessions so that the pupil or pupils builds on work done each time.

Ideally, assistants should be given this opportunity to input some of their own ideas
into class activities when they are at the planning stage. This is because they may have
their own areas of expertise, or ideas which may help the teacher to formulate
activities for pupils. This is especially true for assistants who support individual pupils
with special needs, as there will be some activities in which these pupils need more
structured tasks. You should also be aware of your own areas of weakness: if you know

---

that you will find it difficult to take a group of pupils for an art activity on printing, for example, because you have not done this for a long time, then say so. You should feel comfortable with what you are doing because it is important to be confident when carrying out the activity. If you anticipate any other difficulties in carrying out the plan which the teacher has not foreseen, you should also point these out.

Case study

Adam is in Year 8 and has cerebral palsy. He has an assistant, Mark, who works with him each day and is usually given teachers' plans so that he can make suggestions for how various learning activities can be adapted where necessary. However, during one design and technology lesson a supply teacher is taking the class and although he has been told about Adam, the task which he sets the group to work on is going to be difficult for him to manage. Mark feels that he will be unable to work with Adam and support the rest of the group he has been asked to supervise.

1 What would you do in Mark's situation?
2 What would you do if you were unable to speak to the teacher about the task as they were busy with another group?

Think about it

What opportunities have you been given in the school setting for planning activities alongside the teacher? How often are you involved with planning? If you have not been involved, find out whether this would be possible.

Keys to good practice
Planning learning activities

✔ Ensure you understand the learning outcomes.
✔ Contribute your own ideas to planning sessions.
✔ Include any of your own strengths.
✔ Make sure you have time for what you need to do.
✔ Be aware of relevant policies and guidelines.

Implementing activities

When working with individuals, groups and the whole class, teaching assistants need to ensure that they are aware of the learning objectives of the lesson. The class teacher should always include the learning objectives in their planning, and should also tell the pupils what they are. This is so that they will be able to direct all pupils towards the correct outcome. Assistants should be aware of what individuals and groups of children are working towards so that they can act in a fully supporting role. There may sometimes be problems of time particularly since most classes will take place in different rooms in secondary schools, and assistants may not have opportunities to speak to teachers beforehand. It is often helpful to have either a copy of the short-term planning, or a notebook containing the assistant's tasks for the lesson along with the pupils' learning objectives. Assistants will also then be able to judge how success can be measured when they are evaluating learning activities.

Making use of allocated time

Assistants will need to make sure that they are fully aware of the constraints of time when implementing learning activities. There are many parts of the school day during which time is restricted, and this needs to be considered, especially if there is a large group of pupils to work with on an individual basis. If the work seems unrealistically long for the length of time allocated, you should not try to complete it all and rush the pupils to finish. This will make them feel that their work is less valued. Although time is limited in school, assistants should wherever possible try not to communicate

---

Lesson plan for Food Technology (Year 8)

Learning objective: For pupils to be able to identify some of the more common hazards in the kitchen so that these may be avoided.

Introduction: Short general revision on health and safety. Introduce topic and give the group a short question and answer session.

Main part of lesson: Pupils to work in discussion groups of four and to fill in a chart showing hazards, causes, and ways in which these may be avoided.

Differentiation: Spend time with groups, questioning and finding out whether they understand/clarify any difficulties.

Assessment: Class to discuss their work at the end of the session, talk about their ideas and give examples.

▲ Example of an individual lesson plan for Year 8

this to pupils when they are working on a task. If there is an unavoidable limit on time, you should give the pupil or pupils an opportunity to return to it later the same day if possible.

Case study

You are working with Rajbeer, a Year 10 pupil, on some Spanish, and are helping her to write a short composition about her likes and dislikes. She has been given some ideas and has a plan of what she wants to say, but needs to finish her work before the end of the day as it needs to be handed in.

1 How could you help Rajbeer without making her feel as though she needs to rush?

2 What could you do if the work was not completed by the end of the lesson?

Individual targets

This may vary from school to school, but often individual subject teachers will give pupils targets to work on in their subject. This is to help pupils to be more focused on their own development and to involve them in their achievements.

Knowledge into action

Find out about individual targets which may be given in one of the subject areas you are supporting. How often are they revised? How does the teacher assess whether the pupils have or have not achieved these targets?

Lesson evaluation

Following the lesson, or even while it is taking place, there will need to be some form of evaluation to determine whether the learning objectives have been met and how much the pupils understand. It may be clear during the activity which pupils do not understand the concept and those who are able to explain it.

Where pupils are working independently, their work may be all that is needed to check that they understand what they have been asked to do. Where the work has been practical or verbal, assistants will need to record the names of those pupils who have found it difficult to complete or understand. If assistants find that some of the pupils with whom they are working are clearly finding the work difficult, the teacher should always be told. If any problems arise during the course of the activity, which mean that it cannot be carried out properly, this should also be pointed out to the teacher, for example a distraction which carries on over a period of time. Assistants also need to know exactly how success for each activity is to be measured, for example whether each pupil in the group has fully understood a new concept. When recording or annotating plans, you should be clear about the amount of information which is needed. You also need to be careful about how you report back when the information is verbal. If you have had a difficult session with a group or an individual, make sure you give all the information about the session to the teacher so that they are able to make a balanced judgement. See also record sheet on page 111 for feeding back information to the teacher.

? Think about it

You are working on an activity with some Year 11 pupils to evaluate their IT skills at creating Powerpoint presentations. Some of the pupils are clearly much more confident at this than others, and while you are working with another group one of them insists on coming over to see how they are getting on and tries to intervene and show them what to do.

▶ What would you do in this situation?

▶ Could you make it work to your advantage?

▶ Can you think of any strategies that might work if the pupil was very persistent and disturbed your evaluation?

✔ Keys to good practice
Lesson evaluation

✔ Be clear about what and how you need to report.

✔ Report any distractions or disturbances.

✔ Report strengths and weaknesses constructively.

✔ Be aware of outside influences on the lesson.

Possible problems when planning, implementing and evaluating learning activities

Assistants may find that they come up against a variety of problems when planning, implementing and evaluating learning activities. As already pointed out, it is important to point out any anticipated difficulties at the planning stage if you have the opportunity. Where you encounter problems carrying out tasks, you must act immediately so that pupils do not become distracted from what they are doing.

Possible causes of difficulty when carrying out tasks include:

▷ insufficient time available for planning – unclear requirements of task

▷ insufficient space in area

▷ insufficient subject knowledge

▷ too many/too few pupils for task

▷ bad combination of personalities in group

▷ insufficient time to carry out task

▷ poor or insufficient materials

▷ work too easy/too difficult

▷ differences of opinion when working with others.

When evaluating, the main problem may again be a lack of time for reporting back to the teacher. However, there may also be occasions where there are differences of opinion or ways of reporting which could cause friction between the teacher and assistant. Be careful that you report things to the teacher in a way that is not confrontational.

? Think about it

Look at these two conversations:

Teacher: How did your group get on with their Chemistry investigation?

Assistant: Most of them managed very well once they had worked out how to set up the burette, but Qu and Cameron found it very difficult. I think the task was too hard for them and they didn't really understand the importance of adding the hydrochloric acid in very small volumes. I think you should put them with another group so that they don't have to do such complicated investigations.

Teacher: How did your group get on with their Chemistry investigation?

Assistant: They were all fine except Qu and Cameron, who found it difficult to work through the instructions carefully. Would it help if I wrote out a separate more detailed instruction sheet for them next time they need to carry out an investigation, so that they don't get lost?

▶ Which is a better way of reporting back to the teacher?

▶ Why do you think this example would be preferred by the teacher?

How children learn and the implications for planning and evaluating learning activities

When looking at the planning and evaluation of pupils' work, all staff should remember the variety of needs which exist within each classroom. Some pupils will learn and develop at a different rate, and this will have an effect on how their work is approached. School staff need to be able to cater for a variety of abilities while all the time challenging and motivating pupils to do their best. Unit 3-3 looks in detail at the different ways in which children learn, and gives some ideas about how this will affect planning and differentiation within the classroom.

There will be a spread of attainment which pupils at any age will be expected to achieve, but it is important to take into account those pupils who fall outside this expected level. This will usually be those pupils who the school has put on the Special Needs register, and teachers should plan differentiated work for them in line with their Individual Education Plan (IEP) targets (see also Units 3-13 to 3-16 on special needs, and Unit 3-3.1 on equal opportunities and inclusion). Those pupils who are more able should also have opportunities to extend their knowledge. Teachers will usually cater for this by planning similar activities for them with extension work.

Lesson objective: to analyse a poem and look at the techniques the author uses to gain the reader's attention. To use some of these techniques to write their own poem.

Learning needs of the children: Ryan and Abimbola – School Action Plus, Jack on School Action and Jeannette with a Statement for Emotional/Behavioural difficulties. LSA to support Jeanette and Jack within a larger group. Class teacher to work with Ryan and Abimbola's group.

Introduction: Pupils to fill in blanks in the poem with words written randomly on the OHP.

Middle part of lesson: ask the class for their impressions of the poem. With prompts, if necessary, get them to think about:

▶ unusual imagery using everyday objects
▶ use of rhyme and rhythm
▶ repetition
▶ lack of capital letters and punctuation
▶ what the poet is trying to say and how he says it.

Record these observations, and then ask the pupils to write a poem using some similar techniques, working in pairs (if possible a more able pupil with a less able one).

Plenary: Pupils to report back and some volunteers to read out their poems.

▲ Example of a Year 7 Literacy lesson

As can be seen from the lesson on page 139, the teacher has planned for varying abilities while carrying the same theme through the lesson. When evaluating, you will need to look at whether the pupils you were working with were able to meet the learning objective through their task. If the majority of pupils achieved the objectives but one or two found certain aspects difficult, it would be appropriate to record by exception, i.e. 'were all able to complete the task and had a good understanding but Jeanette was unable to complete the task as she was very unfocused'. Similarly, if a pupil completes the task quickly and is more able than the rest of the group, this should also be recorded.

School, local and national policies and their implication for how you work with pupils

Your school should have a number of curriculum policies which will outline their aims and objectives for different curriculum areas. This will influence the way in which staff teach, both because of the content of what they teach and in how their time is organised. They will be updated in line with the school's School Development Plan which gives priorities for development each year. You should be aware of where to find policies for different subjects, as they should be accessible to all staff. You should also know the layout of your school's policies and how they affect the planning of various activities within the classroom.

Curriculum policies

The school's curriculum policies will also be influenced by local and national guidelines such as the QCA (Qualifications and Curriculum Authority) curriculum documents or exemplars which are published for each subject. These give suggestions for schemes of work to be used in each subject and at Key Stages 1, 2 and 3. Schools may adopt the QCA documents as part of their long-term planning, but this is not obligatory, and schools may use them as reference documents for schemes of work. They may be found on the QCA website: www.qca.org.uk/ and also through www.standards.dfes.gov.uk/schemes3/.

Knowledge into action

Ask a subject teacher to show you a policy for one of the subject areas. Does your school use the QCA schemes of work as a basis for its planning?

Curriculum policies will also be valuable documents as they will outline aims and objectives for each subject and give information about how staff can guide pupils.

Some of the headings within a curriculum policy may be:
 ▷ Aims and objectives
 ▷ Delivery
 ▷ Assessment
 ▷ Policy links.

The staff guidelines may include:

▷ planning advice
▷ teaching and learning
▷ progression
▷ differentiation
▷ assessment, recording and reporting
▷ resources
▷ health and safety
▷ equal opportunities
▷ quality assurance.

Knowledge into action

Find a copy of your school's music policy. Does it include staff guidelines for planning?

At Key Stage 4, teachers will follow the schemes of work which are required for GCSE subjects. These schemes of work are also available through the QCA website.

National documentation to support the curriculum will be sent to schools and local authorities by the DfES and given to staff by the headteacher. They may also be given to curriculum managers at local meetings to pass on to staff at the school's staff meetings.

Evidence collection

Plan, carry out and evaluate a learning activity alongside a teacher. Carry out the activity with a group. Write an account in the form of a report. Your report should:

▶ identify a group of pupils and describe the needs of the group and any specific needs of individuals
▶ identify the activity to be undertaken
▶ show how any school policies influenced what you did in the lesson
▶ review the outcomes of the activity in your evaluation.

End of unit test

1 What might an assistant need to do when helping to plan learning activities?
2 What are the main opportunities for assistants to share information in school?
3 Why is it good practice for assistants to plan alongside teachers?
4 Why is it sometimes difficult to implement?

5 What kinds of problems might assistants experience when evaluating learning activities?

6 Why do schools need to have curriculum policies?

References

National Literacy Strategy: (DfES) Framework for Teaching English Years 7, 8 and 9

Websites

www.qca.org.uk/

Set B

Unit 3.9 Promote pupils' social and emotional development

In this unit you will learn how to promote the social and emotional development of the pupils with whom you come into contact. You will need to know how to help pupils to form positive relationships with others. Pupils will need to learn respect for and rights of others and the importance of acceptable behaviour. They will develop skills of self-reliance and self-esteem as they grow in independence, and also recognise and deal with their own emotions.

How to support pupils in developing relationships with others

In your role as a teaching assistant, you will need to know how to help pupils to develop relationships with others in the school. There are several different groups of people that pupils will need to be able to relate to and form relationships with while they are at school.

Their peers

This can be the easiest group for many pupils to form relationships, but for some it can be difficult. Where pupils have a special need which affects their ability to communicate with others, if they speak English or Welsh as a second language, or if they have different home circumstances from others in the school, they may need to have support to help them to develop in this area. Strategies which may be useful for pupils with these types of difficulties can include the following:

▷ Small groups to develop the types of skills which these pupils need, for example learning the 'norms' of conversation: taking turns and responding to what the other person is saying.

▷ Adult intervention to help the pupil to mix with others, for example playing games with one or two other pupils. These types of activities will help the pupil to gain confidence when socialising.

▷ Small group activities to develop awareness of how people interact with others.

▲ Pupils may need support to develop their social skills

Pupils from different backgrounds and cultures

Pupils will need to be able to mix with others who are from different backgrounds. The school should have its own policies relating to equal opportunities and multiculturalism, which should outline the ways in which pupils' awareness is developed. Some pupils at the school may feel isolated or uncomfortable if they are from a different culture from the majority of pupils. They may be the only one who has to wear a particular item of clothing, for example, and may find that this makes them feel self-conscious. Staff should ensure that they surround pupils with positive images of those from all backgrounds and cultures.

→ Knowledge into action

Find out about your school's policy for multiculturalism. How does the school teach and encourage pupils to find out about other cultures? What kinds of images of other cultures are available or have been brought to pupils' attention through assemblies, visits and so on?

Younger and older pupils

Pupils in a secondary school should also be encouraged to mix with those from a different year group than their own. This may be done through extra curricular activities, or groups of different ages supporting one another and carrying out projects or investigations together. When new pupils start at the school in Year 7, there may be a system which encourages older children to show them around or answer questions about the school. This is helpful for pupils as it encourages them to develop their social skills and learn to respect one another. If they are helping younger pupils, it will be a valuable experience in showing them how to help others.

Knowledge into action

Find out if you can take a small group of pupils to do some work with those of another age group in the school. Ask the older pupils if they can help the younger ones with investigative tasks, such as science or maths activities.

With staff

Children will need to be able to relate to different members of staff with whom they come into contact in school, for example parent helpers, teachers and teaching assistants, midday supervisors and others. It is important that staff are seen as good role models for all pupils. This means that pupils should also see staff forming positive relationships within the school and working effectively together.

Think about it

How often do pupils in your school see staff working co-operatively together?

Other circumstances affecting social development

There may be other issues which make it difficult for pupils to form relationships with others, and if pupils are having difficulties this may need to be investigated by school staff in order to help the pupil.

Home circumstances or upbringing

A pupil who has had a traumatic home background, or comes from a different environment from other pupils, may feel different from them. A pupil who lives in bed and breakfast accommodation, or a traveller pupil, might be very aware of the fact that they live in different circumstances from others.

Physical and emotional health

Pupils who have physical or emotional problems may feel isolated and 'different', which in turn may affect their social skills. If you are an assistant supporting a pupil with a physical disability or emotional difficulties, you may need to help them to mix with other pupils using some of the strategies shown above.

In order to help pupils to develop their social relationships, you will need to be aware of the different stages of social development which can be expected of the pupils with whom you are working (see also Unit 3-1 page 6).

Stages of social development

Years 4 to 7: Pupils coming in from Primary schools will already be aware of how they fit into groups, the co-operation necessary and what acceptable levels of behaviour are. They will be aware of their own achievements and capable of self-criticism. Friendships will already be important to them. Throughout Years 4 to 7 they will be growing in maturity and be able to take on greater responsibilities. They will respond well to small group activities. Leaders should provide reassurances and support.

Years 8 to 10: This age group will be keen to plan activities together and enjoy teamwork. They may enjoy taking part in activities that are away from home.

Years 11 and 12: Give teenagers opportunities to interact in mixed groups. Consistent treatment by staff is important, be willing to listen to and accept each one as an individual.

Effects on pupils' behaviour

Where pupils have difficulties in their social development, this will sometimes result in behaviour problems. These types of conflicts may be minor, in which case pupils should be encouraged to try to resolve them amicably without involving others. The school may have a set of rules to help pupils to think about working and mixing co-operatively with one another and you may need to remind them of these (see Unit 3-1 page 13). However, pupils may resort to more serious kinds of anti-social behaviour, including racist or sexist remarks, that will call for adult intervention. The school may have policies that relate to behaviour management and child protection for pupils when dealing with a range of abusive or anti-social behaviours (see also Unit 3-1). There may also be a scale of sanctions or strategies that are applied by staff when dealing with these behaviours. As a teaching assistant, you should know how to respond in such situations, particularly if they pose a threat to your own safety or the safety of others. However, if you have problems dealing with a situation you should always call on another member of staff.

You are outside during lunchtime when you notice that a group of Year 9 boys have started to taunt two new Year 7 pupils who have recently started at the school. You can hear them shouting racist remarks and following the pupils around.

1 What would you do in this situation?

2 How would you deal with the problem if the situation became more difficult and the older boys refused to stop?

How to contribute to pupils' development of self-reliance and self-esteem

From an early age, pupils will need to start to develop their independence. In school, the development of their self-esteem and self-help skills will be encouraged from Reception, where the Early Learning Goals support pupils in thinking about how they will make their

own decisions. As they become older, pupils will be expected to be able to have a range of self-help skills, which they will need to apply to their own learning. One of the most important roles you will have as an assistant is that of actively listening and responding to pupils so that you can encourage them in their need to communicate their own ideas.

▲ Assistants can help by having positive relationships with pupils

Development of self-esteem in children

Children will begin to develop their self-esteem through the love and care given to them by their parents. If children grow up in a secure and stable home environment with love and affection, they will develop a positive self-image and feel valued. It is important for children that the love given to them by their parents and family is unconditional, and is not dependent on their looks or abilities. At the earliest stages, one of the aims of the curriculum is to 'provide opportunities for all children to succeed in an atmosphere of care and feeling valued'. The National Curriculum for PSHE at Key Stages 3 and 4 promotes the development of confidence and responsibility, and making the most of their abilities. As they grow older, children still need continued love and support to retain a positive self-image and to help their self-development. In school surroundings, we can help pupils to feel secure and valued by giving them routines and responsibilities, and by ensuring that staff are consistent. This will help them to feel confident in applying the skills they have learnt.

(See also Unit 3-15 page 208 for strategies to promote self-esteem in pupils, and Unit 3-1 page 6 for stages of social development.)

Developing and promoting pupils' self-help skills

Self-help skills emerge as pupils start to develop their own independence and choices. They can do this through opportunities to learn skills in:

▷ independent learning – finding out and learning things for themselves through their work

▷ decision-making – thinking about the next step and being responsible for their actions

▷ problem solving – being able to think things through using their learning skills

▷ self expression – being able to express what they feel

▷ exercising choice – making their own choices about what they are going to do

▷ general life skills – being able to help themselves and others.

As a teaching assistant, pupils will ask you for your help with tasks that they may be able to do unassisted. You may need to break tasks down into smaller and more manageable steps, or talk pupils through them. As they become older, pupils may need help with organising themselves and planning their work, but you should be able to encourage them to be independent wherever possible. Your expectations should always be for pupils to succeed at what they are doing, and they should be encouraged and praised as much as possible. In this way, they will continue to attempt to be independent. For example, sometimes you might start something off for a pupil to encourage them to continue it.

? Think about it

Charley is in Year 8 and is a traveller, often out of school for long periods. As you are working with another pupil in his class, he remembers you and you have developed a good relationship with him. He often tries to ask you for help with activities and with organising himself as he can be very disorganised with his work and equipment.

1 What would you say to Charley if he continued to ask for your help?

2 How could you encourage him to be more independent?

You should make sure that you do not make stereotypical assumptions about pupils' self-reliance for any reason such as gender, disability or cultural background. You may not be aware that you are doing it, but by mentioning these issues, pupils' self-esteem and motivation can be easily damaged. You should also make sure that if you hear any pupils making comments about others in negative terms, you speak to them straight away.

Case study

Marek is in Year 7 and has cerebral palsy. As he has poor muscle control, he has difficulty communicating verbally and needs to have a communication aid to help him. You are working with his group when you hear one of the boys saying that Marek will not be able to do the task that they have been set as it is too difficult for him.

▲ Pupils must develop a good self-image in order to fulfil their potential

Levels of self-reliance and self-esteeem

Pupils who are developing normally will show levels of independence and self-reliance at about the stages defined in the tables of social and emotional development (see pages 6, 146 and 153). It is important for staff to help pupils to build up their self-image and self-esteem through giving them tasks that are achievable for their age and stage of development. Pupils' self-image will be largely based on the reactions of members of staff to what they do, which will in turn help them to gain a positive view of themselves. It is vital that pupils develop a good self-image as this will give them greater confidence in their abilities and enable them to fulfil their potential.

? Think about it

Sam is in Year 7 and has to complete a project for RE on different faiths. She has made a general plan about what she is going to do and has been to the library and used the Internet to find information. However, she is finding it difficult to organise the project and asks you if she can show you what she has done during the lunch hour.

▶ How could you encourage Sam with her work?

▶ What would you do if Sam asked you for help in organising her project?

Encouraging and supporting pupils in decision-making

As pupils become more mature, they will be given tasks which require them to make their own decisions and choices. They will need to be given guidance as to how they can think the process through to help them to do this.

The types of strategies you may like to use with pupils could include:

▷ asking them about the different factors which will affect their decision

▷ getting them to think about what will happen if they make a particular decision

▷ thinking about how to test whether this is the right decision

▷ making sure that you listen to their ideas and the reasons for making their choices.

Giving positive praise and recognition to pupils

When pupils are in a learning environment, they will need to be given positive praise and encouragement to build up their self-esteem and to make them feel valued. When this happens, a pupil will be more likely to attempt to gain the same reaction from members of the staff by trying hard next time. If a pupil does not have any encouragement, and staff do not notice when they put in more effort, they will be less likely to do it again (see also Unit 3-1).

When pupils first come into secondary school there might be an emphasis on achievement and behaviour at first so that the pupils gain a clear understanding of each. This will mean that the school gives new pupils clear guidelines on how to behave and what the school and the pupil should expect from one another. Where pupils are conforming and working hard the school should recognise this so that they continue to be motivated. The kinds of rewards which are given will vary from school to school, but may include:

▷ house points
▷ certificates
▷ awards for achievement in different subject areas
▷ merits
▷ written encouragement on pupils' work
▷ special assemblies which recognise pupils' achievements
▷ giving pupils responsibilities.

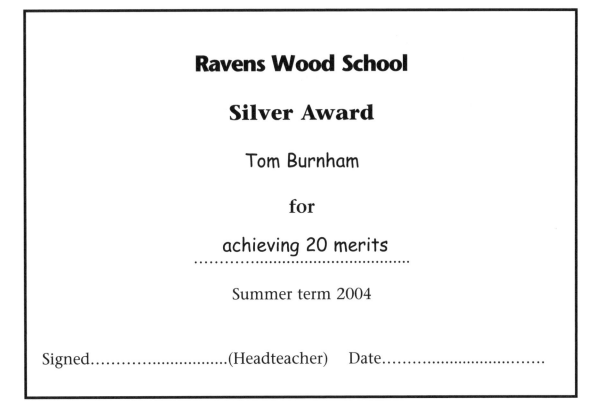

Ravens Wood School

Silver Award

Tom Burnham

for

achieving 20 merits
....

Summer term 2004

Signed...........................(Headteacher)   Date...............................

▲ A school Certificate of Achievement

Think about it

What sorts of rewards and encouragement are given to children at different stages in your school?

Pupils in secondary schools will also be able to run their own clubs and will be responsible for putting on other events such as running school councils and school magazines. Schools will give these kinds of responsibilities to pupils, to show that they are valued and respected as part of the organisation. This may vary from giving pupils a chance to be a prefect, to being captain of the school netball or football team.

You may also find that families have different ideas about what their children will achieve, due to family or cultural expectations. Some families might expect their children to be given responsibilities, as previous siblings have done well, while others may have high expectations of boys rather than girls. Some parents will have low expectations of their children and will not believe that they can do well.

Think about it

Have you had experience of parents or families whose expectations for their children have been unrealistic? How have their expectations been different?

Keys to good practice
Encouraging pupils to be self-reliant and independent

✔ Praise pupils' achievements and their efforts.
✔ Do not talk negatively about pupils.
✔ Support pupils with choices and decision-making.
✔ Always give pupils tasks which they are able to do.
✔ Encourage self-help skills.

Contribute to pupils' ability to recognise and deal with emotions

When you are working with pupils as a teaching assistant, you will get to know them and learn how they are likely to deal with their emotions. Some pupils find this more difficult than others, and will have outbursts and behaviour problems if they feel that they are being treated unfairly. Others may keep their emotions hidden so that you are unable to tell if there is a problem. Emotional development is very closely linked with social development, as pupils are learning to become more confident in themselves. They will need to be able to show how both positive and negative emotions affect them. You must be aware which pupils in the class are likely to find the expression of emotions difficult. It is important for pupils to learn how to recognise and deal with their emotions so that they will grow to have more control over them.

(Stages of social development are to be found in this unit on page 146.)

Stages of emotional development
Years 4–7: Pupils will have a strong need to feel accepted and worthwhile. Set pupils of this age up for success.
Years 8–10: This is a time of emotional swings and the biggest period of challenges to a pupil's self-concept. Staff will need to take time to talk about values with this age group.
Years 11 and 12: Teenagers will be learning to co-operate with others at an adult level. They will need increasingly greater responsibilities to allow for independent thinking and decision making.

School policies and practices for pupils with emotional and behavioural needs

Your school may have a range of strategies in place for supporting pupils who have emotional or behavioural difficulties. As discussed in Unit 3-1, the strategies you may need to use with these pupils should be those which are used by the whole school. It is important that pupils are aware of the consequences of their actions and why these sanctions are necessary.

School policies which relate to **pupils' emotional development** may include:

▷ behaviour policy – this will give staff strategies and guidelines when managing behaviour in school

▷ PSHE policy – this will give details of the way in which staff carry out the National Curriculum with regard to personal, social and health education

▷ inclusion and equal opportunities policies – these policies will promote the school's ethos and procedures in these two areas

▷ anti-bullying policy – since September 1999, schools have been legally required to implement anti-bullying policies

▷ child protection policy – this will have an effect on the way staff are alert at all times for signs of abuse or neglect in pupils. It will give you an indication of the key points which you need to observe and the person you need to go to in order to report any concerns

▷ schools are also now required to have a clear anti-racism policy.

You will need to know the range of strategies the school uses to diffuse and manage pupils' emotions: some pupils may need to be given anger management training.

You may find that teachers use various different strategies for managing negative emotions.

Find out about...

The kinds of strategies used by different teachers with whom you work for managing negative emotions. Do they use school policies? Which of these strategies appear to be the most effective?

Staff will need to know how to recognise the types of activities which will encourage the expression of feelings and emotions. As an assistant, you should be able to support pupils and encourage them to express and discuss how they are feeling. You will need to be:

▷ **observant** – make sure you are always looking out for pupils. The class teacher may not be aware of a pupil who has been particularly quiet – but this could be a sign that there is a problem. There may also be a pupil who is behaving in a different way from usual, for example, is short tempered or seeking attention.

▷ **approachable** – if pupils feel comfortable with you and relaxed, they are more likely to come to you if they have a problem or are upset. They may also want to tell you about something good that has happened which is making them feel positive. You will need to try to develop good relationships with all pupils over time, through being interested and listening to what they have to say.

Teaching tip: Make sure you don't appear to favour only one pupil.

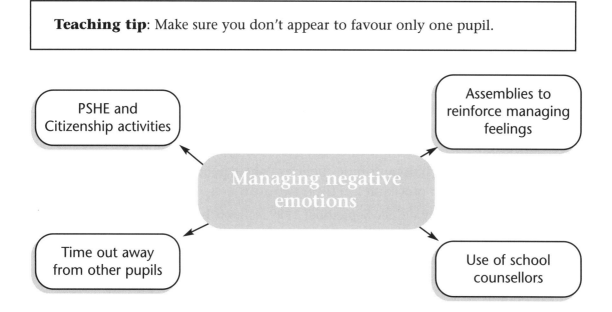

▲ There are different strategies for helping pupils to manage negative emotions

▷ **aware of confidentiality issues** – you must be aware that any information about a pupil is confidential and you should not discuss any issues outside the school environment. The school will also have policies and procedures for ensuring confidentiality, by making sure that computer passwords and files on pupils are only seen by those who are authorised to read them. Alternatively, a pupil with an emotional problem may approach you, or you may feel that they need to discuss something which is upsetting them with a member of staff. In this situation you will need to tell the pupil before they confide in you that you cannot guarantee that you will not tell anyone else, for example, if a pupil is being harmed in any way.

▷ **possible causes of pupils' negative outbursts and reactions** – there is a variety of reasons that pupils may have negative outbursts or react in an uncharacteristic way. It is important that staff are aware of the different factors that can have an effect on pupils' behaviour.

Possible reasons for negative reactions by pupils
Bullying – the pupil may have been bullied intermittently for periods since they have been in school. They may be reluctant to tell staff as they are unsure of the response.
Inability to cope with academic work – the pupil may be finding that they cannot manage their work and need to have extra support, or be diagnosed as having special educational needs. This may be difficult for the pupil to manage emotionally.
Divorce or separation in family – the pupil may be angry with either parent, or be unable to express their emotions. They may also blame themselves for what has happened.
Death or illness in family – this will upset the pupil and could cause outbursts or regressive behaviour, such as withdrawing.
Changing class or school – this may cause pupils to feel insecure and unsure about where they fit in with other pupils.
Substance abuse – pupils may seem to be detached and show signs of neglect or tiredness.
Sexual abuse – this may cause mood swings and changes in behaviour. The pupil may behave differently with other pupils or adults.
Physical abuse – pupils who are being physically abused may be nervous or jumpy around adults. They may find it difficult to trust people and could be quiet or withdrawn and lack self-esteem.
Verbal abuse – pupils who are verbally abused may be very quiet and may also have low self-esteem.
Change in carer – this will have a disruptive influence on the pupil's home life and could affect their self-esteem as they may feel rejected. Pupils may become detached from others because of a fear of this happening again.
Moving house – this may be difficult if pupils need to start at a new school and form new relationships. Even moving home within the same area can be hard for some pupils.

Any of these factors may make it difficult for a child to manage their behaviour and emotions in school. Assistants will need to voice any concerns they have about particular pupils to others within the school.

Problems when dealing with pupils who have emotional difficulties

You may find that pupils are the victims of cultural or gender stereotypes, and are not freely able to talk about their feelings as they are not encouraged to do this at home. Some parents may not feel that boys, for example, should be able to discuss how they feel but should 'put a brave face on it.' This may limit the child's emotional development and make it difficult for them to bring their feelings into the open. If this is the case, you will need to be understanding and reassure them that it is acceptable to talk about feelings and emotions rather than keep them hidden.

When pupils are not able to express how they feel, there may be problems later and behavioural problems could arise, especially if pupils become frustrated by their inability to discuss their feelings.

Keys to good practice
Managing pupils' emotions

✔ Form good relationships with pupils.

✔ Look for any signs of distress/unusual behaviour.

✔ Always remain calm and reassure pupils.

✔ Be aware of confidentiality issues.

Evidence collection

(For this unit you may need to use simulation when obtaining evidence in relation to responding to conflict situations, antisocial behaviour, emotional outbursts and negative reactions.)

You are making your way around the school when you notice a group of girls having an argument in the corridor. There is one girl in particular who seems to be at the centre of the argument. After speaking to the group, you take the girl to one side to find out what has happened and she is clearly very upset.

▶ What would you do next, and in what order?

▶ What school policies would you need to consider when dealing with this situation?

End of unit test

1 What different groups of people should pupils be encouraged to form positive relationships with in school?

2 What are the criteria that can affect the way in which a pupil relates to others?

3 What types of school policies can assist when helping pupils to develop positive relationships?

4 Why is it important for pupils to have a stable and secure home environment?

5 Name some of the different self-help skills we may need to help pupils with in school.

6 What kinds of factors will have an impact on a child's self-esteem?

7 Why might some families have higher or lower expectations of their children than the school?

8 What types of school policies will relate to pupils' emotional development?

9 How can you encourage pupils to come and discuss their emotions if they need to?

10 What kinds of signs may a pupil display who is suffering from emotional difficulties?

References

National Curriculum document (QCA, 1999)

How to stop bullying: Kidscape, Training Guide

Websites

www.dfes.gov.uk/bullying

www.bullying.co.uk

www.childline.org.uk

www.kidscape.org.uk

www.nc.uk.net/index.html

Unit 3-10 Contribute to the maintenance of a safe and secure learning environment

In your role as a teaching assistant you will need to be aware of health and safety issues, both within the school and grounds and while visiting other places on school trips. Health and safety is a responsibility of all staff in the school, and you will need to know types of risks which may occur and to whom you need to report any safety issues.

If you are called upon to take action in the case of an emergency, you will need to know the level of assistance you should start to take, and the types of action you should not. As any other responsible adult who is first on the scene, teaching assistants should always assess the situation and act accordingly. If they are trained in first aid, they should do what they can to remove any immediate danger to the casualty but wait for the first aider or emergency services to arrive.

School policies and procedures for health and safety and your responsibilities within the school

When you first start at a new school, you should have access to or be informed about the school's policy for health and safety. The Health and Safety at Work Act (1974) was designed to protect everyone at work through procedures for preventing accidents. The types of precautions all those in the workplace are expected to observe are as described below.

Report any hazards

You will need to be alert to any hazards which are likely to cause injury to yourself and others in the school. The school is required to carry out an annual risk assessment to determine which areas and activities of the school are most likely to be hazardous, the likelihood of this occurring, and those who are at risk. Pupils and staff need to be vigilant and report any hazards which they notice immediately to the appropriate person. This may be the school's health and safety agent, the headteacher or another member of staff. You should be aware of the designated person to whom you should report health and safety matters.

(See pages 160 and 163 for the types of hazards which may occur.)

Follow the school's safety policy

The school's safety policy should give information to all staff about procedures which the school has in place for ensuring that the school is as safe as possible. All new staff joining the school should be given induction training in safety procedures and what to do in case of emergencies. Safety should be a regular topic at staff and assistants' meetings.

Make sure that their actions do not harm themselves or others

Staff also need to ensure that any actions which they take are not likely to harm or cause a danger to others in the school. This will include tidying up and putting things away after use. It also includes taking no action if they discover a potential danger: this would go against the employee's responsibilities according to the Health and Safety at Work Act.

Use any safety equipment provided

Staff will need to ensure that safety equipment which is provided for use when carrying out activities is always used. This will include safe use of tools which are used for subjects such as design and technology, or gloves when handling materials during science activities. There should be guidelines in the school's policy for the safe use and storage of equipment.

All staff working within a school have a responsibility to ensure that pupils are cared for and safe. The Children Act (1989) also requires that we protect children as far as we can when they are in our care. This includes preventing any risks which may occur.

The types of health, safety and security risks which may occur

(You will also need to read Unit 3–5, page 104 Safe use and care of learning equipment and materials.)

Hazards which may be found in schools

The table below shows some of the hazards which may be found in schools and the action to take for them.

Internal hazards

Type of hazard (indoors)	What to do
Dangerous items left within pupils' reach (scissors, cleaning equipment and materials, kettles, hot drinks)	Remove or put away
Trailing electrical wires/overloaded plugs	Tidy if possible, or report
Untidy areas (things which can be tripped over)	Tidy if possible, or report
Fire doors obstructed	Always keep clear

Schools should carry out regular checks to ensure that these types of risks are kept to a minimum and that staff are aware why they need to be vigilant and what to look for.

There are also other materials and equipment used in schools which may present a risk if not used and stored correctly. Different stages or subject areas may use equipment and materials which are potentially hazardous to pupils or staff, although health and safety issues are relevant through all subject areas and all parts of the school:

▷ **PE** – apparatus use, movement and storage. In PE lessons, pupils will need to learn how to use equipment carefully and safely. Equipment should be regularly checked.

▷ **Design and technology** – tools or equipment. As these tools may not be used often, staff will need to talk to pupils each time about using them carefully.

▷ **Science** – living things, pond areas, use of equipment. Pupils should be taught always to wash their hands after touching animals, and to use any equipment safely.

▷ **Food technology** – cooking areas should be regularly checked and care should be taken with cookers.

▷ **ICT** – computers are in use all the time in schools and should be regularly checked. Office staff will probably be the only people using them for long periods and they should be aware of the importance of taking breaks.

▷ **Other electrical items** – equipment used in school will all need to have an annual safety check. If staff bring their own electrical appliances into school, these should always be checked before use, using a portable appliance tester, to prevent a risk to others.

Find out...

The person in your school who is responsible for checking electrical equipment. Where is this recorded?

Case study

Sue is a full-time teaching assistant who is also the school's health and safety representative and a school governor. She has regular opportunities at staff meetings for mentioning health and safety issues and often has to remind staff about school policy. Some members of staff are not willing to ensure that school policy is followed, for example when putting items of equipment away or making sure that potentially dangerous items are locked out of sight.

1 Why is it important that all staff follow school policy?

2 What would happen if an accident occurred due to negligence?

▲ Materials should always be stored safely

Storing and moving equipment

All items should be stored or moved carefully, and only by those who are authorised to do so. Staff should not attempt to move items which are heavy or difficult to move. Items which may form a potential hazard should be locked away until they are needed. Storing items safely is important as people will often need to find them quickly and they will need to be able to see where they are and be able to reach them. Staff should ensure that storage areas are kept tidy and materials are not piled up to form a further danger.

Accidental breakages or spillages

When breakages and spillages do occur, they will need to be cleaned up as soon as possible to prevent any danger to others. If you are in a situation where an accident has occurred and you are not aware of where to find cleaning equipment, you should not leave the area unattended but send for another member of staff.

Disposal of waste

If you have been carrying out any activities, for example in science, where you need to dispose of waste materials, you should do so in such a way that will not cause harm to others. The school should offer guidance on the disposal of these types of materials. If you are in any doubt you should contact your school's health and safety agent.

Ensuring others are aware of where you are

You should ensure that your line manager knows where you are at all times. This is so that in case of emergency, such as fire or a bomb scare, they will be able to find you. Different schools may have different procedures for doing this, so your line manager should inform you of what to do if you are out of the classroom. It is particularly important if you are taking pupils away from the classroom for any reason.

There may be other hazards which are found outside, for example in playgrounds and pond areas. These will include dangers such as poisonous plants, areas which have not been fenced in, and risk of drowning. If you are taking pupils on a school trip, a member of staff should always visit first to check, among other things, for potential dangers.

External hazards

Type of hazard (outdoor/during school trips)	What to do
Playground areas – broken /faulty equipment – using equipment inappropriately, (e.g. basketball hoops, footballs)	Remove and label or report immediately Warn pupils or remove
Poisonous plants	Fence off area/warn pupils
Litter bins	Keep pupils away from unsafe bins
Danger from animals	Ensure pupils always wash their hands after contact Keep pupils away from animal faeces
Pond area	Ensure any cuts on hands are covered before getting wet (risk of leptospirosis – Weil's disease)

Case study

You are involved with the Duke of Edinburgh Bronze award scheme at your school and have been asked to accompany a group of pupils and staff on a weekend to prepare them for the real thing. Although you have been told about emergency procedures and there is a qualified first aider present, you are anxious about some safety issues but are worried about mentioning them.

What should you do in this situation?

Disability Discrimination Act

With the introduction of the Disability Discrimination Act into schools from September 2002, staff need to be increasingly aware of any increase in potential hazards when taking pupils on school visits. Pupils should not be excluded from any school visit because of their disability.

→ **Knowledge into action**

Investigate an area of your school (indoor or outdoor) for safety. Can you find any potential hazards? What are the school's procedures for reporting these?

School security

Schools need to ensure that they take measures to protect all adults and pupils while they are on school premises. This includes making sure that all those who are in school have been signed in and identified. Schools may have different methods for doing this, for example visitors may be issued with badges. If staff notice any unidentified people in the school, they should be challenged immediately. If you are on playground duty and notice anything suspicious, you should also send for help. Schools may also have secure entry and exit points which may make it more difficult for individuals to enter the premises.

✓ **Keys to good practice**
Minimising risks in the learning environment

✔ Be vigilant.

✔ Use and store equipment safely.

✔ Report anything which is unsafe.

✔ Challenge unidentified persons on school premises.

Minimising risks arising from emergencies

What to do in an emergency

There are different types of emergencies and conditions which can occur in school. You may find that you are first on the scene in an emergency and need to take action. If you are the only member of staff in the vicinity, you will need to make sure you follow the correct procedures until help arrives. It is vital to send for help as soon as possible. This should be the ambulance if necessary and the school's qualified first aider.

Warning! If not trained in first aid, and if at all unsure about what to do, you should only take action to avert any further danger to the casualty and others.

Different emergencies and what you should do

Injuries – check the injury. For minor injuries such as a bump on the head or a graze, you should apply cold water. If the injury is more serious, you may need to take the victim to the qualified first aider in school. All injuries to the head should be recorded.

Epileptic seizure – do not try to move or restrain the patient. If possible, put something soft beneath their head to prevent them from hurting themselves. Clear a space around them.

Burns and scalds – cool the affected area immediately using cold water. Do not remove any clothes which are stuck to the burn.

Electrocution – cut off the source of electricity by removing the plug. If there is no way to do this, stand on dry insulating material, such as newspaper or a wooden box, and push the victim away from the source using something wooden such as a chair. Do not touch the victim until the electricity has been switched off. After this, place the victim in the recovery position (see pages 166–7).

Choking or difficulty with breathing – encourage the person to cough to dislodge the blockage. Bend the casualty over with the head lower than the chest and slap between the shoulder blades five times using the heel of the hand.

Poisoning – find out what the pupil has taken or swallowed if possible. Stay with the pupil and watch for signs of unconsciousness. Take the suspected poison to hospital with you.

Cardiac arrest – if the patient is conscious, place in a half sitting position and support with pillows and cushions. Place another pillow under the knees. Do not give the patient food or water. If the patient becomes unconscious, place in the recovery position (see pages 166–7).

Substance abuse – if you can, find out what has happened so that you can inform medical staff. If the person is unconscious, place in the recovery position (see pages 166–7). Do not try to induce vomiting.

Falls – potential and actual fractures: all cases should be treated as actual fractures. Do not attempt to move the casualty. You will need a qualified first aider to come to the scene. Support a fractured leg by tying it to the other leg, using a wide material such as a scarf or tie. If the knee is broken, you must not try to force it straight. If you suspect a fractured arm, support in a sling and secure to the chest. If the arm will not bend, secure by strapping it to the body.

Faints or loss of consciousness – treat those who feel faint by sitting down and putting their head between their knees. If they do faint, lie them on their back and raise their legs to increase blood flow to the brain. Loosen clothing at the neck and keep the patient quiet after regaining consciousness.

Severe bleeding – it is important to reduce the flow of blood as soon as possible. You should summon the first aider and call for help. Lie the casualty down and remove clothing around the wound if possible. Press down hard on it with any absorbent clean material, or squeeze the sides together if there is no foreign body in the wound. If possible, raise the wound to above the level of the heart. This will slow the flow of blood. Maintain the pressure for up to ten minutes and then place an absorbent material over the wound and bandage firmly. Do not remove the bandage. If there is a foreign body in the skin, do not remove it but bandage around if possible without putting pressure on the object. If you remove the object, it will cause the victim to lose more blood.

Shock – lie the victim down and treat whatever may be causing the shock. Loosen clothing at the neck to assist breathing. Raise the legs if possible and keep warm. Do not give the victim anything to eat or drink in case they need an anaesthetic, but moisten lips if necessary.

Putting a casualty into the recovery position

If you are dealing with an unconscious person, you will need to place them in the recovery position. This will prevent any blood, vomit or saliva from blocking the windpipe. You should always do this unless you suspect that the victim has a fracture of the spine or neck.

1 Kneel beside the victim and turn their head towards you, lifting it back to open the airway.

2 Place their nearest arm straight down their side and the other arm across their chest. Place the far ankle over the near ankle.

3 While holding the head with one hand, hold the victim at the hip by their clothing and turn onto their front by pulling towards you, supporting them with your knees.

4 Lift the chin forward to keep the airway open.

5 Bend the arm and leg nearest to you, and pull out the other arm from under the body, palm up.

If you are treating a casualty, you should be aware of the dangers of contamination from blood and other body fluids. Always wear protective gloves if you can when treating an open wound or if you have contact with other body fluids. Many infections such as HIV and hepatitis can be passed on through contact with these fluids.

You should always stay with the casualty and give as much support as you can, both by giving as much care as you are able and by your physical presence. If you feel that you are not able to deal with the situation, you should always do what you can and reassure the patient as much as possible while sending for help. Where a pupil has been injured badly, their parents or carers should be notified immediately. They will need to know exactly what is happening – if the pupil is being taken to hospital they will need to know where.

Put two fingers under the casualty's chin and one hand on the forehead.

Gently tilt the head back. Straighten limbs. Bend the arm nearest to you so it is at right angles to the body.

Bring the other arm across the casualty's chest. Place the hand against the casualty's cheek – with palm outwards. Pull up the casualty's far leg, just above the knee, using your other hand.

Pull on the far leg and roll the casualty towards you, still pressing the hand against the cheek – until the casualty is lying on their side.

Make sure the casualty's head is well back – to keep airway open and stop them from breathing in vomit or choking on their tongue.

To stop the casualty rolling too far, use your knees as support. Bend the upper leg so that it is at a right angle from the body.

Make sure the upper arm is supporting the head.

▲ Putting a casualty into the recovery position

Religious and cultural restrictions on the actions which you may be able to take

When dealing with an emergency, you should be aware that some religions or cultures may not agree with some treatments – for example, some Muslims may only wash under running water. If you are in any doubts as to what action you can take, always speak to parents first if at all possible.

➡ Knowledge into action

Have you ever needed to deal with an emergency at your school? What kind of treatment were you able to give?

Treating others

If others are in the vicinity at the time of the accident, they may need to have support after the initial danger has passed. This could be due to emotional distress or shock, which can have a serious effect. If you have been involved with treating the victim but another person has now taken over, you should offer what support you can to others in the area. This may include giving them privacy and making the area safe.

Completing accident forms

By law, the school will have procedures for recording and reporting accidents. All accidents, whether they are serious or minor, must be recorded. There may be a school accident book and a local authority accident form. The type of information required will be:

▷ the name of the casualty

▷ what happened

▷ the date and time of the accident

▷ the cause of the accident

▷ the treatment given.

If there has been an accident you should send for the designated first aider straight away, but in the meantime:

▷ remain calm

▷ check there is no further danger to the victim or others.

You should always stay with the casualty and give as much support as you can, both by giving as much care as you are able and by your physical presence.

Your school may give you the opportunity to go on a recognised first aid course to gain a certificate or qualification in first aid. If you are able to attend, these courses are worthwhile and could be beneficial both for yourself and for others.

Sunnymead Secondary School
Accident report form

Name of casualty . . . .

Exact location of incident . . . .

Date of incident . . . .

What was the injured person doing? . . . .

How did the accident happen? . . . .

What injuries occurred? . . . .

Treatment given . . . .

Medical aid sought . . . .

Name of person dealing with incident . . . .

Name of witness . . . .

If casualty was a pupil, what time were parents informed? . . . .

Was hospital attended? . . . .

Was the accident investigated? . . . . By whom? . . . .

Signed . . . . Position . . . .

Other emergencies

All workplaces must carry out regular fire practices so that staff are aware of procedures. In a school, this ensures that pupils also know what to do. These procedures will also apply to bomb scares and any other need for building evacuation. If you discover a fire, you should sound the nearest alarm and ensure everyone leaves the building as quickly and calmly as possible. It is important to remain calm and to check that all pupils and staff have been accounted for. Remember to include any parent helpers or other adults who are in school by checking the school signing-in book.

→ **Knowledge into action**

Are regular fire practices carried out in your school? Are there clear guidelines for evacuation and assembly points?

Fire extinguishers

There are different types of fire extinguishers, and if you need to use one you should make sure that you read the instructions carefully. These will be printed on the outside of the extinguisher.

Water – for wood, paper and textiles

Foam – for wood, paper, textiles, petrol, oil, fats, paints, etc.

Powder – for wood, paper, textiles, petrol, oils, fats, paints, electrical hazards, vehicle protection

Carbon dioxide – for petrol, oils, fats, paints, electrical hazards

Fire blanket – for smothering a fire (usually kept in a kitchen) and putting around someone whose clothes are on fire.

▲ Different fire extinguishers must be used for different types of fire

Evidence collection

The next time your school carries out a fire drill, make sure that you record answers to the following:

▶ How long does it take to evacuate the building(s)?

▶ How does the school ensure that everyone has been evacuated successfully?

▶ Who checks the school to make sure that this has taken place?

▶ As a result of the drill, were any safety issues raised?

End of unit test

1 What are your responsibilities under the Health and Safety at Work Act?

2 Name three hazards which may be found in a classroom.

3 Of what should you be aware when bringing an electrical appliance into school for use?

4 What types of areas may be hazardous outside the school building?

5 What should you do in the event of a burn?

6 When should you put a patient in the recovery position?

7 How can you help others once expert help has arrived to treat the casualty?

8 Why must you be careful with different types of fire extinguisher?

9 What sort of information is recorded on an accident form?

10 Why do you need to be careful when handling body fluids?

References

What to Do in an Emergency (Readers Digest Association, 1988)

Tassoni, P., *Certificate in Child Care and Education* (Heinemann, 2002)

Websites

www.teachernet.gov.uk/visits (good practice guide to health and safety of pupils on educational visits)

Contribute to the health and well-being of pupils

This unit deals with the care and support given to pupils while they are adjusting to a new setting. Assistants will need to show that they support the teacher in the strategies which are used to help and reassure pupils. They will also need to be able to deal with any particular difficulties which the pupil is experiencing in settling in. Where pupils have any medical needs, assistants will need to know the school policies for the storage and administration of medicines and how to care for pupils with signs of ill-health. (For details of what to do in an emergency, see Unit 3-10 page 164.)

How to support pupils in adjusting to a new setting

If you are helping pupils to adjust to a new setting, this may be for a variety of reasons:

▷ the pupils have just started secondary school in Year 7

▷ pupil(s) are joining an existing class

▷ the class is transferring at the start of a new academic year

▷ pupil(s) are re-joining the class after a period of extended absence.

Assistants will need to be able to help pupils in each of these situations to become used to the new setting through a range of strategies. Some pupils may not need to have much staff intervention to help them to settle in, while others may find it more difficult.

Pupils starting school in Year 7

The year group leader, if there is one, class teacher and assistants will all need to discuss the strategies which they will use with the new group of pupils. The school may have set guidelines and procedures that are to be used with all pupils. These may be routine and include:

▷ coming to the school before the start date to meet the class teacher

▷ starting Year 7 at an earlier time than the rest of the school on the first day

▷ being shown around the school so that they are aware of different areas and when they are likely to use them (office, hall/dining hall, playground, etc.).

As the pupils become settled in school, they will gradually learn the rules and routines which they will be expected to follow. This process will take place over time as the pupils become used to being in the secondary school environment.

Pupil(s) joining an existing class

When pupils join an already established class, they may find it quite difficult to come into a class where the majority of pupils already know rules and routines. Assistants and teachers will need to work together to help them to adjust and feel part of the class. The strategies that could be used in this situation would include:

▷ encouraging other pupils to make new arrivals feel welcome through interacting with them and showing them around

▷ showing them around the classroom and class routines

▷ giving them information about the school which you feel would be useful for them to know – playtimes, lunchtimes, location of key areas, school rules

▷ being approachable and available if the pupil needs help in any way.

Class transferring at the start of a new academic year

If you support an individual pupil, you may be in a position where you are moving with all the pupils into a different class. This may make the process easier for them, since they will have a member of staff they recognise who will know them. However, pupils will become more used to changing class each year as they progress up the school, and most will be excited to be moving up into the next year group. If you are a teaching assistant working within a class, you can help the pupils to settle in by:

▷ emphasising the importance of moving into the next year group

▷ showing them the layout of the classroom

▷ encouraging them to join in with class activities

▷ discussing with them any rules or responsibilities which are specific to the year group, e.g. 'Now you are in Year 11, you are allowed to go in first at lunchtime',

▷ being approachable and available for any questions the pupils may have.

? *Think about it*

Have there been any cases in your school where pupils have found it difficult to settle into a new class? What have been the reasons for this? How has the problem been resolved?

Pupil(s) rejoining the class after a period of extended absence

Sometimes pupils may leave the class for a period, for example if they are travellers, or if they have special needs and have required help within another setting for a time. They may find it difficult to adjust to a new environment or be self-conscious about returning and their reasons for being away from the school. You can help them to settle back into the class by:

▷ being available for them to talk through any concerns

▷ support their integration with other pupils

▷ helping them with any specific problems.

▮ *Case study*

Paul is from a travelling family and often misses school for extended periods. He is not unhappy about returning to the school environment but often finds it difficult to settle and focus on his work. How would you encourage Paul to become used to the school and become involved with other pupils?

Factors which may affect a pupil's ability to adjust to a new setting

Sometimes pupils may find it difficult to settle due to external factors. These may include:

▷ the home background of the pupil – the pupil may have a disruptive or traumatic home life

▷ the care history – the pupil may not like change if there have been changes in carer at home

▷ if the pupil speaks English or Welsh as an additional language (see Unit 3-12)

▷ any special educational needs which the pupil has – this may affect the pupil's understanding of what is happening.

You will need to be able to support pupils in all these situations through discussions with teachers, parents and helpers. These pupils may need more reassurance and help and sometimes display challenging behaviour (see also Unit 3-1 for strategies for managing this).

It is vital that the class teacher is aware of any problems or difficulties that a pupil has in adjusting or settling in. If you notice or find out about any issues, or if a parent or other member of staff tells you about a pupil's home circumstances and you do not think the teacher is aware, you must talk to the teacher about it immediately.

School policies and practices relating to medical issues

The school may have a number of policies relating to the medical care of pupils while they are in the setting. These may follow guidelines set out by the Local Education Authority, which should be available to all schools. You should know where to go to ask about them and to find out about your responsibilities.

When the pupil first enters a school, parents will be asked to provide health details which may include whether their child has any allergies, medication and so on (see below).

St Marks Secondary School

Declaration of Health Form

Child's surname . . . . Date of birth . . . .

First names . . . .

Address . . . .

. . . .

Telephone number (home) . . . .

Parent/carer's work/mobile telephone numbers:

Mother . . . . Father . . . .

Name and address of GP . . . .

. . . . Telephone no . . . .

Health Details

Does your child have:

Asthma YES/NO   Eczema YES/NO   Epilepsy YES/NO   Diabetes YES/NO

Any allergies . . . .

Details of medication . . . .

Is there any other information you feel we should know about your child?

. . . .

. . . .

▲ Parents complete a form like this when their child first enters a school

These types of records will be kept in the pupil's file, although if there is any medication which needs to be administered in school, or medical treatment for conditions such as asthma or allergies, these should be kept in a central area such as the school office and treated as confidential. There may be a member of staff who is responsible for administering medication, although this is a voluntary role and should not be expected of staff. If there is not a member of staff who is prepared to administer medicines, parents should be informed in writing and told that an ambulance will be called immediately in the event of an emergency.

Find out...

Is there a volunteer in your school who administers medication to pupils and how often are they called upon to do it. What training have they had?

Common medical conditions

Medical conditions which may require medication to be administered in schools may include the following:

▷ **Asthma** – pupils needing inhalers due to a respiratory condition should have access to these quickly in case of emergency.

▷ **Diabetes** – if hypoglycaemia occurs, the pupil will need to take oral glucose, for example food, glucose tablets or glucose gel.

▷ **Epilepsy** – pupils who are on medication for epilepsy are seldom required to take it during school hours, as it is usually taken twice a day. However, if medication is required three times a day, volunteers in the staff may be asked to administer it.

▷ **Anaphylactic shock** – some pupils have severe allergic reactions to certain substances such as nuts or milk and can suffer anaphylactic shock. The only way in which this can be treated in school is through the administration of adrenalin via an Epipen or Anapen. For this to be administered, staff will need to have had specific training.

▷ **Attention Deficit Hyperactivity Disorder (ADHD)** – school-aged pupils are increasingly being diagnosed with this disorder and the most common form of medication used to treat these pupils is Ritalin.

Schools may also be asked to administer antibiotics and may have a policy as to whether or not they do this. If antibiotics are prescribed to be taken three times a day, it is not necessary to administer them during school time, but pupils who need four doses may need to have one at lunchtime. It is likely that the school will have a policy as to whether or not they will administer medication which has not been prescribed by a doctor. They should also keep a record of medication given. Medication that is to be administered in school should always be correctly labelled and locked in a safe place until required.

Administration of medicines record sheet					

Name of pupil . . . .

Date	Time	Name of medication	Dose given	Any reactions	Signature

▲ Where medication is given, it should be recorded

✓ Keys to good practice
Administering medicines in school

✔ Gain parental consent to administer medication.

✔ Keep a record of medication given.

✔ Store all medication in a safe place and keep labelled.

✔ Keep any urgent medication close to the pupil.

✔ Keep a list of pupils who have medication in school.

✔ Make sure medicines are not out of date.

Access to routine and emergency medical care

In school there must be at least one qualified first-aider who is trained to administer immediate help to casualties with common injuries or illnesses while in school (see also Unit 3-10 page 165). They will be trained to deal with routine medical incidents such as bumps on the head and cuts and grazes. You should be aware of who these people are so that you can send for them in an emergency along with the emergency services. Where pupils have needed medical treatment or have hurt themselves, the school may decide to telephone the parents to tell them what has happened. Any injuries to the head should also be recorded. Staff will need to be aware of the school's confidentiality requirements when recording and reporting health problems.

The school may have to decide whether to phone a parent if the pupil is ill or has been hurt. If the pupil is very ill, distressed or badly injured, the parent will need to be informed immediately by telephone (see Unit 3-10 page 166 for informing parents in cases of emergency). You will need to give reassurance and support to pupils who are ill or suffering from a condition which is distressing to them. The support or advice which you give them will be dependent on the age and stage of development of the pupil.

Case study

Michael is in the first term of Year 7 and has conjunctivitis. The school policy says that he should be taken out of his classes and his parent or carer contacted as the condition is highly contagious. Michael has become quite distressed as he has had to go to sick bay, he is unable to collect his books and other items from the classroom as it is in use and he is anxious about missing classes. You have been asked to go and speak to Michael to reassure him.

1 What would you say to Michael in this instance?

2 Why is it important that you or another member of staff speaks to Michael's mother when she arrives?

School policies relating to health and hygiene issues

The school should have policies relating to the way in which health issues are managed. These will include routines and procedures for everyday health and hygiene, such as washing hands before lunch and after using the toilet. All staff should be aware of how pupils need to be reminded about health issues and how these will affect themselves and others. The school should have a policy for PSHE (personal, social and health education) which will include information about the way in which pupils are taught about health. This may be through cross-curricular activities or taught on its own. Pupils will need to learn about healthy lifestyles and may have visits from people who work in the community such as the school nurse, ambulance service and road safety officer.

If you need to answer any questions from pupils about health and hygiene, you should make sure that you are following school policy.

Case study

Andrea is working with Year 8 on some food technology. The class have just come in from break and are about to start cooking. What sort of policies might the school have in place to ensure that the pupils wash their hands before cooking and are reminded to do this?

You may notice that pupils have different attitudes from home towards health and hygiene issues. Some families may bring their pupils up in more clean and hygienic environments than others and this may be reflected in the pupil's clothing or personal hygiene. Different factors may affect a pupil's personal hygiene habits:

▷ Age – very young children may not yet have established routines for cleanliness and hygiene.

▷ Gender – boys and girls may have different attitudes towards keeping clean.

▷ Cultural/ethnic background – this may affect the importance of cleanliness, particularly if the pupil has a religion which requires them to be extremely clean.

▷ Specific medical conditions – pupils may need particular help, for example if they are catheterised.

These factors may also affect the actions you can take when attending to a pupil's signs of ill-health. For example, if a pupil already has a medical condition and is on medication, you will need to inform any others who come to attend to them.

You will also need to adhere to health and safety regulations and guidelines when you are attending to pupils' health. Guidance on health and safety regulations will be given in the school's health and safety and child protection policies and through information provided by the local authority. The main points to remember are as follows.

▷ If special needs children need to be changed or undressed, following wetting or soiling themselves, they should do this themselves if possible and in private. If staff need to change pupils for any reason, they should not do it on their own but should have another member of staff present.

▷ Where a pupil's necessary medication needs to be administered other than orally, for example through a suppository, staff should again always be accompanied by another member of staff.

▷ Ask for assistance in any situation in which you feel uncomfortable about administering medication or health care unaccompanied by another member of staff.

▷ Always report any possible signs of abuse which you may notice when administering medical or health care (see also Unit 3-1 page 11).

Signs and symptoms of some common illnesses

All staff should be aware of the types of illnesses that may occur in pupils. They should also be alert to physical signs that may show pupils are incubating an illness. This can vary between illnesses, from 1 day to 3 weeks in some cases. General signs that pupils are 'off colour' may include:

▷ pale skin

▷ flushed cheeks

▷ different behaviour (quiet, clingy, irritable)

▷ rings around the eyes.

The Department of Health has issued a useful poster to schools which could be displayed in the first aid area as a quick reference: 'Guidance on infection control in schools and nurseries'. This clearly sets out some common illnesses and their characteristics. Some of these are listed opposite, although this list is not exhaustive.

Common illnesses and their characteristics

Illness and symptoms	Recommended time to keep off school/treatment	Comments
Chickenpox – patches of red spots with white centres (itchy).	For five days from onset of rash. Treat with calomine lotion to relieve itching.	Not necessary to keep at home until scars heal.
German measles (rubella) – pink rash on head, trunk and limbs. Slight fever, sore throat.	For five days from onset of rash. Treat by resting.	Pupil is most infectious before diagnosis is made. Keep away from pregnant women.
Impetigo – small red pimples on the skin which break down and weep.	Until lesions are crusted and healed. Treat with antibiotic cream or medicine.	Antibiotic treatment may speed up healing. Wash hands well after touching the pupil's skin.
Ringworm – contagious fungal infection of the skin, shows as circular flaky patches.	None. Treat with anti-fungal ointment, may require antibiotics.	Needs treatment by GP.
Diarrhoea and vomiting	Until diarrhoea and vomiting has settled and for 24 hours after. No specific diagnosis or treatment, although keep giving clear fluids (no milk).	
Conjunctivitis – inflammation or irritation of the membranes lining the eyelids.	None (although schools may have different policies on this). Wash with warm water on cotton wool swab. GP may prescribe cream.	
Measles – fever, runny eyes, sore throat and cough. Red rash, often starting from the head and spreading downwards.	Rest, plenty of fluids, paracetamol for fever.	Now more likely with some parents refusing MMR inoculation.
Meningitis – fever, headache, stiff neck and blotchy skin. Dislike of light. Symptoms may develop very quickly.	Urgent medical attention, antibiotics.	Can have severe complications and be fatal.
Tonsillitis – inflammation of tonsils by infection. Very sore throat, fever, earache, enlarged red tonsils which may have white spots.	Treat with antibiotics, rest.	Can also cause ear infections.

Staff will need to be alert to signs and symptoms of these types of illnesses, and notice changes in pupils' behaviour which may indicate that they are unwell. Children often develop symptoms more quickly than adults, as they may have less resistance to infection.

Maintaining your own health and safety when dealing with pupils who have health problems

You must remember to think about your own safety when you are dealing with pupils who have health and medical problems. You should make sure that you are aware of the kinds of situations which are potentially hazardous when dealing with first aid situations. Remember good personal hygiene at all times, and that the risk of transmission of infection is minimal if staff adopt sensible precautions:

▷ Cuts to the hands should be covered by a waterproof dressing to minimise risk of infection.

▷ Always wear disposable gloves when dealing with blood and body fluids.

▷ Wash your hands after removing the gloves and prior to eating or drinking.

▷ Any spillages of blood or body fluids must be reported to the caretaker immediately.

Other medical professionals who come into school or ask for information about pupils may include the school nurse, or visitors from medical establishments who come to discuss pupils who have special needs. If pupils have any medical condition which you feel needs to be discussed with another professional, you should speak to the class teacher or SENCo.

Sometimes, pupils may be in a class where there are cases of head lice, ringworm and other conditions which are contagious. The school will usually write to inform parents if there is more than one or two cases. When keeping pupils off school, parents should be aware of the school's normal policies for different illnesses. For example, if a pupil has had sickness or diarrhoea, the school may say they must have been better for 24 hours before coming back.

Contacting parents

The school may have to decide whether to phone a parent if a pupil is ill or has been hurt. If the pupil is very ill, distressed or badly injured, the parent will need to be informed immediately by telephone (see Unit 3-10 page 166 for informing parents in cases of emergency).

Many schools have a standard letter for head lice.

Holy Cross Secondary School

Dear Parent

We have been informed by a parent that one of the pupils in your child's class has had to be treated for head lice. We feel it is important to inform you so that you will be extra vigilant and take the simple steps needed to combat the problem.

In a normal school environment, where pupils work and play closely together, head lice find it easy to transfer from head to head. Remember, head lice prefer clean hair, so the possibility of infection is quite high. Your child has as much chance of being infected as any other.

Fortunately head lice are easy to treat and you should follow the attached guidelines from the health authority to do this.

As a preventative, the only form of treatment is to comb your child's hair thoroughly every day, and if your child has long hair, to keep it tied back.

Yours sincerely,

J A Sampson
Headteacher

▲ A standard letter informing parents of a head lice outbreak

📁 Evidence collection – case study

You are outside during lunchtime when a pupil comes to tell you that she thinks that her friend is having an anaphylactic reaction to a biscuit she has eaten which may have contained nuts. You have not been trained to use an EpiPen and have not heard of this condition before.

▶ What would you do in this situation?

▶ How would you reassure the pupil who was unwell?

▶ How might this incident have an influence on your future training needs?

Write this up as a case study to use for your portfolio.

End of unit test

1 In what circumstances might you need to help pupils adjust to a new setting?

2 What sorts of strategies could you use to help pupils to settle in?

3 What factors would make it more difficult for a pupil to settle?

4 What types of policies may relate to medical issues?

5 Who should administer medicines in school?

6 When would staff need to report or record any medical treatment?

7 Why might pupils have different factors which influence their attitude to personal hygiene?

8 In what kinds of situations would you require another member of staff to be present?

9 Name five common illnesses which may be prevalent in schools.

10 What would a school do if there was no member of staff prepared to administer medication?

References

Stanway, P., *Mothercare Guide to Child Health* (Conran Octopus, 1992)

Websites

Information on infectious diseases: www.phls.co.uk

Health information for teachers: www.wiredforhealth.co.uk

Department of Health: www.doh.gov.uk

Useful addresses

National Asthma Campaign, Providence House, Providence Place, London, N1 ONT (020 7226 2260)

Department of Health, Richmond House, 79 Whitehall, London, SW1A 2NS (020 7210 4850)

Diabetes UK, 10 Parkway, London NW1 7AA (020 7424 1000)

Epilepsy Action, New Anstey House, Gate Way Drive, Yeadon, Leeds, LS19 7XY (0808 800 5050)

Provide support for bilingual and multilingual pupils

This unit looks at the way in which pupils develop their language skills. Pupils from bilingual and multilingual backgrounds will need more support in the classroom when developing these skills. Assistants will need to be aware of the way in which all children process language and the importance for bilingual and multilingual pupils of retaining their identity through valuing and promoting their home language. In this unit, you will identify strategies for promoting pupils' development in speaking and listening, reading and writing in the target language, which may be English or Welsh. You will need to build on the pupils' experience when developing their skills in the target language and encourage them to develop as independent learners.

Processes and stages of language acquisition and how to promote language development

Language and communication skills are crucial to cognitive development, as without the appropriate skills it is impossible to access and process the information that is essential to learning. A bilingual or multilingual pupil may need to have extra support during the development of their language skills as they will be learning two or more systems, although once these are established there will be few problems.

In order to build up a picture of how we learn language, it is important to consider the two different stages which linguists consider all children pass through. These are known as the **pre-linguistic stage** and the **linguistic stage**:

▷ At first, very young children are not able to use a complex system of symbols – it takes time for them to learn the system of their particular home or community language. This happens in stages and is affected by many factors. Physical maturity plays a part in language development, as babies need to have control over their vocal chords, tongue, lips and jaw muscles in order to be able to articulate the sounds necessary to form their first words. The main foundations of language are constructed between the ages of 18 months and four and a half years during which time most children have fully integrated language as part of the thinking and learning process.

The first stages show how a baby will communicate through crying and will start to recognise voices. At 3-6 months babies will start to 'babble' – this is spontaneous and is not social, as babies will babble on their own or with others. This is true for almost all babies. Babies become aware that some of the sounds they make correspond to sounds that others are making, dropping from their repertoire sounds that they do not hear. At this stage, they could pick up any language and enunciate it perfectly – babies in all languages will follow a similar pattern. However, once they have dropped sounds from their repertoire (around 10 months) it becomes very hard for them to pick them up again. Later on, learning languages, it will be hard for us to re-acquire sounds perfectly: this explains why bilingual and multilingual children are able to do it. Importantly, the first year of a baby's life is spent trying to 'tune in' to the language that they are hearing and learning the skills of communication, i.e. making eye contact, responding to others' facial expressions and words. It is often known as the **pre-linguistic stage** and is vital in children's overall language development.

▷ **The linguistic stage** is when babies start to use the words that they are hearing and begin to learn how to make sentences. Children will develop this stage gradually over the next few years so that by the age of around 5 they will be fluent in their home language. Children who are learning more than one language may learn to speak slightly more slowly as they absorb two different systems. This should not, however, affect their overall language development. As children develop language, they will need to have it reinforced through continuous stimulation. As they become older, they will start to ask questions and their vocabulary will expand from around 1000 words at age 4 to 20,000 at age 16.

Age	Vocabulary
Age 4	1000 words
Age 7	7000 words
Age 11	10 000 words
Age 16	20 000 words

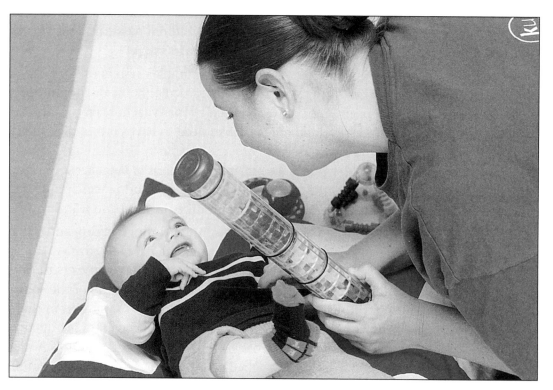

▲ Babies love to communicate from a very young age

The table below shows the stages of language development in children. Adults will need to support children through all of these stages in order to encourage and promote their language development. At each different stage, the role of the adult may be different. For example, a baby will need positive recognition of their attempts to communicate through eye contact and speech. A 5- or 6-year-old may need adults to help them to extend their vocabulary through the use of open-ended questions, or 'what if?' strategies. An older child may need support with organising their thoughts and ideas when speaking. Where children's language progresses more slowly through these stages, there may be other factors involved, such as:

▷ learning more than one language

▷ a communication difficulty such as autism

▷ a speech difficulty such as disordered or delayed language

▷ lack of stimulation from others

▷ a hearing impairment.

Early stages of language development in children

Age	Stage of development
0–6 months	Babies will try to communicate through crying, starting to smile and babbling. They will start to establish eye-contact with adults.
6–18 months	Babies start to speak their first words. They will start to use gestures to indicate what they mean. At this stage, they will be able to recognise and respond to pictures of familiar objects.
18 months–3 years	Children will start to develop their vocabulary rapidly. They will start to make up their own sentences. At this stage, children will enjoy simple and repetitive rhymes and stories.
3–8 years	Children will start to use more and more vocabulary and the structure of their language may become more complex. As children develop their language skills, they will be able to use language in a variety of situations.
8–11 years	Children will continue to develop their language skills. They will be starting to move towards understanding more abstract ideas and their language will reflect this.

Theories of language acquisition

There have been several theories put forward about how children learn or acquire language. In the early part of the twentieth century there were a number of theories with the same broad idea. This was that children acquire language by learning a word together with the thing it means or stands for. Through interacting with adults they will begin to develop sounds which have meaning and which will gain a positive response. This is called the **associationist theory**.

Noam Chomsky, an American linguist working in the 1960s, claimed that we are all born with an innate knowledge of the system of language, or a 'Language Acquisition Device'. In this way, whatever language we need to learn and the accompanying grammar will be decoded by the child. This theory helps to explains how children will often apply grammatical rules which they have heard, sometimes wrongly, because they have not yet learned exceptions to these rules. An example of this might be 'I bringed my drink'.

John Macnamara, working in the 1970s, proposed that children are able to learn language because they have an ability to make sense of situations. This means that they will understand the intention of a situation and respond accordingly. For example, if a child sees that an adult is beckoning towards them and holding out their hand, they will know that the adult's intention is for the child to come towards them. This will be the case even if the child does not understand the words that the adult is saying.

Although there have been many theories about how children develop language, there are still no definite answers about how language development takes place. Staff who work in educational settings will need to be aware of ways in which we can help all pupils to develop their language skills and build on their present knowledge.

Further research has shown that children who are bilingual or multilingual must be able to relate their home language to individuals when they are first learning language. For example, if a child speaks Arabic with their parents, it is important for the child to speak only Arabic with them and not to switch languages when first learning to talk. This is because, for the child, it is important to develop a distinction between languages, which is easier for them if they relate each language to a different person.

Opportunities for developing language

Pupils from all backgrounds, whether they are learning one or more languages, need to be given opportunities to develop their language skills in a variety of different ways. The list below shows the types of opportunities we must give to bilingual or multilingual pupils in school. All of these areas need to be considered in order to provide access to the curriculum.

Keys to good practice
Opportunities for developing language

✔ Creating a secure and happy environment where the pupils feel valued and part of the class and school

✔ Raising cultural awareness in school

✔ Reinforcement of language learning using resources such as dual language texts

✔ The reinforcement of language learning by giving pupils immediate verbal and non-verbal feedback and praise

✔ Making sure that pupils are given time to think about questions before they respond

✔ Creating more opportunities for speaking and listening. These could include opportunities such as paired conversations with other pupils.

Backgrounds of pupils with more than one language and how this can affect their learning and the development of the target language

Where pupils have come from a different background, culture or language to others in the class, entering school may be a challenging experience for them. They may find it difficult due to lack of confidence or self-esteem, and staff will need to be aware of their needs. Sometimes bilingual assistants will be employed, especially where there are a large number of pupils who speak English as a second language. Usually the school will have systems in place when pupils enter school so that they are aware of those pupils who speak English or Welsh as a second language. Parents will have been asked to fill in forms before the pupil enters school and primary schools should also pass on information.

Staff must be aware of the different backgrounds of individual pupils as they come into school, as these will all influence their learning and the development of the target language. It can be very difficult to assess the needs of bilingual pupils, and staff will need to find out whatever they can about the pupil when they first enter school in order to support them fully. The different backgrounds of pupils will influence their behaviour in school and the way in which their language skills develop. When working with bilingual and multilingual pupils we must support and encourage them wherever possible to prevent them from feeling frustrated and isolated.

Educational backgrounds

When pupils enter secondary school at age 11, teachers will have had information passed on from primary schools. This may have been done through meetings with Year 6 teachers, through information forms about each pupil, or other systems. Where there are pupils with more than one language entering schools, this information should have been passed on in this way so that schools are prepared for them.

It is also important to gain as much information as possible about the pupil's previous school if they have transferred after Year 7. The school will be required to send records of assessment and attainment but these may take some time to come through, and subject teachers may need to chase the records through the appropriate channels, particularly if there is an area of concern. Where pupils have come from very different educational backgrounds to others in the class, they may take more time to settle into school, for example if they have come from an area where there are many bilingual children to one where there are very few, or from an area where learning styles are different.

There may also have been other agencies such as speech therapists involved with the pupil's development, and records from these professionals will be useful in finding out about the pupil.

Case study

Mohammed has just transferred from primary school into Year 7 and speaks English as an additional language. He clearly needs extra support with his English and you have been asked to support him for one hour each day to help him during his Literacy class. You have not been told about his background or whether he had additional support at primary school.

1 Would it be appropriate for you to seek further information about Mohammed in this instance?

2 How would you find out about this?

Home backgrounds

These may be varied and will have the greatest influence on the pupil. Pupils whose home backgrounds have been traumatic, such as refugees, may have had wide and varied educational experiences. It would be helpful to obtain as much information as possible about the pupil's background and if possible seek the help of an interpreter so that the school can discuss this directly with the parents.

The experiences that the pupil has had may also affect their behaviour, for example being non-responsive. It may be difficult to obtain information from home and this can cause problems, for example with issues such as sickness notes or forms being completed and returned to school. Pupils who come from backgrounds with a different culture or religion from the majority of others in the school may feel isolated and it is important for them that the school values cultural diversity. Staff will also need to be aware of religious issues which can affect pupils' learning, for example pupils may be fasting during Ramadan. Issues of health and physical development may have been discussed with other professionals, and these checks should be included in the pupil's records.

Language backgrounds

Pupils who come into school with English or Welsh as a second language, or those who are multilingual, may find settling into school difficult due to the development of their language skills in the target language, or to a combination of factors. If staff know that the pupil has never been exposed to the target language before, this knowledge can help them to devise their educational plan. However, pupils who come into school at 11 will need a different level of support from those who come into school at 15. The school will need to ensure that each pupil has an education plan which takes individual learning needs into account.

Language targets – Spring Term 2004
Jamilla Khan – Year 10

Targets:

1 To familiarise Jamilla with the school and routines and start to learn vocabulary relating to school.

2 To learn to be able to use prepositions correctly.

Support:

LSA to work with Jamilla daily on learning.

Review:

End of Summer term 2004.

▲ Example of individual targets to develop language skills

It is very important for all pupils that staff in school are aware of their home language and culture. This is because pupils' self-esteem will be affected by their perception of how others see them and in their confidence when using language. It is important for the pupil to be able to communicate in school and, although pupils will usually pick up language reasonably quickly, this can be a difficult time for them and they may feel frustrated or isolated. If you notice that any pupils are finding it hard to make friends, it is important to discuss this with the class teacher. You may also be able to help them to socialise with others if you are outside during breaks or lunchtimes.

Case study

Saraya has recently started at your school aged 12 and does not speak any English. She is a quiet pupil and you have noticed that she spends breaks and lunchtimes on her own. What sort of strategies could you use to encourage her to socialise and suggest to others, such as midday supervisors?

Strategies for supporting bilingual and multilingual pupils in the classroom and helping them to access the curriculum

School strategies

When supporting bilingual and multilingual pupils, all staff will need to think about how they can promote the development of the target language while valuing the pupil's home language and culture. This is particularly important if the pupil is an isolated learner in the target language. The school should therefore have its own policies and practices for how pupils with English as an additional language are supported. The different types of strategies which the school has in place may therefore include:

▷ school policies to promote positive images and role models

▷ school policies and practices on inclusion, equal opportunities and multiculturalism

▷ identification of bilingual/multilingual pupils – for example, photos in staff room so that all staff are aware (if there is only a small group)

▷ providing opportunities for pupils to develop their language skills

▷ finding opportunities to talk with parents of bilingual pupils

▷ celebrating cultural diversity.

➔ Think about it

What policies does your school have which may be relevant to pupils from bilingual or multilingual backgrounds? How are these made available to parents?

These policies will have been directed by local and national guidelines for schools. Schools must have policies which encourage and promote equal opportunities for all pupils.

Outside support

Pupils who are bilingual or multilingual may have support from a local EAL (English as an additional language) teacher. They may also have an EMAG (Ethnic Minority Achievement Grant*) teacher or assistants who will come into school to help raise standards. These teachers will be able to offer advice and support to both teachers and parents, as well as putting them in touch with other professionals who may be able to help. They will carry out assessments on pupils and may also have centralised resources, such as dual language books, which may be useful to borrow, particularly if schools only have one or two EAL pupils. When pupils' progress needs to be discussed with parents who do not speak English, they may also be able to offer help when finding interpreters. If your school does not have this kind of support but it is needed, it is worth contacting the local authority through the school's representative to find out whether it is available for your school.

Assistants may find that it is often the SENCo (Special Educational Needs Co-ordinator) who is responsible for monitoring and working with pupils who speak English as an additional language. These children do not necessarily have special needs, and may not be on the special needs register or have Individual Action Plans. Occasionally, they will also have specific learning needs which will need to be assessed, but this will be in addition to their language needs.

* This grant was set up in April 1999 to assist schools in their work to address under achievement for all under-achieving ethnic groups, including those learning English as an additional language.

Find out...

Who is responsible in your school for pupils with EAL? What contact does the school have with the local EAL support team?

Strategies for classroom teaching and learning for EAL pupils

Assistants will need to work together with teachers and EAL tutors when supporting pupils in classrooms to enable them to develop their language skills effectively. Planning and development should be clear so that each pupil is encouraged to respond and to further their own knowledge of language. It is necessary to have specific strategies in place so that all staff have clear ideas about how these pupils may be supported. It is also important for staff to consider the abilities and needs of individual pupils and to get to know them, as they may have particular strengths in different curriculum areas.

Find out about...

A bilingual pupil in your school. Are they supported by the EAL service? What kind of input is given through the school? Over time, look at the kinds of strategies which are used to support and develop the pupil's use of language. Comment on the effectiveness of these strategies.

When developing the language skills of bilingual and multilingual pupils, these three areas should be considered:

▷ speaking and listening
▷ reading
▷ writing.

Speaking and listening skills

These skills must clearly be developed in EAL pupils, and assistants may find that they are working with individuals or small groups to facilitate this.

▷ **Finding opportunities to talk** – pupils will need to be given as much opportunity as possible to talk and discuss ideas with others. They will need to be able to develop their language skills in situations which are non-threatening and allow them to explore their own ideas.

▷ **Using physical cues and gestures** – for example thumbs up, thumbs down. This will enable the pupil to make sense of the situation more quickly.

▷ **Using games** – these opportunities are useful as they will help pupils to socialise with others as well as practise their language skills.

▷ **Using practical examples** – these can be used to help pupils when they are being given instructions, for example showing a model when the pupils are going to do group work.

▷ **Discussing with a partner first** – this may help when EAL pupils have to tell their ideas to the class, to help them to gain confidence. They should work with a variety of pupils who will provide good language models.

▲ Games can help pupils with their social and language skills

▷ **Use vocabulary which is appropriate** – staff will need to think about the language that they use with bilingual and multilingual pupils, to ensure that it is appropriate to the pupil's age and level of understanding. If the teacher is talking to the class and has used language which is difficult to understand, assistants may need to clarify what has been said for them.

▷ **Using purposeful listening** – if pupils have come into school with very limited experience of the target language, assistants may be asked to work with them on specific areas of language. For example, the teacher may be focusing on positional words to ensure that the pupil understands words such as *behind*, *above*, *below*, *next to* and so on. You may work with pictures or other resources to help the pupil to develop their understanding of these words.

▷ **Explain the purpose of the activity** – pupils should be aware of why they are undertaking a particular activity and what they are going to learn from it.

Reading and writing skills

Pupils who are learning to speak English or Welsh as an additional language will need to have opportunities to read and listen to books in the target language. This is so that they can associate their developing verbal and written skills with the printed page. Bilingual pupils will also benefit from working with the rest of the class during Literacy lessons. They will be able to share texts with the whole class and with groups of pupils, although teachers may need to use additional strategies so that they maximise learning opportunities. These should be clear to teaching assistants so that they can support the pupils through reinforcing the skills which are being taught.

Such strategies may include:

▷ using repetitive texts

▷ revising previous weeks' work to build confidence

▷ using pictures more in order to point out individual words

▷ making sure they pace the lesson to enable bilingual pupils to have time to read the text

▷ grouping EAL pupils according to their actual ability rather than their understanding or knowledge of English

▷ praise and encouragement wherever possible

▷ use of computer programs to help with reading.

Pupils who are learning to speak English or Welsh may need to decipher the meaning of some words with adult support when they are learning to read. They may need more support during Guided Reading sessions but should benefit from these as they will be able to model good practice from other pupils. As with all pupils, they will need to experience a wide variety of texts, both fiction and non-fiction, in order to maximise their vocabulary. It may be that the pupil is able to read and understand more than has been expected: in this case staff should always continue to extend their vocabulary by discussing the text further.

After consultation with the subject teacher, assistants may find that they need to adapt and modify learning resources which the pupil or pupils are using. This will help them to access the curriculum more fully. Assistants may also need to explain and reinforce vocabulary which is used in the classroom, for example during a particular topic. Often, the types of resources which benefit bilingual pupils will also be useful for other pupils in the class or group.

Problems which may occur when providing support for bilingual pupils

There may be short- or long-term problems which occur when supporting bilingual pupils. If the group or individual which is being supported for a particular activity is finding it too challenging, assistants may need to modify or change plans to accommodate this, as it will not always be possible to speak to the teacher immediately. However, it is important that the teacher is informed as soon as possible in order to inform future planning. Some pupils may take a long time to become confident in a second language, and it will be apparent that they understand much more than they are able to say. This is not unusual, and staff must not push pupils into talking before they are ready. The most important thing to do is to encourage and praise pupils wherever possible, repeating back to them so that they develop a positive view of themselves.

Where pupils have a specific learning difficulty, this can take longer to detect if they are bilingual. This is because staff may feel that they are finding school more difficult owing to their development of the target language. If assistants who are supporting groups of pupils find that a particular pupil is not able to manage the tasks set and is not progressing, they should always speak to the class teacher.

Other problems could include inadequate or unsuitable resources, and disruptions within the learning environment, as outlined on pages 61–62.

Keys to good practice
Teaching bilingual and multilingual pupils

✔ Group with pupils of similar ability.

✔ Use strategies which develop self-esteem and confidence.

✔ Provide visual and physical supports to help understanding.

✔ Model language using other pupils.

Find out whether you can be involved in working with a pupil who speaks English as an additional language over two or three sessions. You will need to be aware of the pupil's background and targets and may also need to discuss the kinds of strategies which you might use with the school's SENCo.

▶ Agree with the teacher the kind of support which you will provide.

▶ Show how you have considered the needs of the pupil when carrying out learning activities.

▶ What would you do if the pupil was having difficulties which you were unable to resolve?

▶ Show how you gave feedback to the teacher on the pupil's responses and progress.

End of unit test

1 What are the stages of language development?

2 What other factors might affect language development?

3 What do staff need to do to encourage language development in pupils?

4 What theories exist about how language develops in young children?

5 Name two opportunities for developing language skills in pupils.

6 Which of these issues are important when looking at pupils' backgrounds:

    a health records

    b home environment

    c language background?

7 What types of strategies may the school have in place for supporting bilingual and multilingual pupils?

8 True or false?

    a The school should educate bilingual pupils separately.

    b Bilingual and multilingual pupils need to be given opportunities to show off their first language to the rest of the class.

    c Pupils who are learning to speak more than one language may take longer to develop language skills.

References and further reading

National Literacy Strategy: Supporting Pupils Learning English as an Additional Language (DfES, 2000)

Managing Support for the Attainment of Pupils from Minority Ethnic Groups (Ofsted, 2001)

Lindon, J., *Working with Young Children* (Hodder and Stoughton Educational, 1997)

Macphee, J., 'Bilingual learners' in *Child Education,* June 2002

Tassoni, P., *Certificate in Child Care and Education* (Heinemann, 2002)

HMI 2003 – More advanced learners of English as an additional language

Key Stage 3 National Strategy, 'The assessment of pupils learning English as an additional language'. (DfES, 2003

Websites

www.becta.org.uk/inclusion/inclusion_lang/community/index.html

QCA scheme: *A Language in common: Assessing English as an Additional Language.* This booklet outlines issues relating to EAL assessment and guidance on profiling and monitoring EAL pupils.

www.naldic.org.uk (National Association for Language Development in the Curriculum). A professional organisation which aims to raise the achievement of EAL learners.

DfES website www.dfes.gov.uk (DfES website). The standards site has a series of publications and documents designed to help those who teach and support English as a second language.

3-13, 3-14, 3-15 and 3-16

Support children with special needs during learning activities

There has been a great deal of development in this area in recent years following the introduction of inclusive education and the new SEN Code of Practice. Many more pupils with special needs are now being educated in mainstream schools, and as a result there will be more assistants employed to support pupils with Statements of Special Educational Needs. (Also see Unit 3-3.1: Provide support for learning activities.) They will be asked not only to support pupils with learning difficulties and enable them to access the curriculum, but also to help them to develop relationships with others. Other pupils in the class will also need to learn to respond appropriately to pupils with difficulties.

For these units you will need to know and understand:

▶ supporting pupils with communication and interaction difficulties (Unit 3-13)

▶ supporting pupils with cognition and learning difficulties (Unit 3-14)

▶ supporting pupils with behavioural, emotional and social development needs (Unit 3-15)

▶ providing support for pupils with sensory and/or physical impairment (Unit 3-16).

Unit 3-13 Support pupils with communication and interaction difficulties

Normal patterns of communication

Where children are developing normally, their language and communication skills will follow a pattern of development. (See Unit 3-12 for stages of language development.) This will mean that they gradually learn and start to reproduce a series of sounds and gestures to help them to communicate with others. Children who have difficulties with communication may develop these skills more slowly than other children, or find it difficult to order their language. They may need to learn alternative methods of communication, or need to have specific learning programmes to help them to develop certain areas of their language.

Characteristics of communication disorders

Assistants may be required to support pupils in school with a number of communication difficulties. These may include problems concerned with:

▷ speech and language

▷ sensory impairment such as deafness or blindness

▷ specific learning difficulties such as dyslexia and dyspraxia

▷ autistic spectrum disorder

▷ moderate, severe or profound learning difficulties.

Speech and language delay and disorders

These may be varied and range from problems such as a stutter, to more complicated disorders where pupils have difficulties in processing their language. Some pupils may require frequent speech and language therapy input to help them develop their communication skills.

Sensory impairment

Pupils with a permanent sensory or physical impairment, such as deafness or deaf/blindness, are at a disadvantage when communicating, and they may not have the benefit of additional cues such as body language. They may need to have access to alternative means of communication such as sign systems, Braille or specialist equipment (see also Unit 3-16).

Specific learning difficulties

Pupils with these kinds of difficulties may have slower language processing skills or have difficulty following instructions. They may also have a limited understanding of non-verbal communication, and find concentrating or organisational skills difficult. As a result, their communication skills will be poorer than those of other pupils.

Autistic spectrum disorder

Autistic pupils will have a developmental disability which affects the way in which they relate to others. This may vary in its severity so that some autistic pupils will seem distracted or quite absent, while others will display quite disruptive behaviour such as frequent interruptions. They will find it difficult to empathise with other pupils and to play imaginatively, and may react inappropriately in some social situations. Autistic pupils will need varying degrees of support in these areas.

Moderate, severe or profound learning difficulties

These pupils have a more general learning difficulty which will affect many areas, including their communication with others. Assistants will need to respond to the pupils' level of language to encourage them to interact with others, while drawing on advice and support from other professionals.

Quite often, pupils will have communication difficulties in more than one of these areas; for example, there may be an autistic pupil who also has input from the speech and language unit. In all of these cases, pupils will need varying degrees of support to enable them to interact constructively with others.

Case study

Michael is an 11-year-old who has Asperger's Syndrome, a form of autism. He finds it difficult to relate to others and regularly plays alone in the playground. In the classroom, Michael particularly enjoys working on the computer and often asks the teacher if he can use it.

1 How could you encourage Michael to develop his social and communication skills with others?

2 What difficulties might you have and how could you resolve them?

School policy for supporting pupils with communication and interaction difficulties

Although the school may not have a policy specifically written for these pupils, the procedures and guidelines for working with them should be incorporated into the school's special needs and inclusion policies. Assistants will need to be familiar with these as they will outline the school's commitment to supporting all pupils. Pupils who have communication and interaction difficulties may have a range of problems and staff should have access to specialist support from outside agencies (see box below).

Specialist support from outside agencies

▶ **Speech and Language Unit** – will give support to pupils with a range of difficulties, from minor speech impairment to more complex language disorders.

▶ **Sensory Support Service** – deals with difficulties such as permanent sensory or physical impairment, including deafness and blindness.

▶ **Complex Communications Service** – will diagnose and advise on disorders such as those in the autistic spectrum.

Assistants should work alongside teachers and also the school's Special Educational Needs Co-ordinator (SENCo). They should work together to set up educational targets for the pupil's Individual Education Plan (IEP). When other agencies come into school to advise and help, support assistants should be given the opportunity to discuss pupils with whom they work as they are often the member of staff in school who spends the most time with the pupil.

Factors which may affect communication

The way in which we relate to others plays a crucial role in the development of our self-esteem. As we develop, we learn to interact with others and in doing this we develop self expression and find our own identity. Pupils who have communication difficulties may find social interactions difficult to the point of trying to avoid them. Other pupils and staff may find them difficult to understand or be unable to relate to them easily. Pupils may have come from another setting and take a while to gain confidence in a new environment. Assistants who support these pupils will need to be able to promote communication between them and others, while encouraging them to be as autonomous as possible.

You can do this by:

▷ ensuring that you have accurate and up-to-date information about the pupil's language and communication skills and are working alongside teachers to develop these

▷ actively encouraging the pupil to participate in learning activities and have an awareness of the planned learning objectives

▲ Pupils may need to have the environment adapted so that they are more comfortable and able to interact with others

▷ reinforcing spoken language wherever possible – this will need to be done through the most appropriate method of communication for the pupil, for example using Makaton, British Sign Language or Braille

▷ encouraging the pupil to respond to the contributions and ideas of others

▷ where necessary, adapting the layout of the room or using any equipment which is needed to enable the pupil to participate more fully in the learning activities, for example a visually impaired pupil may be very sensitive to sunlight or glare from shiny surfaces such as whiteboards.

Other strategies for supporting pupils

Assistants will need to ensure that the pupil who is being supported is given opportunities to develop their independence and self-esteem when communicating with others. They will need to experience a sense of achievement when interacting and may need assistance to encourage this, particularly when they first start at secondary school.

Where pupils need additional communication methods, assistants should be offered some training so that they are able to support the pupils more fully. There may be additional equipment needed to enable them to communicate, some of which may be technical. Assistants may also need to adapt some of the more general vocabulary used by the teacher so that pupils are included in all class activities. Where non-verbal communication is used, pupils should to be encouraged to show other pupils in the class the methods which they use. This will help others to understand how they communicate, and also develop their confidence and self-esteem.

Unit 3-14 Support pupils with cognition and learning difficulties

For effective learning to take place, pupils will need to have developed a range of cognitive skills in order to process and store information. When pupils have cognitive difficulties, there will be an impact on the development of these skills. Pupils will therefore need help in the following areas:

▷ **Language, memory and reasoning skills** – pupils who have cognitive and learning difficulties will take longer to develop language skills. This will in turn affect their learning, as they will be less able to store and process information.

▷ **Sequencing and organisational skills** – pupils may need help and support when organising themselves, as they may find it difficult to follow sequences of ideas.

▷ **Understanding of number** – the abstract concepts of arithmetic may be difficult for these pupils to grasp, and they will need practical help with number.

▷ **Problem solving and concept development** – understanding new ideas may take some time for these pupils, and they may need individual input from assistants.

▷ **Improving gross and fine motor competencies** – these physical aspects of the pupils' development may be affected, and they may need regular practice or therapy.

Assistants who work with pupils with cognition and learning difficulties will need to help them to develop learning strategies and take responsibility for their own learning. Assistants will need to agree areas and levels of support with teachers following advice from outside agencies and specialists. Pupils who demonstrate features of cognitive and learning difficulties may have some of the following special needs:

▷ moderate, severe or profound learning difficulties

▷ specific learning difficulties (e.g. dyslexia, dyspraxia, specific language impairment)

▷ autistic spectrum disorder.

Moderate, severe or profound learning difficulties

Pupils who have these difficulties are said to have a global learning difficulty which means that all aspects of their learning can be affected. They may need help not only in the classroom but in all areas of school, and should have individual learning programmes.

Specific learning difficulties

Pupils with specific learning difficulties such as dyslexia and dyspraxia have a more specific area of difficulty and may have problems with abstract ideas. They will find it difficult to organise themselves in the classroom and will need to have input in these particular areas, sometimes from outside agencies.

Autistic spectrum disorder

Pupils who have been diagnosed as having autistic spectrum disorder may need support in learning activities as they find it difficult to think in an abstract way. They may also rely on routines and set patterns and find it very difficult if these are changed for any reason. Autistic pupils may become obsessive about routine and react strongly to loud noises, which may mean that they can also disturb other pupils.

School policy and procedures for pupils with cognition and learning difficulties

Following the introduction of the Special Educational Needs Code of Practice in January 2002, schools have been required to offer places for all pupils who have a Statement if their school is specified. This means that mainstream schools are likely to have a higher number of pupils with special needs (see also Unit 3-3.1 on inclusion). Teachers must plan for all pupils so that they achieve at their own level within the guidelines of the National Curriculum. Pupils whose difficulty or disability hinders them from achieving at National Curriculum levels will be assessed using the P Targets. These have been drawn up so that pupils who have not reached level 1 can be assessed using a scale which shows their rate of progress, rather than just assessing them at W (Working towards).

School curriculum policies should give teachers guidance on planning and inclusion, and they may also have advice and help when planning educational targets from specialist teachers and agencies, such as the local Sensory Support Service. Pupils with special needs will need to have Individual Education Plans so that they have manageable targets to work on within a set time limit (see below for an example of an IEP). Pupils will be working on the same schemes of work as other pupils, and assistants will need to monitor the pupils' progress and report back to the class teacher (see also Unit 3-8 for more detailed curriculum planning).

Individual Education Plan

Name: Richard Jordan

Area/s of concern: behaviour, concentration   Start date: Jan 2005

Contact teacher: Mrs Fletcher   Year: 8F

Support by: Teaching Assistant when possible   D/O/B: 3/5/92

School Action

Review date: March 2005

IEP no: 4

Support began: Jan 2005

Targets to be achieved	Achievement Criteria	Possible class strategies	Ideas for assistant	Outcome/ review
1. To participate more fully in whole-class activities.	Achieved on 2 occasions out of 3 by review date.	Sit Richard away from distractions. Ensure that he is involved in whole-class activities.	Recognise good behaviour and class contributions.	Not consistent, but much improved – still needs work.
2. To maintain attention in small group activities and behave appropriately.	To participate fully in an activity for 10 minutes.	Ensure Richard is aware of the importance of working together as a group. Give him opportunities to put forward his ideas and also listen to the contributions of others.	Encourage involvement with others.	Now able to share without constant reminders – big improvement.

▲ An example of an Individual Education Plan

A pupil in your school who has a statement of special educational needs. How does the SENCo support teachers so that they are able to plan for this pupil to access the curriculum?

Helping pupils to develop effective learning strategies

Assistants will need to be able to help children to sequence and structure their learning so that they begin to develop independence skills. For example, an autistic pupil will need to be more aware of timetables so that they are aware of what will happen next. With some autistic pupils, it will help if this timetable is visual so that it is clearer and easier to read. If you support an autistic pupil it may be worth asking advice from your SENCo as to whether this is appropriate.

The timetable may or may not need to have the actual time of day but will give the pupil an idea of what to expect. It will also be helpful if there is a change in routine, for example a visitor to the school. The timetable may also benefit other children in the class.

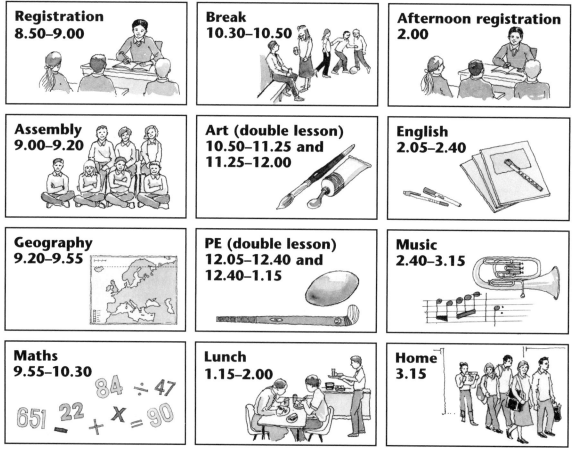

▲ Example of a visual timetable for a Year 8 pupil

Pupils with cognitive and learning difficulties may benefit from 'chaining' activities to help them with their organisational skills. This involves encouraging the pupil to think about the next step when working through a series of actions. For example, if the pupil needs to organise themselves to start an activity, the assistant will need to talk the pupil through what the next step might be and encourage them to think ahead. This will help the pupil to start to develop these types of skills independently.

Case study

Janine is a Year 7 pupil who has dyspraxia and has difficulty organising herself within the classroom. Since starting at secondary school, she has found it particularly difficult as she has had to find her way around the school for different classes and needs to remember her own books and equipment.

1 How could you help Janine to organise herself?

2 Are there any other ways in which you could help Janine without physically shadowing her?

Assistants will need to support pupils with cognition and learning difficulties so that they act in an enabling role, rather than encouraging the pupil to become dependent on their support. This is known as **active learning**, and means that staff should provide opportunities for the pupil to develop skills such as decision-making, problem solving, and exercising choice. It is also important to think about the other pupils in a class or group and how they can work together. Assistants will need to give positive reinforcement and praise to encourage all pupils when working with them on projects, to give them a feeling of achievement and to sustain their interest.

Problems when supporting pupils with cognition and learning difficulties

Assistants may find that they experience problems when supporting pupils with these difficulties. These may be related to the learning environment – for example, if you are trying to work with an autistic pupil and there are loud noises disturbing you from outside. You may also have problems with the resources you are using – although see pages 61–62. You should also be aware if the pupil you are supporting is on any medication, as this may affect their behaviour.

The pupil may have difficulty with the task that has been set, and you may not always be able to speak to the teacher. You will need to be able to adapt to unexpected changes in activities, and be able to modify what you have been asked to do. If you know the pupil well, and are aware of other areas which have been targeted in the IEP, you may need to change the focus of the activity to another which will benefit the child. Where possible, however, you should always try to aim towards the intended learning outcomes of the activity.

Keys to good practice
Supporting pupils with learning difficulties

✔ Ensure you have up-to-date information about the pupils' needs.

✔ Check that you have details about the planned learning objectives.

✔ Liaise with teachers and modify work where necessary.

✔ Monitor pupils' responses to learning activities.

Unit 3-15 Support pupils with behavioural, emotional and social development needs

This unit explores the reasons for antisocial behaviour in school and how assistants can manage pupils' behaviour in the learning environment. You will also need to read Unit 3-1, Contribute to the management of pupil behaviour, and Unit 3-9, Promote pupil's social and emotional development. Pupils with these difficulties will need to learn to develop their self-help and self-control skills, and assistants must be able to encourage and foster these, as well as helping them to develop relationships with others.

In addition to a policy on inclusion (see page 59), the school should also have a behaviour management policy (see also Unit 3-1, page 15). Assistants should be aware of this since it will give the school's guidelines for managing pupil behaviour. You will also need to know the types of strategies and sanctions which the school uses when there are problems with behaviour, and should agree these with the teacher. Pupils should be aware that these are to be consistently applied at all times, as they may attempt to play staff off against each other if they find that this is possible. Where there are pupils in school with particular behaviour, emotional or social difficulties, all staff should be aware of these pupils and their needs.

You will also need to be familiar with the levels of behaviour and social development to expect of pupils at different ages and stages. (See table in Unit 3-9 page 146.)

Pupils' backgrounds and the impact of their experiences on their self-esteem

Pupils who have emotional and behaviour problems may have had traumatic experiences during their lives, or be experiencing a difficult time at the present. They will often feel different or less valued, and may have low self-esteem as a result. In order for pupils to learn, their self-esteem will need to be developed, as their negative opinions of themselves will damage their ability to learn. Their behaviour is often a way of seeking attention, and even though this may be negative as a result, to these pupils some attention is better than none at all. Such pupils need to start to feel valued again and gain positive experiences from their time in school. It is important for staff to find out as much as they can about a pupil's background to enable them to work with parents and help the pupil in school (see also Unit 3-1 page 8). Staff must also be careful not to have stereotypical assumptions.

Case study

Aaron is a Year 8 pupil who has always had minor behavioural problems in school, but this behaviour has recently become more disruptive. You are working with Aaron alongside a group of other pupils when he says that he is not going to continue with the task and refuses to carry on.

1 Why might Aaron have recently become more disruptive in school?

2 What could you do to encourage Aaron to re-engage in the task?

Pupils who have experienced negative emotional experiences in their early years may find it difficult to form relationships with staff or their peers. They will need to have good role models in school to encourage them to develop their social and behaviour skills. Staff should always model the behaviour they would like to see in school and show respect and consideration towards others. Where you see good behaviour, it is important for this to be recognised, either verbally or through a reward system.

You will need to be able to recognise the kinds of behaviour patterns which may indicate forms of abuse such as child abuse or substance abuse, or bullying (see Unit 3-1 page 11). If you are at all concerned about any aspect of a pupil's behaviour you should always report these to the teacher.

Strategies to promote self-esteem

Assistants will need to be aware of ways in which they can develop self-esteem in pupils and encourage them to be more self-reliant. Some of these include the following ways:

▷ Giving responsibility to pupils to enable them to gain attention and approval without seeking negative means. This is an ideal opportunity to give the pupil a chance to do well while giving staff a chance to praise good behaviour. It may be necessary for the pupil to partner another to start with, to ensure that they are able to manage the responsibility. Ensure that you are aware of any differences in family or cultural expectations which may have an influence on the use of responsibility.

▷ Use strategies which reward and recognise pupils' efforts in school. These will need to be in line with the school's strategies and guidelines. Some schools may issue certificates for good behaviour and effort, while others may prefer to reward the class as a whole.

▷ Always listen to pupils and give them your attention when speaking to them. If a member of staff is clearly showing that their thoughts are elsewhere, and they are not interested in what is being said, this will damage the pupil's confidence and self-esteem.

▲ Group activities can promote children's self-esteem

▷ Encourage pupils to think about their behaviour and take responsibility for their own actions.

▷ Group pupils carefully, as the other pupils with whom they work can have an effect on pupils and how they work. If they are with a group of pupils with whom they have had negative experiences, this can prevent effective learning and damage their self-esteem.

▷ Staff will need to show that they notice positive as well as negative effort and behaviour. If a pupil is trying hard to achieve their individual targets and this effort goes unnoticed, it will make it less likely for the pupil to continue to work at it. There are different ways in which staff can show approval, apart from verbally, to boost a pupil's self-esteem (see also Unit 3-9: Promote pupils' social and emotional development).

? Think about it

A pupil in your class has been diagnosed as having Attention Deficit Disorder, which means that it is very difficult for her to sit still and concentrate for any length of time. You notice that she is sitting over on the other side of the classroom and has been working hard at her task for some time. She looks up and catches your eye.

▶ How could you show your approval at what she is doing without talking?

▶ What else could you do to follow this up later?

Establishing relationships with others

Pupils who have emotional and behavioural difficulties will sometimes need encouragement to help them develop relationships with others. This does not only mean other pupils within the class, but all other individuals such as parents, carers and teachers. It may be difficult for pupils, and sometimes staff, to develop these social skills, and assistants may have to help them to establish contact and relationships. You can do this by:

▷ ensuring that pupils are encouraged to interact positively with others

▷ giving pupils opportunities to work co-operatively with others in groups and pairs

▷ showing that pupils are able to work with others by giving them tasks which are appropriate to their age and ability.

Managing conflict and anti-social behaviour

You may find that you have to deal with situations of conflict when managing challenging behaviour. This may involve aggression or abuse in the form of racist or sexist remarks. If you have not been in these sorts of situations before, you will need to be prepared for them and ensure you protect your own safety and that of others. You may also need to rebuild damaged relationships between the two parties following areas of conflict, which may involve negotiations and discussions with both sides.

The situations you may find yourself in may escalate due to the needs of the pupils with whom you are working. They may find it more difficult to control their feelings than other pupils, or sometimes display aggressive behaviour. If they are on medication, this can also affect the way they behave.

Ways in which to manage conflict

Talking to pupils – where there has been a disagreement or argument between pupils, the first way to calm the situation should always be through listening to both sides to try to establish the cause of the problem.

Negotiating – this is a way of teaching pupils to talk to one another and try to resolve the disagreement sensibly, through talking about their responsibilities towards one another and reminding them of school policies.

Positive handling – it is better to manage conflict in a non-aggressive way and try to discuss the issue rather than to become angry with pupils. In this way, pupils will be more likely to put forward their own views and problems.

Time out – this may be a last resort and will be to remove one or both sides from the situation to calm down.

If you are in a situation where you feel that it is necessary to use physical restraint, this should only be used in circumstances where pupils are likely to cause harm to others or yourself. You should always seek help as soon as possible in this situation, by sending another pupil if necessary. If you are on your own with the pupil, try to move to another area if possible where there is another member of staff who can act as a witness. Your school or local education authority may have guidelines for the use of restraint.

 Find out about...

Your school's policy for child protection and the use of physical restraint.

Unit 3-16 Support pupils with sensory and/or physical impairment

The Disability Act 2001 amends the Disability Discrimination Act 1995 and strengthens access to mainstream school education for all pupils.

From September 2002 all schools must:

▶ 'not treat disabled pupils less favourably, without justification, for a reason which relates to their disability

▶ make reasonable steps to ensure that disabled pupils are not placed at a substantial disadvantage compared to other pupils who are not disabled

▶ plan strategically for and make progress in improving the physical environment of schools for disabled children, increasing disabled pupils' participation in the curriculum and improving the ways in which written information which is provided to pupils who are not disabled is also provided to disabled pupils.'

From *Inclusive schooling – Children with Special Educational Needs: Nov 2001*

Assistants who support pupils with sensory and/or physical impairment will therefore need to be prepared to manage a range of special needs for pupils with hearing, visual and physical impairment. You will be expected to enable these pupils to participate in learning activities alongside other pupils as far as possible, and be prepared to implement structured learning programmes alongside the class teacher.

The school should now have a policy for inclusive education, (see also Unit 3-3.1 page 9 and Unit 3-5 page 98) and assistants should be aware of their role in relation to this. Your responsibilities will include:

▷ making sure that you have up-to-date information about the nature and level of the pupil's needs

▷ ensuring that you have detailed information from the class teacher about the planned learning tasks and objectives

▷ adapt the learning environment and materials where necessary to enable pupils to participate in the planned tasks

▷ assist and encourage pupils and give positive reinforcement.

Apart from subject teachers, there will be others both within and outside the school who will contribute to the support of pupils with sensory or physical impairment. You may also have access to written information and reports from these people:

▷ **The school's SENCo**, or Special Needs Co-ordinator, will be available to support subject teachers and support assistant in the development of Individual Education Plans.

▷ **Specialist teachers** – these professionals may be available from the local Sensory Support Service to offer advice and equipment and to visit the pupil from time to time.

▷ **Physiotherapists/occupational therapists** – may be able to visit the school, or pupils may have to go on a waiting list before they are able to see them. They will develop individual programmes for pupils to use at home, with advice for activities they can work on in school.

▷ **Other professionals** – these may be inside or outside the school, but may have experience of dealing with pupils who have physical or sensory impairment.

You will also need to provide these people with information about the pupil's progress and participation in learning activities, whether these are cognitive, creative or physical.

The impact of a primary disability on pupils' learning and social, emotional and physical development

There may be differences between the disabled pupil and his or her classmates in several areas of their development. Pupils with these impairments may be less able to concentrate than their peers. They may find that they tire easily, or become frustrated if they are unable to complete tasks as quickly or as well as they would hope to. If their condition is progressive, they have to take medication, or they are in pain, these pupils may find it difficult to be responsive to learning activities on occasions. It is important that assistants are able to reassure them and give them encouragement to sustain their interest and enthusiasm. This can be done by praising them for their efforts, and by giving them levels of assistance which are consistent with their abilities. If too much help is given, pupils will not experience a sense of achievement and independence, but if too little is given, they will become frustrated and lose interest. Assistants should be able to encourage the pupils to use their other sensory and physical functions to help them to achieve.

Case study

Garry is in Year 11 and has a hearing impairment. The teacher and assistant both need to use a microphone so that he is able to hear them clearly. Garry has individual support for 10 hours a week. He has many friends in the class, but the other pupils sometimes have trouble understanding what he is saying. He is working with a group of other pupils on an activity to gather information and present it in the form of a graph. You feel that Garry may need some extra support with this as he will not be able to hear the responses of all of the group, but are not sure whether to intervene.

1 What would you do in this situation?

2 Is there anything you could do to support Garry to develop his relationships with other children?

If pupils take medication, this may also have an effect on their abilities and behaviour. Pupils may seem to be less able to concentrate or find it difficult to sustain their physical effort. If it is clear that it is difficult for a pupil to carry on, you should always stop the activity and carry on if appropriate at another time.

Selecting and using appropriate materials and equipment

Assistants will need to select and use the correct kinds of equipment when working with pupils with sensory and/or physical impairment. You will need to know the kinds of equipment which are appropriate to use to help the pupil with whom you are working. You may be given some advice and equipment from outside agencies, such as Brailling machines and auditory aids. The school may also be visited by professionals such as the local institute for the blind, who may give advice on equipment which could be used in school. They may also advise on how the school could assist pupils, such as making certain areas more visible by painting them – for example, the edge of the playground, or the edge of steps.

Pupils may be accustomed to using some equipment and so may also be able to show assistants how to use it: this would be another way of developing their self-esteem. Ideally, they will become used to managing some of their own equipment, for example if they need a sloping desk they may be able to go and get it independently.

Pupils who have **visual impairment** will need to sit as close as possible to the class teacher. They will be affected by lighting and should not be facing bright and direct sunlight, or be in an area which is too dark. If teachers use whiteboards, these may be difficult to see as the light will glare, and staff may be advised to use paper to avoid this. Where Brailling machines are used, other pupils in the class should also be introduced to the machine so that they are aware why it is being used. Pupils who use Braille may also be able to teach simple messages to other pupils in the class.

Pupils who have **auditory impairment** should also sit close to teachers to enable them to lip-read if necessary. They may require the use of specialist equipment such as hearing aids and microphones to help them, and be sensitive to acoustics within rooms such as dining areas. If they use sign language or Makaton, they may also teach some of the signs to others. The impact of showing and teaching other pupils will be to make the pupil feel less isolated within the classroom.

Pupils who have a **physical impairment** may need to sit away from the teacher so that they are able to access any larger equipment. They may also need to use computers and other specialist equipment to enable them to complete learning tasks.

If pupils are less independent due to physical impairment, assistants may need to help with physical management such as lifting. However, you should ensure that you have proper training before being asked to carry out lifting on pupils.

You may need to lift a pupil in a wheelchair. In this case you will need to make sure that the brakes are applied before you start, and that the pupil is sitting well back in the chair (1). Ensure that the wheechair does not have detatchable parts such as arm rests which will come off if you attempt to use them as you carry the chair. Support the chair from each side and carry as shown (2). Never carry a wheelchair by the wheels.

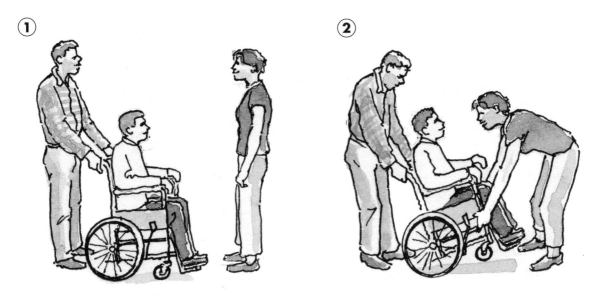

When lifting a pupil from a wheelchair, the bearers will need to bend at the knees and grasp each others wrists as shown, beneath the pupil's legs (3) using the four-handed seat. The pupil will then need to put an arm around each of the bearer's shoulders (4). The bearers should then stand up together.

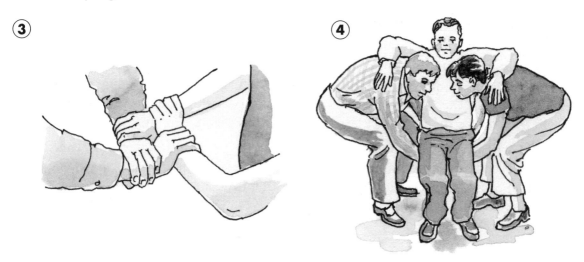

▲ Safe lifting methods

Evidence collection

Ask your SENCo if you can work with a pupil who has special educational needs if you have not done this before. What kinds of needs does the pupil have? How do you go about supporting these needs? Write about the pupil and the kinds of support that are available in schools including any equipment. Remember you will need to think about confidentiality when writing about the pupil.

End of unit test

1 What types of communication difficulties might children have?

2 What outside agencies might be involved with pupils who have communication difficulties?

3 Why should pupils who use non-verbal communication systems show others how to use them?

4 What skills do pupils need in order to develop effective learning?

5 What is 'active learning'?

6 Why is good self-esteem important in children?

7 How might schools develop self-esteem in pupils?

8 How can you encourage the formation of positive relationships between pupils with social and emotional problems and others?

9 Name three ways in which you could manage conflict.

10 When should you use physical restraint?

11 What is inclusive education?

References

Collins, M., 'How to deal with Autistic Children' in *Five to Seven* (Vol. 8, Dec. 2001)

McNamara, S. and Moreton, G., *Teaching Special Needs* (David Fulton, 1993)

Planning, Teaching and Assessing the Curriculum for Pupils with Learning Difficulties (QCA) General guidance plus individual guides for each National Curriculum subject.

Websites

www.nas.org.uk (National Autistic Society)

http://inclusion.ngfl.gov.uk

www.dfes.gov.uk/sen

www.nasen.org.uk (National Association for Special Educational Needs)

Set C

Unit 3-17 Support the use of information and communication technology in the classroom

Information and communication technology (ICT) plays a major role in the school curriculum, as it can be a part of all subject areas. The National Strategy for Key Stage 3 states that schools should provide one hour per week of dedicated time for ICT in Years 7, 8 and 9, and that this should be supplemented by opportunities to develop ICT skills in other subject areas. This means that assistants should be able to support pupils when using a range of ICT equipment in school. Although secondary schools have dedicated ICT departments, assistants should nevertheless be familiar with the equipment. This unit is about ensuring that such equipment is available and ready to use when required and that you know how to support teachers and pupils when preparing and using equipment safely.

The types of ICT equipment you will need to use in the classroom

When working as an assistant in a secondary school, you will be expected to know how to prepare and use different ICT equipment. This may range from setting up computers in classrooms and computer suites to knowing how to operate recording equipment. You should make sure that you are familiar with the different equipment you will need to use. This may include the following:

▷ **Classroom computers and related equipment such as printers.** There are many different computers and printers available, and you will need to know how to operate those which you are expected to use. In secondary schools, computers will be kept in dedicated computer rooms or suites, although some computers may also be kept in individual classrooms or departments. You should make sure you know how to operate interactive whiteboards if your school uses them.

▷ **Recording and playback equipment.** Most departments will have access to tape recorders, CDs, video recorders and digital cameras. You will need to know where these can be found and how to book them in advance. You should also know where to find extension leads and the keys to the storage cupboard if necessary.

Preparing equipment for use in the classroom

Computers and peripheral equipment

If you have been asked to prepare computers for use, you will need to find out whether you need to book or timetable them for use by your class. Your school may have

▲ You will be expected to use a variety of ICT equipment

procedures for this and you may need to find out about these from the subject teacher or ICT subject manager. You will also need to make sure that you have set up any computers which are used in your own classroom, and are able to access any CD-ROMs or printers which are needed. If you are going to use computer suites with or without the subject teacher, you will need to know how to access the equipment and use any passwords. Always make sure that there are no safety issues which need to be addressed, for example the length of time a pupil should spend looking at a screen.

Recording and playback equipment

You will need to make sure that you have access to this equipment when it is required and that you know how to use it. You may need to prepare recording equipment such as video cameras for use in the classroom; this may involve booking or unlocking from storage, and finding the correct place on the tape. Most pupils will be familiar with tape recorders. However, pupils' experience with other equipment such as digital cameras or video cameras will vary greatly. You may therefore need to teach groups of pupils how to use these, and they in turn may teach the others.

Overhead projectors and screens

You may be asked to prepare overhead projectors for use in the classroom or other areas in the school such as the hall or staff room. This will involve removing the equipment from wherever it is stored and setting it up so that it is ready for use. You will need to ensure that there are no safety issues to be addressed, such as trailing cables around the projector.

Checking for and reporting equipment faults

Electrical equipment which is used in school should always have an annual safety check, but if you find any faults in the equipment while preparing it for use, you

▲ Children need to be given opportunities to develop their ICT skills in the classroom

should always report them, however minor. The school should have its own procedures to follow, such as writing in a maintenance book, but you should also inform the teacher and whoever is responsible for repair or maintenance. Faulty equipment should then be labelled and isolated from any power source.

Following manufacturers' instructions

It is important to ensure that instruction booklets for individual items of equipment are easily accessible. Teaching staff need to be sure that equipment is being set up and used correctly, and it is also useful to be able to use a troubleshooting section if there are any problems.

✓ Keys to good practice
Preparing equipment

✔ Check availability of equipment and accessories.

✔ Ensure that you know how to use all required equipment and have all the information needed.

✔ Check that you have switched on and the equipment is ready to use.

✔ Ensure you know the location of any consumables, e.g. printer ink, batteries.

✔ Make sure any safety issues are reported to the teacher and maintenance officer.

Make a note of the different ICT equipment available for use in your school, and the procedure for booking or allocating this equipment. Write down where you can find accessories and consumables such as mice or printer paper, as well as instructions or information. Finally, note down the procedures for reporting faulty equipment.

Supporting the use of ICT equipment in the classroom

When supporting pupils in the use of ICT, assistants should know the types of skills which are being developed in pupils of different ages. At Year 7 in particular there may be a marked difference in pupils' experience and skills, and assistants should find out as soon as possible about individual pupils' levels of attainment. However, there should be a clear progression from the expectations of the Foundation Stage, through Key Stages 1 and 2, to Key Stage 3 and beyond.

The National Framework for Teaching ICT capability: Years 7, 8 and 9

The National Framework for Teaching ICT capability for Years 7, 8 and 9 sets out the skills to be developed in Key Stage 3.

By the end of Key Stage 3 all pupils should be able to use ICT securely, creatively and independently, be confident enough to keep their skills up-to-date and be able to generalise from their ICT experiences. The knowledge, skills and understanding that they need in the subject are closely intertwined and may be summed up as follows:

▷ **Knowledge:** Pupils need some knowledge of the technology, for example, that a computer requires different driving software to control peripherals such as printers or scanners, or that Internet search engines use different methods to find information, which affects results from a search. They also need to know the technical terms associated with the ICT facilities that they are using.

▷ **Skills:** To handle information efficiently, pupils need both technical skills in using ICT facilities, such as how to use a particular software package to reorganise information for a new purpose, and information skills, such as skimming and sifting. They also need interpersonal skills, for example, in co-operating with others, both present and remote, in an ICT-based task.

▷ **Understanding:** Pupils need to understand the concepts that underpin effective use of ICT, for example, when and when not to use ICT for a given

be improved, for example, to make it more efficient, versatile, interesting or robust. Understanding helps pupils to become reflective and responsible users of ICT, with an awareness of its impact on daily life and society.

The National Curriculum programme of study for ICT in Key Stage 3 groups the knowledge, skills and understanding that pupils need to acquire into themes. These themes, which characterise what people normally do when they work with ICT, are:

▷ **Finding things out**
▷ **Developing ideas and making things happen**
▷ **Exchanging and sharing information**

A critical feature of the development of ICT capability, which needs to be integrated into each theme, is:

Reviewing, modifying and evaluating work as it progresses

Elements of all the themes are likely to occur in most units of ICT work. Schools will often teach certain units earlier in the year so that pupils are familiar with ICT tools and techniques required by teachers of other subjects.

From *Framework for teaching ICT capability: Years 7, 8 and 9; Section 2: The ICT curriculum at Key Stage 3* © Crown copyright 2002

Find out about...

How teaching assistants in your school are used to support activities in ICT. Perhaps you could devise a questionnaire to find out the following:

▶ How much training is available to them? Would they use it if more were available?
▶ Do they feel confident when they are asked to work in a computer suite or with groups of pupils using other equipment?
▶ Are there any other issues they have which they would like addressed concerning ICT?

School policy for the use of ICT

The school should have an ICT policy which will give guidelines for using and working with ICT in the classroom. There may be set routines or guidance for all users of ICT equipment. For example, pupils may have to sign a checklist to say when they have used equipment. The school policy should give the aims and objectives of the school with regard to the pupils' experiences and opportunities in ICT.

There will also be requirements for safety, and for storage and security of ICT equipment. There may be a borough or school policy on use of the Internet and the availability of websites which are suitable for schools.

Legislation and regulations relating to the use of ICT

Several legal requirements exist which are relevant to the use of ICT in schools. Assistants should be aware of these and make sure that any information which is confidentially held or seen is not passed onto others. If you have access to school computers containing information about pupils for example, it is important that you only use them as they are intended, and do not leave computer screens on for others to read.

Relevant legislation for the use of ICT in schools

Data Protection Act 1998 This has implications for the use of data which is held on school computers and how it is used. Individuals have the right to know what information is held, and any information about the children in the school should only be used by the school and not passed on to a third party (see also Unit 3-6 page 116). Any data which the school holds should be protected against unauthorised access by appropriate security measures.

Child Protection The 1989 Children Act outlines a set of principles which everyone should follow when children are involved. These are to ensure that the welfare of the child will always come first. The local authority may have guidelines for child protection and how information is kept on computers. Staff should ensure that any information which is held about pupils is kept confidential within the school, and any work or results which are published do not contain pupils' names or other personal information.

Copyright If the school has CD-ROMs and other software, these must only be used by the school and not by other parties, and multiple copies of programmes should not be made.

Software licensing This is important in the case of schools as they should be aware of which licences they should have with regard to software held in school. There are different kinds of licence depending on the intended use of the software, for example single use or across a network.

How to support the development of ICT skills in pupils

Staff will need to understand and follow the National Curriculum for ICT when working with pupils. They shoud also be familiar with the ICT requirements of other areas of the curriculum. Subject teachers will have long-term, medium-term and short-term plans (see Unit 3-3, page 54) which will highlight the skills to be taught in ICT and how pupils should be supported. Assistants should support pupils while building their confidence and independence when using ICT equipment. They should do this by developing a variety of skills including the following:

▷ **Basic user skills** – sometimes it is tempting to intervene when pupils are using computers and other equipment, especially if they have not had much experience using them before. For example, some pupils may have experience of giving multimedia presentations, whilst others will not have come across the equipment. You should try to ensure that you guide them while allowing them to operate equipment independently. You can do this by guiding them through the task verbally, or by showing them first and then asking them to repeat what you have done. In this way they will start to develop skills such as using a mouse or keyboard, switching on and closing down equipment, and following on-screen instructions.

Think about it

You are working with a group of Year 9 pupils on a media unit. Their task, in pairs, is to design and compose the front page of a newspaper on the subject of school life, using images and text. The pupils have used a digital camera to take pictures around the school, and now have to import those images into their front page. The first two pupils with whom you work have obviously used this kind of equipment before at home, but the second pair have not and are having difficulties.

How could you help the pupils with their publishing skills without doing the work for them? Do you think this kind of work is appropriate for Year 9 pupils? Why?

▷ **Selecting and using appropriate software packages** – subject teachers should give guidance when selecting software for use in the classroom as it will be related to the work pupils are currently doing. For example, pupils may be using presentation software such as word processing or desktop publishing programs, web-page creation software or other creative software tools in areas like music, graphic design or textiles. Pupils may also use simulation or modelling software to look at, for example, coastal erosion in geography, battle strategy in history, molecular structure in science. Pupils will often use databases and spreadsheets for mathematical tasks. You will need to use their own existing knowledge as a starting point when helping them to use appropriate software for the task. The program selected should be straightforward for the pupils to use and not too time-consuming or too short for realistic use in the classroom. Some programs are unsuitable as they take too long to complete, while others are too complex and require too much expert support and intervention.

▷ **Accessing and using learning programs** – you will need to be able to use computer programs without needing assistance, in order not to interrupt either the teacher or the pupil you are supporting. This means that prior planning and preparation with the ICT or other subject teacher is crucial. Some of these programs will be CD-ROMs and programs already on the school's computer, but there will also be a selection of useful materials available on the Internet. Pupils may need support when accessing learning programs from CD-ROMs and computer disks, and you should provide this by talking them through each stage if they are unsure. Some pupils may like to write themselves reminders for accessing programs.

▷ **Accessing information** – pupils will need to learn how to access information from computer files, CD-ROMs and the Internet. They will need these research skills in a range of subject areas and will require help in learning to assess information sources for relevance, usefulness and bias. It is most important that pupils at Key Stage 3 learn to assess information sources critically.

▷ **Using electronic communication systems** – most pupils will have begun to use the Internet and email in primary school. These can be a useful way to support learning, though, again, pupils should be encouraged to be critical about the kinds of information they access. Pupils must also be made aware of the potential dangers of email communication: they should be taught never to give away their names and addresses or to arrange meetings with unknown email correspondents. In particular, they should be warned of the dangers of Internet chat-rooms and taught not to assume that correspondents are trustworthy.

Safety when using ICT equipment

When using all these methods to develop ICT skills in pupils, assistants should also be aware of the risks associated with using equipment and how these can be minimised. Equipment should be safe as long as it is used properly and checked regularly. Pupils should always be taught to shut down computers correctly after use as they can be damaged if turned off incorrectly.

✔ Keys to good practice
Using ICT equipment

✔ Check the equipment regularly and report any faults.

✔ Use only the correct accessories with each item of equipment.

✔ Never overload plugs.

✔ Ensure that the equipment is being used safely and intervene when it is not.

✔ Store equipment safely when not in use.

📁 Evidence collection

Make a list of ICT tasks you have supported in the classroom. For each of these tasks, write down what knowledge you needed in order to do this, for example, how to use the program, how to minimise risks, school policy for internet use etc.

End of unit test

1 What sort of ICT equipment might be found in secondary schools?

2 What should you consider when preparing ICT equipment for use?

3 What types of ICT skills would you expect from a pupil at the end of Key Stage 3?

4 What sort of ICT programmes might secondary school pupils use across the curriculum?

5 What skills will staff be helping to develop in children in the use of ICT?

6 What should you do if you find any faulty equipment?

7 What relevant legislation exists for the use of ICT in schools?

References

National Curriculum Document (QCA, 1999)

National Strategy for Key Stage 3, Framework for Teaching ICT (DfES, 2002)

Scheme of Work for Information Technology (QCA, 1998)

The *Times Educational Supplement* has an IT section which has useful and up-to-date websites and information.

Websites

BECTA (British Educational Communications and Technology Agency): www.becta.org.uk/technology/software/curriculum/licensing/

National Curriculum Website: www.nc.uk.net

Children Act 1989: www.fnf.org.uk/childact.htm

Data Protection Act: www.legislation.hmso.gov.uk/acts/acts1998/19980029.htm

Guidance on the use of ICT in the classroom: www.mape.org.uk

www.standards.dfes.gov.uk/keystage3/publications

Unit 3-18 Help pupils to develop their literacy skills

This unit will help you to support pupils when developing reading, writing and speaking and listening skills. You will need to know the different ways in which teachers plan learning activities both within English lessons and across the rest of the curriculum, and the support you are required to give to different groups and individuals. Assistants will need to work under the direction of subject teachers to help pupils achieve the learning objectives of each lesson. They will need to report back to the teacher on pupils' achievements in reading, writing and speaking and listening.

The structure of literacy instruction in secondary schools

As with other subjects, the school's English policy will relate to local and national frameworks and policies for English. It will cover pupils' reading, writing and speaking and listening skills. The National Strategy for Key Stage 3, *Framework for teaching English* sets out a recommended framework for the teaching of literacy skills:

Key Stage 3 **English**				
Word level	**Sentence level**	**Text level**		
		Reading	**Writing**	**Speaking and Listening**
• Spelling • Spelling strategies • Vocabulary	• Sentence construction and punctuation • Paragraphing and cohesion • Stylistic conventions • Standard English and language variation	• Research and study skills • Reading for meaning • Understanding the author's craft • Study of literacy texts	• Plan, draft and present • Imagine, explore, entertain • Inform, explain, describe • Persuade, argue, advise • Analyse, review, comment	• Speaking • Listening • Group discussion and interaction • Drama

This structure allows the teacher to plan the curriculum, drawing together objectives from each level. It also allows assistants to understand the scope and purpose of the tasks they may be required to undertake with pupils.

> **1** Short lesson starter activity (e.g. spelling, vocabulary) 10-15 minutes
> **2** Introduce main teaching points (e.g. teacher exposition or questioning)
> **3** Develop the main teaching points (e.g. through group activity)
> **4** Plenary to draw out the learning (e.g. through feedback and presentation) 5-10 minutes

▲ Recommended lesson structure from the Framework

The interactive use of speaking, listening, reading and writing

When pupils are developing their language skills, they are learning to communicate with others. The three areas of language interact with each other to promote self-expression and imagination, thought and learning.

Most explicit literacy instruction will take place within English lessons, but pupils need good language and literacy skills for all areas of the secondary curriculum. In recent years this need has been addressed by whole school training in literacy across the curriculum, and schools should have a designated member of staff with responsibility for promoting and coordinating programmes. You should make sure you know who is responsible for literacy across the curriculum in your school, and what policies and procedures staff are expected to follow. (See also Unit 3-20, Helping pupils to access the curriculum.)

➡ Knowledge into action

Locate a copy of the National Strategy for Key Stage 3, *Framework for teaching English*. Find a medium term plan for a year group with which you regularly work, e.g. Term 2 in Year 7. Can you find examples of literacy skills which you have covered in class with your pupils?

Help pupils develop their reading skills

Basic principles of reading skills

Assistants should have some idea of the basic principles by which children learn to read so that they are able to support their reading in the learning environment. In primary schools, children are taught a range of strategies to enable them to make sense of what they are reading. However, as pupils progress through secondary school, less time can be allocated to explicit teaching of the more basic strategies. Assistants may need, therefore, to give extra help to those pupils who have not mastered these skills.

▷ **Phonic cues** – pupils start by learning initial sounds so that they can begin to word build using phonics at an early stage of reading and writing. They should be taught sounds using phonics rather than letter names so that they are able to 'sound out' words.

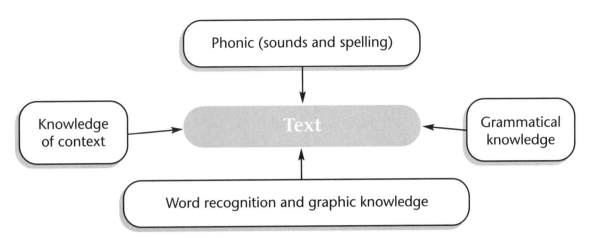

▲ Strategies for learning to read (from *National Literacy Strategy Module 4 – Teacher's Notes*. DfES 1998)

▷ **Contextual cues** – pupils will also learn by thinking about the setting of the text and the kinds of words which may be used as a result. For example, in a book about animals they may recognise the word which follows 'the cat ran after the' simply because they know cats chase mice, and that the sentence will then make sense. This technique also works with more complex texts and ideas.

▷ **Grammatical knowledge** – pupils will be able to make sense of the text through their knowledge of grammar and syntax.

▷ **Picture cues** – these are generally used at the early stages of reading as they give the child more confidence when tackling a text. Pictures can also be useful when preparing differentiated work for pupils with weak reading skills or for whom English (or Welsh) is an additional language.

This is known as the Searchlights model, as each of these cues illuminates meaning in the text.

? **Think about it**

Look at this sentence:

The brig was waffling snickerly at the linp.

Can you find the subject, object, verb and adverb in the sentence?

Although the sentence does not make sense to you, you will understand who is doing something to something else, through the way in which the sentence is constructed. Through the kinds of strategies we teach pupils learning to read, we are building up these skills so that they can make sense of the text, even if they do not understand some words.

All of these cues will help the pupil to decipher the text through forming a system through which they can decode the meaning.

Expected level of reading skills

Teaching assistants will need to know exactly what reading skills are expected of the pupils whom they support. The Framework for teaching English sets this out very clearly.

By the end of Year 9, each pupil is expected to be 'a shrewd, fluent and independent reader':

▷ orchestrating a range of strategies to get at meaning in text, including inferential and evaluative skills

▷ sensitive to the way meanings are made

▷ reading in different ways for different purposes, including skimming to pick up quickly the gist of a text, scanning to locate specific information, close reading to follow complex passages and re-reading to uncover layers of meaning;

▷ reflective, critical and discriminating in response to a wide range of printed and visual texts.

These skills are a prerequisite for the kind of study that will take place during Key Stage 4, and are also crucial to learning in other subject areas.

The different types of reading activities in English lessons

Even within English lessons, reading will occur in a variety of situations:

▷ **Shared reading** – this will take place in the class situation and all pupils will be working on the same text.

▷ **Guided/group reading** – this consists of group teaching while other pupils work independently. It may be preparation for a written task or for a speaking and listening task such as a presentation.

▷ **Independent reading** – this may be individual, paired or small group work. It may be a 'time out' activity during whole class teaching. Other independent reading sessions may take place in the school library. Pupils will choose their own books and may often be required to discuss and keep a record of their reading.

Teaching assistants may occasionally be asked to take charge of a whole-class session while the teacher works with a small group on a guided reading activity.

✓ Keys to good practice
Strategies for supporting reading at Key Stages 3 and 4

Pupils at Key Stages 3 and 4 will need to use their reading skills in a variety of ways. These may be categorised as follows: research and study skills, reading for meaning, understanding the author's craft, and the study of literary texts.

Teaching assistants may be able to offer the following kinds of support:

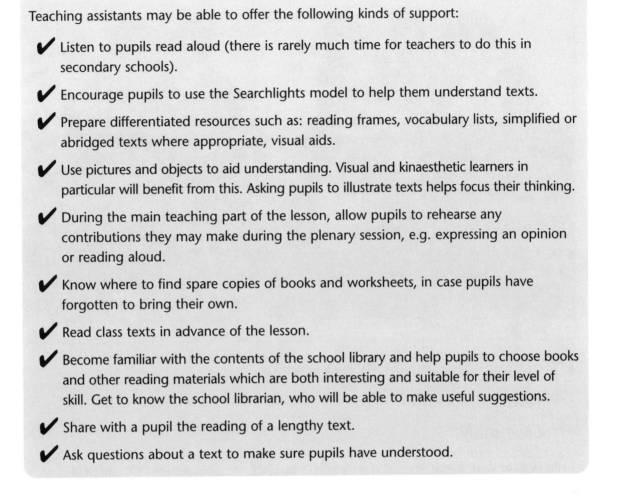

✔ Listen to pupils read aloud (there is rarely much time for teachers to do this in secondary schools).

✔ Encourage pupils to use the Searchlights model to help them understand texts.

✔ Prepare differentiated resources such as: reading frames, vocabulary lists, simplified or abridged texts where appropriate, visual aids.

✔ Use pictures and objects to aid understanding. Visual and kinaesthetic learners in particular will benefit from this. Asking pupils to illustrate texts helps focus their thinking.

✔ During the main teaching part of the lesson, allow pupils to rehearse any contributions they may make during the plenary session, e.g. expressing an opinion or reading aloud.

✔ Know where to find spare copies of books and worksheets, in case pupils have forgotten to bring their own.

✔ Read class texts in advance of the lesson.

✔ Become familiar with the contents of the school library and help pupils to choose books and other reading materials which are both interesting and suitable for their level of skill. Get to know the school librarian, who will be able to make useful suggestions.

✔ Share with a pupil the reading of a lengthy text.

✔ Ask questions about a text to make sure pupils have understood.

Working with groups

When supporting groups, it is important to remember to use strategies to involve all the pupils, particularly those who are quiet and reluctant to discuss their reading. Praise and encouragement will help to build up their confidence, and will help develop the courage they need to offer answers and opinions in a whole class situation. If necessary, divide the group, placing more able with less able pupils. In this way, they can support each other, and potential disruption is averted. You should, however, always consider the personalities and dynamics within any group you set up.

Working with individuals

If you are supporting a particular pupil in a class, you will need to ensure that you understand your role within the classroom situation. You should be clear on the needs of each pupil you are supporting; for example, if a child has Special Educational Needs, you should know what these needs are. Specific language targets may be worked on, for example, while hearing the pupil read. A partially sighted pupil may need resources such as a magnifier or enlarged text to enable them to use the school's resources.

▲ Shared reading is a valuable whole-class activity

Case study

Michael, in Year 9, has special needs and is at stage 'School Action' on the SEN register. He is a reluctant reader and can rarely find a book that interests him enough to persevere with it. Most books for his ability level he finds too 'babyish'. You have been asked to support him during independent reading sessions in the library.

1 How could you help find reading material that matches both Michael's interest and his ability?

2 What strategies could you use to help Michael develop his reading skills?

Evidence collection

You are working with a group of Year 8 pupils who are reading a short, comical play together. Most of them find it funny and enjoyable. One of the pupils, Ana, has poor reading skills and cannot keep up, losing her place, and missing her cues. She is beginning to get upset, and the other pupils are starting to show their frustration with her.

What strategies could you use to support Ana with her reading and keep the group working together?

Tackling problems when supporting reading

You may find that while you are supporting pupils in the learning environment, you face problems to do with the resources you are using, the environment, or the pupil's ability to learn. If you find that there are difficulties which mean that you are unable to continue with your task, you should speak to the class teacher if possible. If the teacher is busy or elsewhere you may have to decide what to do.

If there is a problem with resources, for example you do not have enough copies, you may need to organise sharing or obtain further copies. Do not forget to speak to the teacher afterwards. If there are problems with the learning environment, such as too many distractions, it may be best to move to a quieter area, out of the room if necessary. If a pupil is finding a text too difficult, tell the teacher so that extra support may be planned. Similarly, if a pupil is finding a text too easy, you and the teacher will need to devise ways of challenging that pupil. If behaviour problems are causing concern, do not attempt to continue unless the behaviour improves. Involve the teacher if the behaviour does not improve.

Case study

You are working with a group of six Year 10 pupils who are looking at bias in newspaper reports. They have two articles on the subject of asylum seekers, one from the *Daily Mail* and one from the *Guardian*. The pupils' task is to distinguish fact from opinion in these articles, and show how each newspaper uses particular vocabulary and linguistic styles to support its own political viewpoint. Two pupils are finding this task very difficult, partly because texts are a little too difficult for them.

How could you help the pupils work as a group to identify bias in each article?

Supporting pupils who have English or Welsh as an additional language

Pupils for whom English or Welsh is an additional language have different needs from native speakers. Some may be literate in other languages, and become fluent very quickly; others may not be literate in any language or may have other special educational needs. Some pupils may not need extra support; others will require a language support teacher and differentiated activities. Assistants may be able to use dual language texts: speak to the local EAL (English as an Additional Language) unit about borrowing some of these if your school does not possess any. It is also helpful to use commercially or school-produced stories on tape so that the pupils may see and hear what is being read at the same time. If appropriate, allow groups of EAL pupils to discuss their reading in their mother tongue before they formulate a response in English. Always remember to allow extra time for these pupils to process their response and produce an answer. For other ideas see also Unit 3-12, Supporting bilingual and multilingual pupils.

Resources available

Schools should have a variety of books and resources which are accessible and relevant to the age range. Pupils will be able to spend time in the library and borrow books to take home. Other resources may include:

▷ variety of fiction and non-fiction texts

▷ poetry and plays

▷ 'spoken word' books and tapes

▷ dual language texts

▷ simplified or abridged editions of novels and stories

▷ newspapers and magazines

▷ computer programs

▷ CD-ROMs

▷ suggested reading lists for different age-groups.

Help pupils to develop their writing skills

You will be required to support pupils with their writing in English lessons and all across the curriculum; sometimes with note-taking or answering questions, sometimes with planning and drafting a longer piece or producing a polished final draft. (At GCSE level it is particularly important that you do not 'do it for them', as this not only fails to help the pupils learn, it is also cheating.)

Extract from Larkmead English faculty handbook:

Targets to improve writing

Paragraphs

- Introduce paragraphs with a topic sentence and group connected ideas together
- Expand main points or ideas in the paragraph with details, points or examples
- Vary the lengths of paragraphs and connect ideas inside them in a logical way
- Link paragraphs clearly, using connectives
- Begin and organise paragraphs in varied ways

In sentences

- Use conjunctions in addition to *and* and *but*
- Use subordinate clauses and punctuate more correctly
- Use compound and complex sentence structures
- Use sentence of different lengths
- Use the passive voice in formal writing
- Use subordinate clauses in different positions for effect
- Use noun phrases in different positions for effect
- Use adverbial clauses in different positions for effect

Expected level of writing skills

The way in which pupils learn to write differs from reading as they need to remember a greater amount of information. In reading, pupils have the cues on the page in front of them, but in writing they need to formulate and structure ideas for themselves.

By the end of Key Stage 3, pupils are expected to be:
  ▷ able to write for a variety of purposes and audiences, knowing the conventions and beginning to adapt them.
  ▷ able to write imaginatively, effectively and correctly
  ▷ able to shape, express, experiment with and manipulate sentences
  ▷ able to organise, develop, spell and punctuate writing accurately.
From *National Strategy for Key Stage 3*, Framework for teaching English

The skills needed to become this kind of writer are again broken down into word level, sentence level and text level categories. Specific teaching objectives for each Year Group can be found in Section 2 of the *Framework for teaching English*.

A structure for teaching writing

The *Framework for teaching English* recommends a ten-step 'teaching sequence' for carrying out writing activities:

1 Establish clear aims
2 Provide examples
3 Explore features of the text
4 Define the conventions
5 Demonstrate how it is written
6 Compose together
7 Scaffold pupils' first attempts
8 Independent writing
9 Draw out key learning
10 Review

➔ Knowledge into action

Ask to observe a writing lesson.
▶ Where do the teaching and learning activities you observe fit into the teaching sequence above?
▶ How can teaching assistants support pupils and teachers in each of the different steps of the teaching sequence?

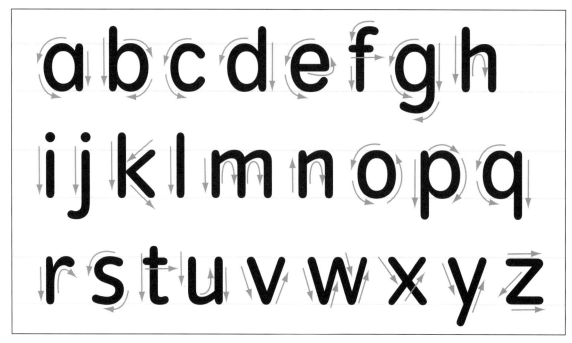

▲ Letter formation is important from an early stage

Handwriting

Correct letter formation is crucial in developing fluent, legible handwriting. By the time pupils are taking their GCSE exams, they will need to be able to write clearly at speed. Often, pupils have fallen into bad habits and do not form their letters in the correct way. This is not always obvious from looking at the finished work, but incorrect letter formation does impede their writing. Teaching assistants are well placed to observe handwriting and to work with individual pupils on any problems they may have. Pupils who have problems with handwriting need to show enormous patience and application to break bad habits; teaching assistants should offer as much encouragement as possible.

Spelling

Many schools now provide pupils with a booklet containing spelling lists for key words across all subject areas. Teaching assistants should make sure they are familiar with all the words in that list and remind pupils to refer to it when necessary. There may also be class lists of words on the wall, or dictionaries or word banks. Helping pupils learn to use a dictionary is a helpful activity.

Different people learn to spell in different ways. Some benefit from the 'look, cover, say, write, check' method whilst others prefer to use mnemonics, learn rules, or use magnetic letters to learn new words. Find out what spelling resources your school has and be ready to use a variety of strategies to help your pupils. If a student has problems with spelling, do not necessarily correct every mistake as this could be disheartening. Instead, focus on two or three different points, such as 'too/to/two', and 'there/their/they're'.

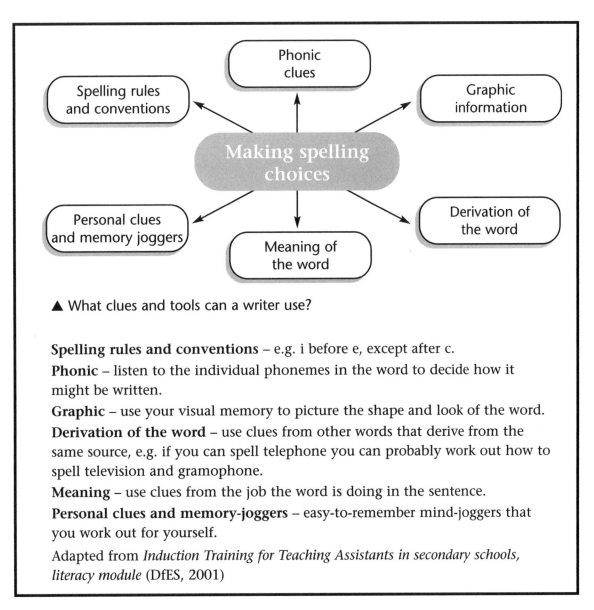

▲ What clues and tools can a writer use?

Spelling rules and conventions – e.g. i before e, except after c.
Phonic – listen to the individual phonemes in the word to decide how it might be written.
Graphic – use your visual memory to picture the shape and look of the word.
Derivation of the word – use clues from other words that derive from the same source, e.g. if you can spell telephone you can probably work out how to spell television and gramophone.
Meaning – use clues from the job the word is doing in the sentence.
Personal clues and memory-joggers – easy-to-remember mind-joggers that you work out for yourself.

Adapted from *Induction Training for Teaching Assistants in secondary schools, literacy module* (DfES, 2001)

Strategies for supporting pupils' writing

Assistants will need to help pupils with both the technical aspects of writing, such as spelling and punctuation, and also with the intellectual process of composing particular kinds of text. Strategies for doing so may include the following:

▷ **Acting as a scribe** – There are two cases for doing this. First, the student may need help taking down instructions or notes before beginning a task. You may choose to write in the student's book. Alternatively, you could write on a piece of paper, so that the student may copy without having constantly to refocus his/her eyesight from the board to the page on the desk. Second, if the student is composing a longer piece of text, he or she may dictate it to you. In this way, the composition process is not impeded by the technical problems involved in writing it down. The student may always copy or type up the writing later.

▷ **Using pictures** – Pupils who have difficulty writing might do better to produce a picture or series of pictures with captions prior to or rather than several paragraphs of continuous text. It is less useful (though more decorative) for pupils to 'illustrate' text that they have already written. Pictures may also be used as prompts to stimulate writing.

▷ **Cloze procedures (filling in the blanks)** – These may be used, again, as an alternative to producing continuous text. It is also a useful way to test comprehension or to consolidate new vocabulary.

▷ **Using artefacts** – pupils whose preferred learning styles are visual or kinaesthetic (learning through the use of gestures and body language) may benefit from having objects and artefacts to look at and touch as a stimulus for writing.

▷ **Key words and phrases** – Pupils may be provided with a list of key words and phrases that are useful in a given context. For example, when writing formal letters, pupils may need to be taught phrases such as "I write with reference to", "please find enclosed", "I would be most grateful if…" This helps pupils get started on a task and also encourages them to use the correct degree of formality, or register.

▷ **Writing frames** – These are help pupils structure their ideas, and make the composition of a text less daunting. These should allow pupils enough space to fill in their thoughts, ideally half to one side of A4 paper. The writing frame could be structured like this:

I think that
because
The reasons for my thinking this are, firstly
so
Another reason is
Moreover
because
These (facts/arguments/ideas) show that

▲ Example of a writing frame. (David Wray, University of Warwick)

▷ **Tables or grids** – These are similar to writing frames. Pupils often find it helpful to fill out a table or grid either prior to writing an essay or instead of composing a long piece of text. It is particularly useful in 'compare and contrast' type activities.

▷ **Flow charts and concept maps** – These consolidate learning by providing visual approaches to a topic. They may also be used as memory-joggers or when revising. Pupils can also create charts, diagrams or maps when trying to structure their own ideas.

▷ **Visualisation** – Recent research into brain function suggests that visualising both the process of writing, and the way the finished product will look fires the same pathways in the brain as actually completing the text. Encouraging the pupils to imagine themselves writing, and to imagine what their finished piece looks like helps take away the fear of the blank page and gets pupils started on their task.

▷ **Writing with the pupils** – Pupils often find it helpful to watch the teacher or assistant go through the same writing process as the class. This strategy both provides a model of writing and the writing process for the pupils, and also acts as a motivating psychological boost.

▷ **Using cards** – This is another technique useful for visual and tactile learners. Cards may be used to sort ideas into categories - this helps with the skills of paragraphing and ordering information. It also teaches pupils to order and structure their thoughts. Alternatively, cards may be used to work on word and sentence level skills, for example, grouping synonyms or constructing sentences using particular parts of speech.

▷ **Using music** – Music may be used as a stimulus for writing. Some pupils may also like to have music playing as they write. Recent research suggests that this may be helpful rather than distracting, provided that the music is instrumental rather than vocal.

Case study

John is a Year 10 student who has difficulty with reading, writing and organisation, though he has not been given a statement of special educational needs. The class has been discussing the issue of fox-hunting for a week, gathering information and formulating arguments. John has found it difficult to take notes in class, and since he rarely brings his folder, has scraps of paper with odd notes crumpled at the bottom of his bag. He has lost all his handouts. Pupils are now asked to write a letter to their local MP arguing their side of the debate.

How would you help John with this task?

Problems when supporting pupils during writing activities

These may be the same kinds of problems as those during reading activities, concerning resources, the learning environment, or pupils' behaviour and ability to complete the task. Where you have any concerns you should always speak to the class teacher.

Supporting SEN pupils

If a pupil you support has Special Educational Needs, you must make sure that you know what these needs are. You could ask the SENCo or individual subject teachers. You should always agree the strategies to be used with pupils who need extra help, or who have specific educational targets or an IEP. If the pupil has problems with writing skills, these strategies may be addressed by individual help on points which have been covered in class.

Supporting bilingual and multilingual pupils

Pupils who speak English as an additional language will probably need more encouragement and support when undertaking writing activities. Their oral skills may be further advanced than their written skills and they may need more time to think about the task. These pupils benefit from hearing text read aloud slowly, since it can be difficult to segment a stream of sounds and hear the individual words within it. It can be useful to highlight key words in a written text. Previous work should be consolidated before moving on. Where appropriate, allow pupils to discuss a task in their mother tongue before beginning to write. It may also help them to have a model or writing frame before starting, so that they can clarify what they have been asked to do. (See also unit 3-12, Supporting bilingual and multilingual pupils.)

Resources

▷ Spelling banks and vocabulary books.

▷ Dictionaries.

▷ Thesauruses.

▷ Spelling and grammar checks on word-processing programs. (These can, however, be unhelpful. Spell checks will not pick up wrongly used homophones; grammar checks do not help pupils to learn from their errors, and may mean that they do not understand what they have written.)

▷ Good pens. Fibre-tip or roller ball style pens often help pupils to write neatly.

▷ Line-guides for writing on blank paper.

▷ Your own notebook for copying text so student can copy from the desk rather than the board.

▷ ICT: some pupils may have the use of laptops or specially designed computer equipment to help them.

▷ Other computer software for developing writing skills.

✓ Keys to good practice
Supporting reading and writing in the classroom

✔ Confirm the pupils you will be working with and agree organisation.

✔ Clarify your understanding of pupils' learning needs with the teacher.

✔ Agree any strategies to be used.

✔ Obtain any resources needed.

✔ Encourage and praise the pupil where appropriate.

✔ Monitor pupils' progress and report back to the teacher.

Help pupils to develop their speaking and listening skills

Expected level of skill

By the end of Key Stage 3, each pupil is expected to be 'an effective speaker and listener:

▶ with the clarity and confidence to convey a point of view or information

▶ using talk to explore, create, question and revise ideas, recognising language as a tool for learning

▶ able to work effectively with others in a range of roles

▶ having a varied repertoire of styles, which are used appropriately.'

From the *National Strategy for Key Stage 3, Framework for teaching English*.

The value of talk

Years ago, it was thought that the buzz of chat in a classroom meant that little learning was taking place. Now, the value of talk in learning is properly understood and most lessons will contain opportunities for speaking and listening. Dyslexic pupils will often perform well in these sessions, and the value of discussion for pupils learning English as an additional language is immense. Pupils whose learning style is auditory will often learn more from these sessions than from writing activities. However, all pupils benefit from properly structured speaking and listening activities.

School's English policy, objectives for speaking and listening

Larkmead English Faculty
Teaching and Learning

Our aim is to challenge pupils to think for themselves and empower them to make those thoughts articulate.

Our objectives are
to develop students' acquisition and control of language
• as speakers and listeners through group, paired and individual opportunities
• as readers to respond to what is written and to understand how language is manipulated in text
• as writers to control and manipulate language for effect

(extract from Larkmead English Faculty Handbook)

Providing opportunities for speaking and listening

All classrooms offer opportunities for speaking and listening, but staff need to know how to make this beneficial for all pupils. Some pupils are enthusiastic in their contributions, but others may be reticent or extremely anxious about speaking in class. These anxieties may be due to a range of factors:

▷ Physical or emotional factors. Pupils may find it difficult to speak openly if they have a physical condition or speech difficulty which makes it hard for others to understand them. Staff may need to support them by repeating back what they have said to the group after they have finished speaking. You should not interrupt the pupil or finish sentences for them.

▷ Lack of self-esteem. Pupils who do not feel able to speak in front of others may lack self-esteem due to their experiences at home and school. Staff need to develop self-esteem in pupils by giving them opportunities to succeed and to praise their achievements (see also Unit 3-13 page 207 about developing self-esteem).

▷ A pupil's special needs. Pupils with special needs may lack confidence or feel 'different'. Assistants who work with individual pupils will know their pupil and may be able to encourage them to talk through particular interests or experiences which they have had.

▷ Pupil may speak English or Welsh as an additional language. If the child is not confident in the second language, this may prevent them from contributing.

Strategies for encouraging pupils when speaking

Pupils who are not confident when speaking need to know that others value what they have to say. We can show that we are interested by:

▷ giving them eye contact when they are speaking to us (unless there is a cultural reason for not doing so)

▷ smiling or encouraging to continue while they are talking

▷ repeating back what they have told us, e.g. 'So you think that the poet is actually expressing fear in this verse'

▷ asking open questions to encourage them to respond in more detail.

Teachers and assistants can also help by:

▷ giving pupils plenty of time to think about questions and formulate responses

▷ asking pupils to explain their reasoning

▷ providing opportunities for pupils to rehearse their contributions in advance

▷ modelling the particular language structures needed in the context and allowing pupils to practise them; using sentence starters and talk frames.

Strategies for encouraging pupils when listening

Many pupils find listening to others much harder than speaking. Pupils in Year 7 may still be at the stage where they need to be heard immediately, and find it hard to wait their turn. Older pupils may find it hard to concentrate and either switch off or begin to talk amongst themselves. They may also make disparaging comments to their classmates. Assistants can help in whole class speaking and listening situations by using behaviour management techniques. (See Unit 3-1.) Pupils may find this kind of activity more productive in smaller groups, particularly if one or several of the group members has the responsibility of reporting the group's discussion back to the class. As a teaching assistant you can help by establishing a climate of security and respect, where all contributions are valued.

Case study

You are working with a group of five Year 7 pupils. They have been asked to discuss the issue of school uniform, making a list of its pros and cons before reporting back to the class. They have fifteen minutes to complete the task. One of the pupils is a speaker of English as an additional language and arrived in the UK only six months ago: he has contributed nothing so far. One pupil is attempting to distract another group. The others run out of ideas after three minutes and the conversation turns into a discussion of the sorts of clothes they like and dislike.

What strategies can you use to keep this group on task?

Speaking and listening skills may be developed in many different situations, not necessarily in planned events. Older pupils may enjoy discussions and debates on set topics, and will be expected to adapt their spoken language according to the purpose and audience. Drama, improvisation and role play activities are useful for all age groups and in a range of contexts. Activities which involve movement will help those pupils who find it hard to learn when sitting still behind a desk.

Humanities – protecting the environment: what should you do to help?

English – Julius Caesar: role play a modern-day political journalist quizzing Brutus over his decision to assassinate his friend.

PSHE/citizenship – debate: should cannabis be decriminalised?

▲ Examples of discussion opportunities in secondary schools

Some kinds of talk are more productive than others. The following are the kinds of interactions that staff should plan for and encourage.

Productive talk behaviours

▶ Making suggestions or introducing new ideas

▶ Supporting others' suggestions by building upon them, clarifying them or modifying them

▶ Challenging ideas so that others reflect upon their validity

▶ Reasoning or justifying ideas

▶ Asking questions to seek clarification and elaboration

▶ Summarising to move the discussion on

▶ Analysing and evaluating to make explicit the strengths and weaknesses of own and others' ideas

From DfES training module *Literacy Across the Curriculum*

Knowledge into action

Classroom talk may be organised in many different ways, e.g. whole class discussion, pair talk, envoys (where groups send one member to another group to compare ideas) etc. Over the course of a week, make a list of all the different ways of organising talk that you come across. What are the advantages and disadvantages of each type?

Keys to good practice
Developing speaking and listening skills with children

✔ Make eye-contact with pupils.

✔ Listen carefully to what they are saying.

✔ Ask open-ended questions.

✔ Praise pupils for appropriate language.

✔ Give a variety of opportunities for pupils to use their language skills.

✔ Be aware that certain topics are contentious or may touch on the personal experiences of some of the pupils. Be sensitive in your approach to these topics.

Evidence collection

Make a list of some of the speaking and listening tasks you support in the classroom. What strategies do you use to support each of these activities?

End of unit test

1 What skills are covered by the term 'literacy'?
2 What are the three levels into which literacy skills are broken down?
3 Name some of the cues we use when learning to read.
4 Name some of the ways that reading is tackled in school.
5 What should you do if a pupil you are supporting has Special Educational Needs?
6 Why might a Year 10 pupil need help with handwriting?
7 Name some strategies that are useful when supporting writing activities.
8 What is a writing frame?
9 Why is it important for pupils to learn to listen to one another?
10 Why might pupils feel uncomfortable speaking in front of others?
11 How can we show pupils that we value what they have to say?
12 What opportunities can we give pupils to develop speaking and listening skills?

References

Framework for teaching English (DfES, 2001)
Language for Learning (QCA, 2000)
Literacy Across the Curriculum (DfES, 2001)

Websites

www.alite.co.uk
www.dfes.gov.uk
www.literacytrust.org.uk
www.standards.dfes.gov.uk/keystage3

Unit 3-19 Help pupils to develop their numeracy skills

This unit will help you to support pupils when developing numeracy skills. You will need to know the different ways in which the teacher plans for learning activities within Key Stages 3 and 4. You will also need to know how to work under the direction of the teacher to help pupils achieve the learning objectives of the lesson. Assistants will need to report back to the teacher as to pupils' achievements in numeracy activities.

What is numeracy and how is it taught?

Numeracy is more than basic arithmetic. It involves developing 'confidence and competence with numbers and measures'. (*Framework for teaching Mathematics*). Pupils learn about the number system and will develop a range of mathematical techniques to use in different situations, both quantitative and spatial. Pupils also learn about ways in which data is gathered and presented, for example, counting and measuring, graphs and charts.

The *Framework for teaching Mathematics* is part of the National Strategy for Key Stage 3 and builds on the work of the primary-based National Numeracy Strategy. It offers guidance on how to plan and deliver effective mathematics teaching and learning.

Some features of the Key Stage 3 National Strategy

▶ Planning based on clear teaching objectives from the *Framework for teaching Mathematics*: Years 7, 8 and 9.

▶ Structured mathematics lessons.

▶ Regular opportunities to develop oral, mental and visualisation skills.

▶ Focus on direct interactive teaching of the whole class and groups.

▶ Emphasis on the development of key vocabulary and mathematical language.

▶ Promotion of continuity between Key Stage 2 and Key Stage 3 by building on pupils' achievements in primary schools

▶ Catch-up programme for pupils entering Key Stage 3 below level 4

Adapted from *Mathematics Induction Training Module for Secondary Teaching Assistants* (DfES, 2002)

Assistants should be aware that mathematics may be taught in a very different way to their own experiences in school. Mental calculation is considered central to number work, but estimation, exploration and thinking around the issues are also crucial. For example, rather than asking, "What is 19+17?", a teacher may say, "The answer is 36. What is the question?".

Other subjects offer opportunities for mathematical development, and schools should have a designated member of staff responsible for co-ordinating numeracy across the curriculum. (See also Unit 3-20, Helping pupils to access the curriculum.)

The *Framework* offers a model structure for mathematics lessons:

> ▶ An oral and mental starter (about 5 to 10 minutes): whole-class work to rehearse, sharpen and develop mental skills, including recall skills, and visualisation, thinking and communication skills
>
> ▶ The main teaching activity (about 25 to 40 minutes): combinations of teaching input and pupil activities; work as a whole class, in pairs or groups, or as individuals; interventions to identify and sort out misconceptions, clarify points and give immediate feedback
>
> ▶ A final plenary to round off the lesson (from 5 to 15 minutes): whole-class work to summarise key facts and ideas and what to remember, to identify progress, make links to other work, discuss the next steps, set homework

The school's mathematics policy should give a breakdown of the aims and objectives of the school's teaching of maths. Staff should refer to the maths policy and to the *Framework for teaching Mathematics*, which give guidelines for the way in which maths is to be taught in school.

➔ Knowledge into action

Find out how the Mathematics department in your school uses the *Framework for teaching Mathematics* to plan for and teach pupils in a particular Year group. Looking at a copy of the *Framework*, locate the key objectives and teaching programmes for use with that Year group.

Expected level of numeracy skills

The *Framework for teaching Mathematics* lists key objectives for Key Stage 3. These build on the objectives of the numeracy strategy for primary schools, and lead pupils to the skills they need for Key Stage 4.

> These are just some of the skills pupils are expected to have developed by the end of Year 9. They are expected to be able to:
> ▶ have a sense of the size of a number and where it fits into the number system
> ▶ recall mathematical facts confidently
> ▶ calculate accurately and efficiently, both mentally and with pencil and paper, drawing on a range of calculation strategies

- ▶ use proportional reasoning to simplify and solve problems
- ▶ use simple formulae and substitute numbers in them
- ▶ measure and estimate measurements, choosing suitable units, and reading numbers correctly from a range of meters, dials and scales
- ▶ explain methods and justify reasoning and conclusions, using correct mathematical terms
- ▶ judge the reasonableness of solutions and check them when necessary
- ▶ give results to a degree of accuracy appropriate to the context.

Help pupils to develop their understanding and use of number

Teaching assistants are required to work with groups of pupils and individuals to help them understand and use number. Assistants should work with the subject teacher to ensure that they understand the learning objectives of the lesson, and the ways in which the activity will be taught.

The teacher is responsible for informing the assistant of learning objectives, key vocabulary and the learning needs of individual pupils. Assistants will need up-to-date information about pupils' current ability to understand and use number. This information can come from the class teacher, from their own observation and knowledge of the pupil, or from written records and assessments. Assistants should be familiar with any number targets or strategies specified on individual education plans. The strategies to be used with groups and individuals should be agreed in advance with the teacher.

The teaching assistant should offer feedback to the teacher at the end of the lesson, and also during the lesson if appropriate. Teachers need information as to pupils' responses to the learning activities so that they may plan properly for subsequent sessions and maintain their records and reports. Assistants can also usefully report back any common mistakes or areas of confusion, so that these may be addressed in the plenary and clarified before the end of the session.

Helping pupils to interpret and follow instructions

For a variety of reasons, some pupils may not understand what they have been asked to do. During whole class oral work teaching assistants should position themselves near any student who may need extra help. They should be ready to repeat the teacher's instructions or explain them in terms more suited to that pupil's learning needs. They should observe carefully any pupils they will be working with in order to decide upon the type of support they will need to provide. In the main teaching part of the lesson, assistants should ascertain how much the pupil has understood and be able to clarify the teacher's explanation. Clearly, the need for assistants to have a thorough understanding of the lesson objectives is crucial.

Case study

The class in which you are working has been asked to perform a series of mental addition calculations, using both 're-ordering' and 'partitioning' techniques, saying in each case which strategy they found easier.

Re-ordering: changing the order of the numbers to make the calculation easier.

Partitioning: splitting numbers into tens and units, or hundreds, tens and units in order to make the calculation easier.

You are working with Jack, who has grommets in his ears and found the instructions difficult to understand as he did not hear clearly. How would you go about explaining the task to Jack?

Questioning and prompting pupils

Various types of questioning may be used by assistants in maths lessons. During whole class oral work, assistants may prompt shy or reticent pupils to offer answers. During group work, assistants can use questioning to encourage the participation of all group members.

The *Framework for teaching Mathematics* also refers teachers and teaching assistants to the booklet 'mathematical vocabulary'. Although this booklet is part of the National Numeracy Strategy for Years 1-6, it is also useful for those working with Key Stage 3 pupils who have Special Educational Needs, who speak English as an additional language or who simply need some extra help in mathematics. The booklet includes an introductory section on the use of questioning in mathematics lessons and suggests the following types of question:

▷ Recalling facts, e.g. "What is 8 times 9?"

▷ Applying facts, e.g. "How would you measure the area of the school playground?"

▷ Hypothesising or predicting, e.g. "Estimate the number of pupils that can fit, sitting down, in the school hall."

▷ Designing and comparing procedures, e.g. "How could you divide 732 by 63?"

▷ Interpreting results, e.g. "What does this graph tell us about the Year Group's favourite football teams?"

▷ Applying reasoning, e.g. "How many different ways could you rearrange the furniture in this room so that all 30 pupils can still see the board without having to turn around?"

Try to maintain a balance of open and closed questions. When using open questions, prompt the pupils to give several possible answers. It is a good idea to build up a bank of questions so that you can be ready to use them as and when they are needed.

Assistants should remind pupils of teaching points made earlier in the session or in previous lessons. They should also prompt pupils to explain their methods as this helps them to clarify their thinking.

Teaching Assistant's Handbook

Think about it

A Year 7 pupil is finding it hard to understand the idea that speed equals distance over time. For example, if you travel 14 miles in 2 hours, you are travelling at 7 miles per hour. How could you question this pupil to help her get to grips with the concept?

Helping pupils to select and use appropriate resources

Assistants may be asked to use a variety of mathematical resources and should ensure that they know where these resources are to be found. Pupils may need help using some of these resources so assistants should familiarise themselves with them in advance.

When supporting activities which develop understanding of number, assistants working with older pupils may find that most work is paper-based. However, working with younger pupils or pupils with special educational needs, assistants may need to be familiar with the following items: number cards, number lines and squares, place value charts, calculators, games and puzzles, computer software programs.

If unsure, assistants should always ask the class teacher to explain how these resources are used. Assistants and teachers should encourage pupils to dispense with these resources as and when they are ready.

Reinforcing mathematical vocabulary

Assistants may need to reinforce the use of mathematical vocabulary which has been used by the teacher while explaining new concepts. This vocabulary is crucial to the

▲ There are various resources to help with different maths activities for pupils with special educational needs

---

understanding and application of mathematical ideas, and by Key Stage 4 may appear highly technical to assistants who may not feel sure of their own mathematical ability. Assistants should refer to the National Numeracy Strategy document, 'mathematical vocabulary', as well as to any school vocabulary lists that may be given out to pupils. In addition, Appendix 3 of the DfES training module Numeracy Across the Curriculum provides a mathematical glossary for non-specialist teachers at Key Stages 1-4. Again, assistants should ask the maths teacher for any help they need in understanding and applying these terms.

Introducing follow-on tasks to reinforce and extend learning

Assistants may be asked to use follow-on tasks for those pupils who finish their work early and have grasped the concept thoroughly. For example, a student who has just finished a series of exercises may be asked to carry out a problem-solving investigation based on the same topic. There are many good websites containing examples of such problems: with guidance from the teacher you may be able to locate particularly useful tasks for pupils in your classes.

Knowledge into action

Pick a topic which one of your classes will soon be covering in maths lessons. Do this by asking the mathematics teacher or looking at the termly plan for that Year group. Find out what follow-on tasks the mathematics department has prepared for lessons within that unit of work. When the time comes, ask for the chance to work with more able students on one of these activities.

Using praise to promote further learning

Pupils may easily become discouraged if they find a concept hard to understand, so it is crucial to use praise and encouragement to motivate them and boost their spirits. Pupils need to experience success – whatever their level – in order to remain motivated and on task. The teaching assistant should therefore provide positive, constructive feedback to help pupils build upon what they know and encourage them in their work.

Case study

You are working with a student who is carrying out a series of calculations. You notice that several of his answers are wrong. What techniques can you use to help him identify where he has gone wrong without discouraging him altogether?

Think about asking, "how did you work that out?". Why might this question be particularly useful?

Using calculators

The use of calculators is a whole school issue and assistants should find out about the policy in their own particular school.

All pupils should be able to decide when it is and is not appropriate to use a calculator. They should be able to decide which method of calculation is most appropriate: mental, written or using a calculator.

During Key Stage 3 pupils will be taught:

▶ how to select from the display the number of figures appropriate to the context of the calculation

▶ how to enter numbers and interpret the display when the numbers represent money, metric measurements, units of time or fractions

▶ the order in which to use the keys for calculations involving more than one step

▶ how to use facilities such as the memory, brackets, the square root and cube root keys, the sign change key, the fraction key, the constant facility, and so on.

By the end of Key Stage 3, pupils should have the knowledge and skills to use a calculator to work out expressions such as 3250×1.05^5 or $(7.82^2 - 2.91^2)$

Evidence collection

Make a list of the different resources available in your school for supporting pupils who have difficulty with numbers. How are each of these resources used?

Help pupils to use and understand shape, space and measures

The terms 'shape, space and measures' apply to a range of mathematical activities.

At Key Stage 3, pupils will be building on the basic, practical work on shape, space and measures which they carried out at Key Stage 2. Work at Key Stage 3 takes the pupils' intuitive understanding of geometry and teaches them to prove geometric facts analytically. For example, pupils 'should be able to explain why the angle sum of a quadrilateral is 360°, and to deduce formulae for the area of a parallelogram and of a triangle from the formula for the area of a rectangle'. This so-called 'deductive reasoning' is central to shape, space and measures work at Key Stage 3. Pupils must have developed these skills before they can move on to the 'proofs' that are introduced in Key Stage 4.

ICT may be used to develop geometrical reasoning and an understanding of shape and space, for example, by using the programming language Logo.

Pupils will be expected to develop an awareness of the degree of accuracy of measurements. They will learn about speed and density. At Key Stage 3 pupils' work on perimeter, area and volume will be applied to varied and more complex shapes. Much work will be done on triangles. This leads on to Pythagoras' theorem and, at Key Stage 4, trigonometry.

Assistants will need to make sure that they understand the learning outcomes required if they are to support pupils effectively in mathematics lessons. They should be thoroughly briefed by the class teacher as to the learning objectives of each lesson or series of lessons, and should ask for further explanations of the concepts if necessary.

Building on prior knowledge

As with all subjects, work in mathematics constitutes an extension of the skills and understanding which the pupils already possess. Assistants will need to know the stage pupils have reached in order to build on the skills they have. For example, before a pupil can understand how to perform calculations with triangles using Pythagoras' theorem, he or she must be familiar with the term 'hypotenuse'. Assistants can find out about pupils' previous levels of understanding in the following ways:

▷ Through the teacher, who can tell assistants about work already completed

▷ Through observing the pupil

▷ Through teacher or class records. Pupils may already have been given specific targets relating to shape, space and measures. Assistants should make themselves aware of these targets and any particular strategies to be used when working towards them.

Support strategies when working on shape, space and measures

Assistants will need to use the same types of strategies when supporting work on shape, space and measures as they do when supporting work on number. Questioning and prompting are particularly important tools. Other strategies should be agreed with the teacher. Assistants should ensure that there are sufficient resources to carry out activities, and that they know both the location of these resources and the departmental procedure for borrowing them. Such resources might include diagrams, small whiteboards for jotting, individual ICT resources, measuring equipment, compasses and so on. Assistants should make sure that they and the pupils know how to use these resources before tackling the specific learning objectives of the lesson.

Some of the strategies for supporting pupils with special educational needs are equally useful in supporting other pupils in the mathematics classroom. See below for further suggestions.

▲ A variety of measuring equipment will be needed

Working with pupils who have special needs

Pupils who have a Statement of Special Educational Needs may be working at a very different level from the other pupils in the class. The special needs which you may encounter in mainstream schools vary widely, and it is not possible to cover them all here. Some pupils may need extra help with mathematical vocabulary; some may have visual impairments which makes it difficult for them to use mathematical equipment; others may need to use individualised ICT resources. Subject teachers should seek advice from the SENCo and from outside agencies in order to select the best strategies to use with particular pupils.

The *Framework for teaching Mathematics* suggests that written work be kept to a minimum, but obviously some tasks will need to be worked out or recorded on paper. Teaching Assistants should be ready, under the direction of the teacher, to differentiate learning activities and homework tasks for pupils who have special educational needs, or those who work slowly through mathematical tasks.

Keys to good practice
Strategies for supporting numeracy for pupils with special needs

✔ Present worksheets in large print format.

✔ Give instructions orally if pupils find visual instructions problematic.

✔ Help pupils interpret and respond to oral instructions if they have difficulty hearing.

✔ Tape record instructions for homework tasks.

✔ Provide extra diagrams, illustrations and worked examples.

✔ Obtain apparatus usually used by younger age groups (e.g. mirrors, geometric shapes) to compensate for difficulties in managing visual information.

✔ Select key questions from textbook exercises rather than requiring pupils to tackle several complete sets.

✔ Offer help with the recall of mathematical facts if long- or short-term memory is a problem.

Assistants should always be aware of the particular needs of the pupil, and should always agree strategies with the class teacher, referring to the pupil's Individual Education Plan as appropriate.

Pupils who speak English or Welsh as an additional language

The techniques used to support these pupils across the curriculum are equally useful in maths lessons. These techniques include highlighting key vocabulary, practising words, phrases, signs and symbols in English or Welsh, using visual clues and gestures. Assistants may also:

▷ encourage pupils to bring in and explain mathematical games and puzzles from different cultures

▷ model good mathematical language; allow pupils to watch and listen until they are ready to give oral explanations

▷ encourage pupils to demonstrate their reasoning using a whiteboard, without forcing them to speak aloud as they do so

▷ allow groups of pupils to use their home language when carrying out practical tasks

▷ remember that high mathematical ability may be disguised by weak language skills; check understanding regularly.

Tackling problems when supporting mathematical development in number and shape, space and measures

The problems you may encounter when supporting pupils with mathematical tasks may be related to any of the following:

The pupil's own concept of working on mathematical tasks

Mathematics can and should be presented as fun. However, pupils can become disheartened when they have trouble understanding a concept and for this reason maths has in many quarters gained a reputation for being difficult or boring. It is crucial that assistants - whatever their own experiences of mathematics education at school - counter these stereotypical views of the subject and model an interested and enthusiastic response to work in mathematics lessons. Assistants are well placed to listen to any concerns that a pupil might have, and can work with the teacher to build those pupils' self-esteem and confidence with maths.

Case study

You are working with Hiab, a Year 9 pupil, and the class has just had a lesson on the properties of triangles. Hiab does not have enough confidence to put up her hand when the teacher asks whether there are any questions. You are later working with her group and notice that she is having difficulties.

1 How could you talk to Hiab without damaging her self esteem?

2 What would you say to the class teacher?

▲ Some pupils may find mathematical tasks intimidating

The pupil's ability to learn

A pupil may be unable to complete a task because it is too difficult, or it may be that the pupil has special needs which make the task hard to complete. Assistants may need to adapt the pupil's work so that they have a realistic chance of completing it and of maintaining their confidence and self-esteem.

Case study

Jessie in Year 7 has an autistic spectrum disorder, though she does not have her own support assistant. You are working with her group, who are estimating the answers to sums before using a variety of strategies to work out the answers accurately. Jessie needs the certainty of accuracy and precision, and is made anxious by the notion of estimating.

1 How could you reassure Jessie?

2 What would you do with the rest of the group if Jessie needed to be removed from the activity?

The learning environment

Pupils need to work in an environment which maximises the opportunity for learning. There needs to be sufficient space for everyone to work comfortably, and a minimum of noise so that everyone can concentrate. If there is insufficient space or too much noise, pupils will be disturbed and effective learning will not take place. Encouraging pupils to work independently and quietly will minimise the risk of disturbance. Sometimes it may be possible to find another space for a group or groups of pupils to work.

Resources

Pupils must have access to the equipment and resources they need to carry out their work. They may forget to bring equipment from home, such as pencils, rulers, compasses and calculators, and assistants may be able to locate spares for the pupils to borrow. Some items are kept at school, either in the classroom or centrally in a department office or stock-room. Assistants should report any broken or missing items immediately so that no time is wasted during lessons.

Evidence collection

What are the main difficulties pupils experience when working on shape, space and measures? How have you, as a teaching assistant, helped pupils to overcome these difficulties?

End of unit test

1 What is the suggested structure of a maths lesson at Key Stage 3?
2 Name three mathematical skills that pupils should learn by the end of Year 9.
3 Which skill is considered central to number work?
4 What sort of strategies might assistants use when working with pupils on number activities?
5 What are some of the questioning strategies assistants might need to use?
6 What do 'shape, space and measures' refer to in mathematics?
7 How might assistants find out about pupils' previous level of understanding?
8 What equipment can be used to support pupils in mathematics lessons?
9 How might assistants find out how to help a pupil who has a Statement of Special Educational Needs?
10 What types of problems might you face when supporting pupils with mathematical tasks?

References

Framework for teaching Mathematics (DfES, 2001)
National Numeracy Strategy, Mathematical vocabulary (DfES, 2000)
Numeracy Across the Curriculum (DfES, 2001) (download only)

Websites

www.dfes.gov.uk
www.teachernet.gov.uk
www.smilemathematics.co.uk

Unit 3-20 Help pupils to access the curriculum

This unit is aimed at assistants who provide literacy and numeracy support to help pupils to access the curriculum. Pupils need skills in literacy and numeracy before they can participate fully in learning activities in other curriculum areas. Assistants will need to help both individual pupils and groups with their literacy and numeracy skills, whilst also helping to develop pupils' subject knowledge and skills across the whole curriculum. Assistants should be aware of and able to resolve the problems that may occur when providing learning support to these pupils.

How the school's policies and procedures support pupils with literacy and numeracy related learning needs

Every school should have a range of policies setting out the ways in which pupils with literacy and numeracy related learning needs may be supported. Teaching assistants should familiarise themselves with these policies, which may include:

▷ **English policy** – this provides information about the way English is to be taught within the school; see also Unit 3-18, page 241, for an example of an English policy.

▷ **Mathematics policy** – this provides information about the way mathematics is to be taught in the school.

▷ **Literacy and numeracy policies** – these differ from English and Mathematics policies, since they deal with literacy and numeracy across the whole curriculum.

▷ **Marking policy** – there may be a whole-school marking policy which sets out the ways written work should be marked.

▷ **Special Educational Needs policy** – this provides information about the way the school provides for pupils with Special Educational Needs across all curriculum areas.

▷ **EAL and EMA policies** – these provide information about the ways in which the school provides for speakers of English as an Additional Language, and promotes Ethnic Minority Achievement.

▷ **Other curriculum policies** – these provide information about the ways in which all subjects are to be taught within the school. They may also set out curriculum links between different subject areas.

The different policies which exist in your school and which of these you think are particularly relevant to your work with pupils.

Planning and implementing learning activities

Subject teachers will normally plan and provide for pupils within their classes, some of whom may have special needs and individual learning targets. In a busy secondary school, where assistants may work with a large number of pupils and teachers, it can be difficult for teachers and assistants to plan together. However, joint planning is valuable for several reasons:

▷ You will be able to contribute your own ideas.

▷ You will have more time to consider your approach to the planned learning activities.

▷ You will be better prepared for your contribution to the learning activity

▷ You will gain a greater understanding of the reasons why pupils are asked to carry out particular activities.

▲ Planning with the subject teacher will give you more opportunities to prepare for learning activities

▷ You may be able to prepare extra resources or modify existing learning materials.

▷ You will be more confident in carrying out tasks effectively.

▷ You will be better placed to assess the extent to which pupils achieve the learning objectives set out in the plan.

▷ Both you and the subject teacher will have a clearer idea of your respective roles in the classroom.

When planning, assistants will need to have up-to-date information about pupils' learning needs. Planning with the teacher allows for discussion about individual pupils' progress. It is also advisable to gather more information about individual pupils by looking at records and speaking to the Special Educational Needs Co-ordinator (SENCo). You may need to discuss some of this information with others in the school.

How to provide literacy and numeracy support to help pupils to access the curriculum

The term 'literacy' is used to describe the skills of reading, writing, speaking and listening in schools. It encompasses not only basic skills but also the skills of understanding and manipulating the conventions of language. 'Numeracy' incorporates not only the use of number but also a variety of other topics such as shape, space, measures (of time, space, weight, speed etc.), handling data and algebra. Pupils need to be able to use their literacy and numeracy skills in all subject areas.

When pupils are not making the kind of progress in literacy and numeracy which is necessary for them to achieve in all their subjects, assistants may be asked to support them. These pupils may or may not have a statement of Special Educational Needs. Support may take place either through a structured programme such as the Literacy Progress Units, or through other interventions within and outside English and Mathematics classes.

See also Unit 3-18, Help pupils to develop their literacy skills and Unit 3-19, Help pupils to develop their numeracy skills.

Literacy Progress Units (LPUs)

Pupils who have not achieved Level 4 in English by the time they enter Year 7 will struggle to keep up with work all across the curriculum. These students may be withdrawn from class and given special catch-up sessions known as the Literacy Progress Units, or LPUs. These were first piloted in September 2000 as part of the Key Stage 3 National Strategy. Taught in small groups, these lessons are fast-paced and intensive, covering writing organisation, information retrieval, spelling, reading between the lines, phonics and sentences.

Sometimes, teaching assistants are asked to deliver these sessions; however, if you are asked to do this, you will be entitled to proper training and support.

Reading Challenge, Writing Challenge

These are two separate schemes designed to help pupils whose reading and writing skills are about two years below expectations. These may include Year 7 pupils working at Level 3, or Year 8 pupils working at Level 3-4. They are not designed for pupils with specific learning difficulties in literacy or those with statements of Special Educational Needs.

Each pupil on the scheme is allocated an individual coach. Coaches may be teaching assistants, adult volunteers or senior pupils. A half-day's training session is provided for all coaches. A key reading or writing target is identified for each pupil, and the coach then helps the pupil work on that target on a one-to-one basis. Progress is recorded in the pupil's Log Book and the coach's record book.

Find out about...

Whether LPUs, the Reading Challenge or the Writing Challenge, have been implemented in your school. How successful have they been in enabling pupils to 'catch up' with their literacy skills?

Other strategies for supporting pupils' literacy needs

Pupils who have literacy needs may need support with one or more of the three areas of speaking and listening, reading and writing. These areas interact with and support one another, and assistants will be required to help pupils develop these skills within the classroom. Since language is the basis for learning, these pupils may have educational needs beyond literacy.

Speaking and listening

Clearly, pupils need to have good speaking and listening skills in order to access the school curriculum. Difficulties in this area may be due to a number of reasons:

▷ Shyness. Pupils may be afraid of 'getting it wrong', or they may feel that their contributions are not valid. They may also dislike being the centre of attention, however briefly. Teachers and assistants should be aware of these pupils, offering them encouragement and providing opportunities for speaking in smaller, less threatening groups.

▷ Difficulty listening to others. Some pupils are happy to put across their own ideas but less interested in listening to others respectfully. It is vital that these students are taught to wait for others to contribute, and to give due credit to others' ideas and opinions.

▷ Special Educational Needs. These pupils may have a range of difficulties which make speaking and listening problematic. Pupils who have speech problems may be reluctant to proffer opinions in case others find them difficult to understand. Others may rely on signing or other forms of communication to understand what is being said or to get their own ideas across. If you work with a pupil who has special needs in this area, it is important to provide them with as many opportunities as other children to put their ideas forward.

▷ Pupils who speak English or Welsh as an additional language. These pupils may not have been speaking English or Welsh for very long and hence may lack the confidence to express themselves in front of large groups. Smaller groups may provide a less threatening environment for them to practise their spoken English. Assistants should ensure that they understand any oral or written instructions given out, and should also allow them extra time to process what they hear and formulate a response. Sometimes, it may be appropriate for groups of EAL pupils to get to grips with a concept using their mother tongue. However, EAL pupils should be encouraged to use English as the language of learning unless the subject teacher has specified otherwise.

Assistants may also:

▷ use effective questioning, both to ensure that pupils are able take part in the learning activity and also to extend and develop their thinking

▷ require pupils to explain their reasoning

▷ model subject-specific vocabulary and language structures correctly

▷ practise subject-specific vocabulary and language structures with pupils

▷ allow pupils to rehearse their contributions to plenary sessions.

? Think about it

Think about pupils in your classes who do not contribute as much as the others. What might the reasons be for their reticence? How do subject teachers try to involve them in whole class discussions and group activities? Can you think of other ways in which you could encourage them to participate without making them feel more self-conscious?

Reading and writing skills

Reading and writing skills are important in all areas of the curriculum, and school work can be very frustrating for pupils who have difficulties in this area. These pupils may be sensitive about requiring extra support, so assistants should bear this in mind when working with them. Assistants should always remember to use praise and encouragement so that pupils do not feel their efforts and achievements go unnoticed.

The support you are asked to give with reading and writing could include the following:

▷ Helping pupils interpret and understand instructions. Pupils may have difficulty reading and interpreting instructions if they have not been reinforced orally. You should make sure that these pupils have a clear idea of what they have been asked to do.

▷ Helping pupils read and understand larger chunks of text, such as novels or articles in English, source materials in History, explanations in Science textbooks. These texts can often be daunting for weaker readers.

▷ Looking out for situations which could prove difficult for pupils in need of literacy support. Think about whether these pupils will be able to complete the tasks independently, and, if not, what kinds of support you can offer.

▷ Observing and monitoring pupil progress. Subject teachers may ask you to watch and record how pupils manage when left to work independently.

▷ Differentiating work and modifying tasks where necessary. Assistants may sometimes need to simplify what pupils have been asked to do, or to try a different approach.

→ Knowledge into action

Ask for the opportunity to observe writing in a variety of subject areas. Make a note of the different forms and purposes of writing students are asked to undertake. Which forms of writing are common to several subject areas, and which are subject-specific? To what extent do subject areas other than English contribute to the teaching of literacy skills?

▲ Assistants may be asked to help or support children who speak English or Welsh as an additional language

Strategies for supporting pupils with numeracy needs

Numeracy skills are developed primarily in mathematics lessons, but are also used in many other areas of the curriculum. As well as having literacy needs, pupils may have difficulties carrying out mathematical tasks in these other subject areas. Poor numeracy skills will hamper pupils' progress and damage their self-esteem.

The strategies assistants use to help these pupils will depend upon the nature of the difficulties encountered. For example, a pupil with autism may find it difficult to explain the methods they have used to complete a calculation. A pupil with a speech and language disorder may find the same calculations difficult because of finding it hard to associate symbols with the type of calculation required.

Pupils with Individual Education Plans may have specific numeracy targets which differ from those set for the whole class. Assistants should ensure that they are familiar with any individual targets set for their pupils. In addition, the DfES document *Assessing the National Curriculum for Mathematics* provides examples of what pupils with Special Educational Needs working at different levels should be able to do in mathematics.

Pupils who need support with numeracy activities may need help in any of the following areas.

Numbers and the number system

Pupils who have difficulty with number may be said to have 'dyscalculia'. This affects the ability to acquire mathematical skills. Pupils with this condition often suffer from dyslexia as well, and have difficulty understanding and learning number facts. This will affect their progress in many subject areas, but particularly in Science, Design and Technology and Geography. These pupils may find it helpful to learn patterns in number to be used as a memory aid. Other pupils find it difficult to process number and should be given visual aids (such as number lines and grids) as well as plenty of practical experience.

Calculations

Calculation skills will be used in a variety of subject areas, but again, Science, Design and Technology and Geography require a high degree of proficiency in this area. In Science, for example, pupils may have to calculate means and percentages; in Food

Technology they may have to work out cooking times. Some pupils may be able to perform calculations without being able to write them down; others may be unable to perform them mentally. Pupils often like to resort to calculators, but should be encouraged to try other methods first. Assistants should check school policy on the use of calculators.

Problem-solving activities

These may be difficult for pupils and it is important to ensure that the problem is realistic so that pupils are able to relate it to their own experience. Pupils should also be encouraged to develop an awareness of the use of mathematics in the workplace. When tackling a problem-solving activity, think first about the types of mathematical skills that the pupil will need, then help the pupil to break the task down into more manageable chunks.

Shape, space and measures

Ideas of shape and space are key in subjects like Art and Design and Technology. Patterns and constructions in a variety of cultures are based on spatial ideas and the properties of shapes. Ideas of symmetry and geometry may be applied in Religious Education when looking at, say, Islamic patterns and cathedral rose windows. Pupils will use a variety of measuring techniques across the curriculum, ranging from height, distance and time in athletics, through weights and times in food preparation to measurement of rates of change in Geography, History and Science. Assistants may be able to remind students of skills they have learnt in maths lessons whilst tackling shape, space and measures activities in other subjects.

Data handling

Data handling skills are regularly used in other subject areas. In ICT, for example, pupils are expected to collect and classify data, use data handling software, produce graphs and tables, and to interpret and explain their results. They will also be expected to demonstrate spreadsheet skills, and use numeric, algebraic and graphical skills to construct formulae and to generate sequences, functions and graphs.

Many subject areas demand a range of mathematical skills and assistants can remind pupils of the relevant terminology as well as providing extra consolidation of the techniques pupils will need to apply.

Assistants will not always have extensive numeracy skills themselves and can sometimes feel daunted by this aspect of the curriculum. If you feel that there are gaps in your skills which prevent you from providing effective support to your pupils, you should of course approach the relevant subject teacher. In addition, Appendix 3 of the DfES document *Numeracy Across the Curriculum* provides a mathematics glossary for non-specialist teachers in Key Stages 1-4.

Programmes to support the development of numeracy skills

Springboard 7 is a non-statutory programme designed to help Year 7 pupils who are performing below level 4 catch up with their peers. It is the numeracy equivalent of the Literacy Progress Units. The programme is offered in the autumn and spring terms of Year 7 and consists of ten units, each tackling a different aspect of numeracy, as well as revision and assessment sessions.

Mathematics Challenge offers individual help in developing numeracy skills. The programme is organised on the same basis as the Reading Challenge and the Writing Challenge. (See page 262.)

Working with teachers to support literacy and numeracy needs

In order to ensure that all pupils have full access to the curriculum, you should be aware of the learning objectives of each lesson. You will also need to have a clear understanding of the literacy or numeracy demands of any activities undertaken, so that you will be able to target those children who find those areas difficult. You will need to work with teachers to make sure that you are aware of specific areas which pupils may find difficult. You may also be able to provide teachers with useful information about the literacy and numeracy skills of particular pupils; this information can then be used when planning particular learning activities.

Pupils who speak English or Welsh as an additional language

These pupils will have different learning needs from others in the class, particularly if they have recently started to learn English as a second language. You may find that they understand more than they are able to speak, and staff must be careful when giving them tasks that they are being sufficiently challenged and are grouped by ability rather than knowledge of English, particularly during mathematical tasks. It is important to remember that these pupils do not have learning difficulties (and indeed may be very bright) but will have different learning needs from other pupils. (See also Unit 3-12 Provide support for bilingual/multilingual pupils for strategies for supporting them.)

In order to distinguish between these different types of learning support, it is important that staff consider the difference between bilingual children and those who have learning difficulties. Although some areas will overlap, such as the development of vocabulary and language skills, some may be specific to EAL pupils:

 ▷ development of self-esteem through social and cultural reinforcement

 ▷ giving pupils more time to listen and process information

 ▷ providing dual language texts to enable pupils to develop verbal and written language together

 ▷ using pictures to support comprehension.

Bilingual pupils will need to have support not only with academic areas but also with social issues so that they are able to retain their own identity. Staff should monitor whether the support given for bilingual pupils is showing clear progress within their individual targets. If pupils have had a good deal of support over time, and are not seen to be making progress with their language skills, it is possible that they have a learning difficulty. In this case it is advisable to speak to the school's SENCo to see whether an assessment is possible with the educational psychologist.

Problems when providing learning support in literacy and numeracy activities

The problems which may be found when supporting pupils with literacy and numeracy activities have been looked at in Units 3-18 and 3-19. You may also find that pupils have difficulty relating the work that they are doing in other curriculum areas with literacy and numeracy. However, if you find that a pupil is experiencing difficulties which you do not feel able to resolve, you must inform the teacher as soon as possible.

Evidence collection

Think of a pupil you work with who has numeracy-related learning needs. Make a note of some of the subject areas other than maths where these needs lead to difficulties. What resources and strategies can you use to help he or she access the curriculum?

End of unit test

1 What are the policies which you should be aware of when supporting pupils' curriculum needs?

2 Why should assistants be involved with planning as much as possible?

3 How can you find out about pupils' learning needs?

4 Why do pupils need to develop their literacy and numeracy skills as much as possible?

5 What are the LPUs?

6 How might you involve pupils who are reluctant to contribute in class?

7 How can you support pupils who have reading and writing difficulties?

8 Why might pupils who have numeracy difficulties need different strategies to support them?

9 Why might a bilingual pupil still need support after receiving it after a period of time?

10 What should you do if you feel that you do not have enough knowledge or experience to deal with a particular problem when supporting a pupil?

References

Framework for teaching English (DfES, 2001)

Framework for teaching Mathematics (DfES, 2001)

Literacy Across the Curriculum (DfES, 2001)

Mathematics Challenge pack (DfES, 2003)

Numeracy Across the Curriculum (training folder) (DfES, 2001) (not available to order; download only)

Reading Challenge, Handbook for school organisers (DfES, 2003)

Writing Challenge, Handbook for school organisers (DfES, 2003)

Websites

www.dfes.gov.uk
www.standards.dfes.gov.uk/keystage3
www.smilemathematics.co.uk

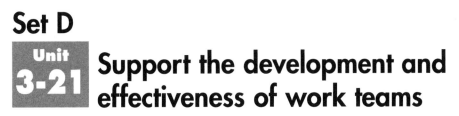

Set D

Unit 3-21 Support the development and effectiveness of work teams

In this unit you will learn about the importance of taking an active role as part of a team. Teams in schools may be different groups of people who work together in order to achieve shared objectives for supporting individuals or groups of pupils. You will need to be able to contribute to the effectiveness of the team and work alongside others for the benefit of pupils. This means that you will need to be aware of the ways in which you can recognise and respond to issues affecting team effectiveness. You should also be able to contribute in your own way to the development of the team through providing support and advice to others.

Principles underlying team effectiveness

There have been many different areas of research surrounding the effectiveness of work teams. Most agree that there are certain stages which groups pass through before they can operate effectively. One of the most succinct definitions has been reached by Tuckman (1965) and others, who believed that all groups need to go through a process of maturing before they are able to function efficiently. The process has been divided into four stages: Forming, Storming, Norming and Performing. (See also the section on development of groups on page 39.)

▷ At the **Forming** stage, members of the team are just starting to get together and a leader emerges. Members of the group will need to have a clear sense of identity and purpose.

▷ When **Storming**, members will start to view themselves as more of a team and will have reached an understanding of what is expected of them. There may be a challenge to the leader during this stage. Individuals will need to have clear roles and opportunities for participation within the group.

▷ **Norming** defines the stage at which the team organises itself into work groups and starts to develop different areas of activity. At this stage, the group will need to establish a culture around shared norms and values that they all agree on.

▷ **Performing** is the ideal state to which all teams aspire. The group are comfortable with one another and work effectively together.

These four stages may not have clear boundaries and teams may sometimes become 'stuck' at a particular stage, or go backwards and not develop fully. John Adair, in his book *Effective Teambuilding*, suggests that there may also be a fifth phase of development, the **Dorming** phase, when the group may fall into a state of complacency about its achievements and does not continue to move forward. This is usually avoided through consistent planning.

 Think about it

Think about different groups in which you may have worked in the past.
What might it feel like to be in a group at each of the four different stages?

Skills that are needed when working within a team

Within the team, individuals will also need to have effective communication, interpersonal and collaborative skills. This will enable the team to function more efficiently.

Effective communication skills

Good communication is an essential part of working as a team. The principles of effective communication include the following:

▷ Listening to what others have to say. This is important: often people listen to one another but do not really hear what others are saying. This may be because they are thinking about something else or are too eager to put their own point of view across.

▷ Making sure that you contribute to team discussions. You may not feel confident in volunteering your ideas: perhaps you are new to the team or find it difficult to put ideas forward. You should remember that all contributions are important, and your point of view is as valid as anyone else's.

▷ Providing regular opportunities for talk. This is important in a school, where everyone is busy and may not have time for discussions when one member of the team needs to talk about a particular issue. For teams to communicate effectively within a school, there will need to be systems in place which contribute to this. These may be through clear staff structure and clearly defined roles, which will make it easier for individuals to see where they fit into the school as a whole and how their role is defined. It should also take place through meetings between different groups within the school, for example the senior management team, the teaching staff, the year group, teaching assistants, individual support assistants and those working within a particular class or subject area. These meetings provide regular opportunities for discussion and exchange of information, which may be written or verbal.

▲ Meetings will give individuals within a team opportunities to contribute their ideas

Effective interpersonal skills

These are sometimes the most difficult skills to have as within any team there will be a number of personalities. Individuals will need to have the skills to relate to one another well and be sympathetic, supportive and helpful. Members of the team should be sensitive to the needs and feelings of others, and encourage those who they know are finding work challenging or difficult. This may be due to other issues which they have to deal with outside school.

There may be a combination of factors which makes it difficult for individuals to focus and tackle problems in the work environment. This may mean reading others' body language at times or realising that now may not be a good time to approach another member of the team with a problem. There may also be a member of the team who is much more of a speaker than a listener. This can be a problem if the person does not give others the chance to have their say.

? Think about it

Have you ever been in a group, perhaps when you yourself were at school, where one or a group of individuals was always the first to put their ideas forward? What kind of effect did this have on you and others within the group?

▲ Issues outside school may make it difficult to concentrate on problems in the work environment

Effective collaborative skills

Members of the team will need to be able to work together. In his *Team Development Manual*, Mike Woodcock outlines nine 'building blocks' which lead to team effectiveness. These are:

▷ have clear objectives and agreed goals

▷ be open about facing issues and resolving them

▷ work in an atmosphere of mutual support and trust

▷ have appropriate leadership which suits the task, team and individual members

▷ conduct regular reviews to reflect on their performance as a team and their performance as individuals

▷ have good relationships with other groups

▷ have sound procedures for working together and taking decisions, with all members being consulted and involved

▷ encourage and foster individual development of all team members

▷ work together cohesively but be free to disagree when necessary, i.e. allow both co-operation and conflict to get results.

Teams within a school should be able to apply these skills to their own environment and experience to ensure that they are supporting other members of their team. It is important to remember that although you are working as a team, individuals will have their own strengths and should be valued.

▲ Collaboration is an important part of team work

? **Think about it**

John is a teaching assistant in a secondary school. He has been told that he is to have a staff appraisal the next day but has not been told about appraisal before. How could the school have adapted some of the building blocks into their practice to help John as a team member to prepare for appraisal?

Helping and advising others

You may find that you are in situations where other team members need your help and advice. If you are the most experienced teaching assistant, others may come to you in this situation. You should always think about your role and theirs within the team when doing this, while remaining supportive. Where you do not feel that it is appropriate for you to deal with a particular issue, you may need to refer to someone else within the team. You must remain non-judgemental about others and not allow your own opinions to intrude or cloud any decisions you may have to make.

Hilary is an individual support assistant in a secondary school. She supports Simon, who has Asperger's Syndrome, for some of the time and also Ramina, who is partially sighted, for several hours each week. As the school is large and there is little time for planning with teachers, Hilary is finding it difficult to work with the pupils and to support them effectively as she has no time to prepare resources. She feels that she is not doing her job properly as she is unable to devote adequate time to their needs. She has discussed this with you, another individual support assistant, as she feels that you are the closest member of the team.

1 What advice would you give to Hilary?

2 How do you think the team could help Hilary in this situation?

The relationship between your role and the role of others within the team

You may find that there are a variety of different teams in which you work within a school on a short-, medium- or long-term basis. Although your role may be the same within each, these different teams will be focusing on different areas within the school. These may be:

▷ supporting a particular pupil – assistants who work with individual pupils may work alongside others such as the SENCo, or other professionals who come into the school to support a pupil who has Special Educational Needs (see Unit 3-4, page 82-3 for the types of professionals who may come in to schools)

▷ within a class – assistants will work with the class teacher but there may also be other members of staff within the class who work together

▷ within a year group – the school may be large and have 3 or 4 classes within a year group. Year groups may work very closely together and support one another in planning and moderating pupil's work

▷ within the school – all members of staff within a school are part of a team and will support one another. For example, the maths co-ordinator will be able to offer help and advice to any member of staff on any maths activities.

In each of these situations, members of the team will need to understand their role and how it fits in with the role of other members of the team. The most important part of any role within a team is communicating effectively with others. There should be clear and consistent methods of communication so that all members of the team feel that they are valued. (See also Unit 3-4, page 83.)

Interpersonal relationships and how these work within a team

Individuals within a team will have a range of personalities, but will need to be able to work together in order to achieve different goals. Because there are different personalities, there may sometimes be areas of conflict or disagreement which may occur at different levels. This can cause problems where individuals have very different ideas about how things should be done (see page 278.) Having good relationships with others means being able to listen to others and respect their ideas and opinions. Your own personal feelings about people should not interfere with your role as a member of the team.

→ Think about it

Think about your own experience of working within a team. Do some members of the team always put their ideas forward while others are very quiet?

Working together for the benefit of the team

Although you will have your own agenda, you will also need to be aware that other members of the team should have information about what you are doing in case they need to take over from you. In a school where there are good systems in place and planning and reviewing take place on a regular basis, there should be information for others to use if they need to. Similarly, if you find that you have information which may be of help to another member of the team in what they are doing, you should be willing to share this information.

Understanding different ways of working

All schools will work slightly differently and it may take some time for you to become used to different styles of teaching and learning. You may also be moved to a different class or classes within the school and have a variety of teachers to work with who may also have slightly different approaches. It is important to be able to work in different situations.

Case study

Rob has been working as a teaching assistant supporting the same subject area for three years. The subject manager has left the school and Rob has to work with another teacher who will also be his manager. The new teacher suggests to Rob that it will be helpful for everyone if he is able to spend Thursday lunchtimes planning for the following week, but Rob is not paid for working in his lunch hour and is unwilling to stay.

1 Do you think that Rob should speak to the teacher or another member of the subject area? Why?

2 How would you suggest that this problem be resolved?

Professional and personal relationships

When working with others as members of a team, it is important to be able to recognise the difference between working and personal relationships. When individuals work together as professionals, it is important to establish good working relationships first, although people often become friends through working together. In order to establish good working relationships with others, you will need to ensure that you consider the keys to good practice (see below).

You will also need to be aware of ways in which you contribute to the development of that team. Apart from areas already discussed, such as being aware of how you can support others, you will need to be able to develop other strategies for your contribution to the team.

✓ Keys to good practice
Establishing good working relationships within a team

✔ Be considerate towards others within your team.

✔ Carry out your duties well and cheerfully.

✔ Do not gossip or talk about other people in your team.

✔ Speak to the appropriate team member if you need help.

✔ Prepare for and contribute to meetings.

✔ Acknowledge the support and ideas of other team members.

? Think about it

How much do you feel part of a team as a teaching assistant? Do you tend to mix only with other support staff or do you feel part of the school as a whole? Why do you think this is?

Problems which may occur when working in teams

Apart from clashes of personality, there are other areas which may cause problems within a team. One of the main areas is that of conflict. Members of an effective team will need to confront any differences they have rather than ignore them. In his book, *Managing Disagreement Constructively*, Herbert Kindler identifies four main areas of conflict which occur within teams. He defines these as follows:

▷ Having inaccurate or incomplete information – in this situation, members of the team may have access to different information and feel that they have not been fully informed as to what is happening. This may also cause them to interpret information in different ways. This emphasises the importance of openness within teams.

▷ Having inappropriate or incompatible goals – staff may feel that they do not agree on strategies for managing one area of their work. However, if everyone in the team ensures that they have the same aims at the outset, these types of conflicts should be avoided.

▷ Having ineffective or unacceptable methods – it is important for the team to have shared values so that some members do not seem to say one thing and do another. This again makes it important for members of a team to share values and be consistent in their practice.

▷ Having antagonistic or other negative feelings – this is usually due to left over resentment which has built up over time. Conflict which is caused by old wounds is difficult to diagnose for this reason and often difficult to heal or resolve.

The school may have policies and procedures in place for dealing with difficulties and conflicts within working relationships. This will include areas such as confidentiality and all members of teams should be aware of issues surrounding the exchange of information. You should be aware of who you need to speak to on a professional level if you find that there are problems within your team or group which are affecting your work. Kindler also states that conflict exists at six levels:

▷ **Conflict within the individual** – this means that one person has to choose between actions or goals which are incompatible with one another; for example, an assistant who has been offered ICT training after school each Thursday but has other commitments at home.

▷ **Conflict between two people** – this may be when individuals disagree about joint outcomes. It is most likely if members of the team do not have the same ideas about the team's objectives when working together.

▷ **Conflict within a group** – members of the group or team may disagree on important issues, such as which topic or area to plan for the term.

▷ **Conflict between groups** – different groups or teams within the school may disagree about the way in which something is done; for example, year groups who would prefer to do things in a different way from one another.

▷ **Conflict within an organisation** – a school may find that members of staff do not agree with a particular decision which has been made.

▷ **Conflict between organisations** – this is not so relevant to schools, but an example might be when two schools which are geographically close together have an area of disagreement.

If you find yourself experiencing conflict or difficulty, try to identify what level it is and be ready to articulate it to the right person so that the problem doesn't fester and become worse.

Evidence collection

Consider the different kinds of 'teams' you may be part of within your school: for example, support assistants, staff members, professionals dealing with a special needs pupil, subject specialists.

▶ What kinds of opportunities do you have to meet other members of your team?

▶ How do you support one another so that you all carry out your duties more effectively?

▶ Have there been any issues within your team and how have they been resolved?

End of unit test

1 What are the four main stages of team development?

2 What skills do team members need to have for the smooth running of the group?

3 How can team members ensure that they are communicating effectively?

4 What should you do if another team member approaches you for advice?

5 What types of different teams will you find within a school setting?

6 How is a working relationship different from a personal relationship?

7 Why does conflict occur within teams? What are the different types of conflict which occur within organisations?

8 How can you ensure that you establish good relationships and working practices within a team?

9 How can you ensure that there is a good system for the exchange of information within teams?

10 What should you do if someone within your team approaches you with a problem you do not feel able to resolve?

References

Adair, J., *Effective Teambuilding* (Pan, 1987)

Kindler, H. S., *Managing Disagreement Constructively* (Crisp Publications, 1996)

Woodcock, M., *Team Development Manual* (Gower Publishing, 1989)

Unit 3-22 Develop and maintain working relationships with other professionals

In this unit you will look at the ways in which assistants can support the work of other professionals in schools. You will need to be able to work with others in a way that is likely to inspire confidence and trust. You should also make sure that you make the most of any opportunities that become available to you to observe the good practice of others so that you can extend your own knowledge. Assistants must be able to maintain positive relationships with others and be willing and able to share their own knowledge.

Your role and the role of others inside and outside the school

When you are working in a school environment, you will find that there are many different professionals who work both inside and outside the school. Depending on how much you are involved with a particular pupil, you may get to know some of these people on a regular basis. Alternatively, working as a classroom assistant and having limited hours in school, you may find that you come into contact with very few people other than teaching and other support staff. You will need to be able to show that whoever you work with feels that you are a trustworthy and competent member of staff. (See also Unit 3-4 for more detail on the role of the teaching assistant and others within the school.)

Members of staff with whom you may come into contact regularly

▶ Other assistants – you may meet formally and informally to discuss issues

▶ Teaching staff – you will work with on a daily basis

▶ Year group leaders – you may meet to discuss ideas as a year group

▶ Special Educational Needs Co-ordinator – you may have regular contact with the SENCo if you are working as an individual support assistant

▶ Assistants' manager or co-ordinator – you should have regular meetings with other assistants to discuss school issues

▶ Headteacher/deputy head – you should have some contact with senior management which may take the form of meetings and exchanging information

---

Professionals from outside agencies will probably visit the school in order to work with and advise on pupils who have Special Educational Needs. If you are an individual support assistant, you may be asked to join in with meetings and discuss the pupil's progress. Professionals from outside school with whom you are likely to come into contact may include:

▷ speech and language therapists

▷ educational psychologists

▷ English as an additional language (EAL) support tutors

▷ sensory support tutors

▷ learning support staff

▷ behaviour support staff

▷ specialist teachers, for example for pupils with autism

▷ occupational therapists and physiotherapists – may also offer advice but will usually work with pupils outside school.

(See Unit 3-4 for a description of the roles of these professionals.)

As there are many different aspects to the role of teaching assistants in schools, your role will need to be written down clearly in your own job description so that you are aware of the different responsibilities you will be expected to undertake. There have been many changes in the role of the teaching assistant in recent years that have moved away from the traditional role of supporting the teacher to a more 'teaching' role in supporting children's learning. The National Occupational Standards for teaching assistants, published in April 2001, provide a framework that schools can use to draw up job descriptions (see www.lgnto.org.uk for National Occupational Standards for Teaching Assistants). You will need to be clear about the duties that you will be expected to perform, and should also be aware of your own limitations within your role.

 ## Case study

Carol has just started work at her local secondary school as a learning support assistant. She has been working with Josh, who has learning difficulties. At a school fundraising event, one of the parents asks whether Carol can come and volunteer to work in the school.

1. Do you think Carol should feel obliged to volunteer?

2. What would you say in her position?

Observing and demonstrating good practice

Observing others

As part of your own professional development, you may be given specific opportunities to observe other teaching assistants in their role. However, you will also be in situations where you can observe good practice when working with others on a day-to-day basis. This will give you the chance to extend your own knowledge and to give you a greater understanding of how to work with pupils. In secondary schools, this will include opportunities for assistants to observe different teachers and note the kinds of strategies they use, for example when managing classroom behaviour. You may not realise it, but often you will pick up on good practice by simply being around other members of staff.

You may also be asked to be present at meetings and discussions with professionals from outside the school, particularly if you support an individual child. It is good practice to make as much use as you can of opportunities to observe others' expertise. In this way you will develop your understanding of others' professions, and how they affect your own work.

→ Knowledge into action

If you are in a situation which always requires you to always be in school at the same time and for the same subject, ask your mentor or line manager whether you can come in at a different time to observe different members of staff working or to support children in different subjects.

Demonstrating good practice

You may also be asked whether other members of staff can observe your work with pupils. This is a regular occurrence between teaching staff, but at time of writing is less likely to happen with teaching assistants. However, it is a useful exercise, as all staff will need to have opportunities to observe one another and look at different strengths. If you are asked whether you can be observed, you should not be anxious or wary of others observing you, as they will be looking at your skills and not being critical. It is also useful for observing and demonstrating good practice, if it is viable, for classroom assistants to 'shadow' one another for a day or more. Students might find this is a valuable exercise.

How to establish and maintain good working relationships with others

When you are working with other professionals, you will need to be able to work in an environment that is one of mutual support. In school surroundings, you will not be able to work independently of others, nor would it be practicable to do so. (See also Unit 3-21: Support the development and effectiveness of work teams.)

The support you will be required to give others will be on several levels:

▷ **Practical** – you may be working with others who are unfamiliar with the classroom or school surroundings and need to have help or advice with finding or using equipment and resources.

▷ **Professional** – you may be in a position to support or help others with issues such as planning, or you may be asked whether others can observe your work with pupils.

▷ **Informative** – you may need to give support to those who do not have information about particular issues. Alternatively, you may be asked to prepare and write reports about particular pupils.

▷ **Emotional** – it is important to support others through day-to-day events and retain a sense of humour!

> **?** **Think about it**
>
> Which of these types of support have you needed to give during the last two weeks? Why do you think they are important?

If you are working with others and are unable or unwilling to support them, you will be unlikely to be carrying out your own duties effectively. This is because you will not be working as part of a team.

> **?** **Think about it**
>
> Sasha has just started as a teaching assistant at your school. She is working in the same key stage as you. How could you help her to settle in and ensure that she starts to feel part of the school team straight away?

Providing information

When you are asked to provide information and reports about a particular pupil, you will need to do so in a professional manner. This means that you should always respond willingly to any requests for information and ensure that they are complete, accurate, up-to-date and reliable to the best of your knowledge. Reports and other requests for information should only be given to those who are authorised to receive them and you should remember to observe the school's policy on confidentiality.

There may be occasions when you are approached by professionals from outside the school who need to have access to information about a pupil with whom you are working. It is unlikely, however, that they will approach you directly, and you will be more often asked by the SENCo to produce reports. If you find that you are unable to produce a thorough report and do not feel that you have sufficient information, or if you are unsure about any aspect of what you have been asked to do, you should speak to the member of staff who has requested it. You will also need to make sure that any contact you make with professionals outside the school goes through the usual channels. If the school usually writes to inform others about meetings, it will be good practice to continue to do this rather than make a phone call. It is also useful to maintain written records of contacts made.

Keys to good practice
Providing information

✔ Provide any information requested promptly.

✔ Remember confidentiality.

✔ Ensure that details are complete and accurate.

✔ Follow the usual school routines.

Evidence collection

Make a list of the other professionals with whom you come into contact in your school (see page 281 for examples of these). What are their roles within the school context? How do you share information with them?

End of unit test

1 Name some of the visiting professionals with whom you will come into contact when working in schools.

2 How has the role of the teaching assistant changed over time?

3 Why should you make use of opportunities to observe others?

4 Why is it important to ensure that you are aware of your own area of responsibility?

5 When are you likely to be involved with meetings with other professionals?

6 What sort of support will you be required to give others in school?

7 When are you likely to be asked for information about a particular pupil?

8 What should you remember to do if you are asked to provide information?

References

Working with Teaching Assistants: A good practice guide (DfES, 2000)

Fox, G., *A Handbook for Special Needs Assistants* (David Fulton, 1993)

Websites

National Occupational Standards: www.lgnto.org.uk

Liaise effectively with parents

In this unit you will learn about the contact you have with the parents and carers of the pupils with whom you work. You will need to think about your responsibilities when sharing information with parents about their children, and how you promote positive relationships between themselves and the school. It is important that you remember to show consideration for pupils' home backgrounds and to report any problems in communicating information to parents with teachers. You will also need to know how to share the care of pupils with their parents. It is important to see the relationship between parents/carers and the school as a partnership.

School policies and procedures for communicating with parents

Parents are the primary carers and most important attachment that children have before they come to school. They play the most central role in the care and welfare of their children and know them better than anyone else. It is vital that good lines of communication are established and maintained between parents and staff throughout a pupil's time in school. This will be beneficial to everyone concerned.

▷ **Beneficial for the pupil** – their main role models will be seen to be forming a positive relationship, both through a formal and informal exchange of information.

▷ **Beneficial for the parents** – they will be reassured in the knowledge that the school has as much information as it can about their child. They will also know that the school is up to date with their needs.

▷ **Beneficial for school staff** – staff will need to build up an accurate and up-to-date picture of each pupil. Through exchanging information as much as possible, staff will be more aware of issues and when they arise.

There may be many different ways in which the school has contact with parents and exchanges information. When the pupil initially enters secondary school, there may be a series of forms for parents to complete, as the school will need to collect information about the pupil's background. The DfES also requires that schools request information about ethnic origins, cultural background and home language.

Information provided by the school

▷ Written information such as newsletters
▷ Noticeboards

▲ There should be as many opportunities as possible for schools to exchange information with parents

▷ Prospectuses
▷ Home–school agreements
▷ Policies, for example for curriculum subjects such as history, or for issues such as behaviour
▷ School reports (annual)
▷ Information about activities the pupils are going to undertake
▷ Parents' meetings
▷ Parents' evenings

Information provided by parents and carers

▷ Initial information forms such as medical/allergies/emergency numbers
▷ Specific information which is relevant to the pupil's welfare, for example if the pupil is in foster care
▷ Any special needs which have been diagnosed before the pupil enters the school

Much of the information provided by parents will be kept by the school on file or in the computer systems, so that it is accessible when needed. It is confidential and only used by staff within the school. If the school needs to pass any information onto other parties, such as outside agencies, parents should always be informed.

Other opportunities for exchange of information

Secondary schools may seem less approachable than primary schools to parents, simply because their children are more independent and there is less need for such frequent communication between home and school. However, schools will welcome and encourage contact with parents and will usually communicate through letters and contact books.

There will also be other opportunities for verbal communication between parents and staff, which may take place at specific times during the school year. It is important for the school to make use of any time that exists for communicating with parents. These may be either formal or informal, but they are good opportunities for parents and staff to meet and talk to one another. In your role as a teaching assistant, you may find that you are involved in some of these events more than others.

> **?** **Think about it**
>
> Think about the times where you have been involved with the type of events shown in the diagram below. Does your school offer any other opportunities for communicating with parents?

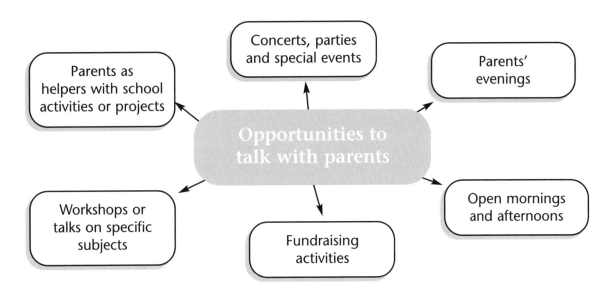

▲ It is important that contact between staff and parents is maintained

Your role when communicating with parents

In your role as a teaching assistant, you may have some contact with parents, particularly if you can support an individual pupil. However, it is important for you to remember that teachers should be the main point of contact for parents. This is because teachers will need to have all available information at all times, and the more people that are involved in passing information, the more likely it becomes that information will be lost.

Case study

Jackie is an individual support assistant for Katrina in Year 7, who has learning difficulties. On the way into the school one morning, she bumps into Katrina's mother, who asks her to tell the school that she will be needing to take Katrina out of lessons in the afternoon as she has an occupational therapy appointment. When they reach school, Jackie has so much to do that she forgets to inform the class teacher or the office, so that when Katrina's mother arrives they have some difficulty finding her.

1 Do you think that this situation was Jackie's fault?

2 What could she have done to avoid this happening?

Sometimes, you may be given information by parents which needs to be passed on to another member of staff. You may find that you are given written material to pass on, or you are asked to communicate a message to someone else. It is always best to request that the parent either writes to or contacts the person directly if possible. If you are required to pass on information, you will need to do it as soon as possible, for two reasons – first because it may be important, and secondly so that you do not forget. If there is any danger of you forgetting or not being able to pass it on immediately, then write it down.

You may also be asked by a parent if you can arrange a meeting with another member of staff, such as the SENCo or the headteacher. If a parent needs to speak to another member of staff, it is better for them to go direct to that person, or arrange a phone call through the school office. If it is an urgent request, you may be able to ask them to wait so that you can find the member of staff.

Care, confidentiality and school procedures

There may be occasions on which you have access to information about pupils which is confidential. This may have been given to you because it is in the pupil's interest that you are aware of it, for example if there is an issue of child abuse. You will need to be sure that you do not pass on any sensitive information, even if you feel that the person you are talking to is unlikely to tell anyone else. If you do not know who else is aware of this information or has access to it, you should ask the member of staff who passed it on to you.

School procedures for communicating with parents

You will need to make sure that when you are communicating with parents, you observe the school's normal procedures for doing so. This may involve making sure that any information you give to parents is:

▷ agreed with the teacher

▷ presented in a way that is easy to understand and does not include 'jargon'

▷ consistent with your own role within the school

▷ consistent with confidentiality requirements.

? Think about it

Are you aware of any school procedures for passing information to parents? Find out whether your school has a written policy or what the normal procedures are. What kind of information are you able to communicate to parents in your role as a teaching assistant?

Addressing parents

Staff should make sure that when addressing parents, they use the preferred name or form of address. Nowadays there are many different types of family structure and staff should not assume that pupils are living with two parents who are married. Some parents may be married, but prefer to be known under separate surnames – some mothers would rather not be known as 'Mrs'. Other parents may have titles or modes of address which are important. These details will usually have been noted down on forms when their child enters school.

You should also be aware that in some cultures, it is not acceptable for individuals to be addressed by their forename. When writing parents' names, their surname may sometimes need to be written first. If you are in any doubt, you should always check such details in the school's records.

Difficulties in communicating with parents

Sometimes there will be problems when the school needs to communicate information to parents. There can be several reasons for this:

▷ The pupil may not have passed on important information, either orally or through letters: to avoid problems the school could also display important information on noticeboards and in windows, or have a set day for sending home letters so that parents always ask their child on a Thursday, for example, if there are any letters.

▷ Telephone numbers or addresses may not have been updated: parents often forget to inform the school of changes, particularly in telephone numbers. Send home regular reminders or keep a prominent notice on a noticeboard.

▷ Parents may not be able to read letters which are sent home, either because they are unable to read or because they speak English or Welsh as an additional language (see below).

▷ Contact books are not regularly checked by parents or staff. The school needs to make sure that there is a policy for checking these books to ensure that important information is not missed (also see below).

If you find that important information has not reached a parent, you may need to seek advice from the relevant person within the school about how best to deal with the problem. Usually, assistants will not need to contact parents directly, although if working with an individual pupil, you may have a source of communication such as a contact book, which is completed regularly. Schools may also have other books, such as homework diaries, which parents and staff need to sign or fill in on a regular basis. This will be useful if you seldom see the parent and wish to let them know about things which have happened at school. Similarly, parents may need to inform you about what has taken place at home. You may need to telephone parents if they have not returned forms or requests for information. If you need to do this you will need to make sure you address the parent correctly and observe school policy.

If you have an 'open door' policy, you may find that some parents are over-keen to come into the school, and this can become a problem if it happens too often. If you have a problem in the area in which you work, you may need to refer to another member of staff, but as an assistant you should not speak to the parent about it.

Parents who speak English or Welsh as an additional language

Where you need to communicate with a parent or group of parents who find it difficult to speak and understand English or Welsh, care must be taken so that the parents do not feel isolated from others in the school. This can happen very quickly, particularly if the parents' cultural background is also different. The class teacher or another member of staff may need to refer to your local support team for those who speak English or Welsh as an additional language.

If the parents come to the school regularly with their children, it would be good to encourage them in to help and become involved with the school so that they form positive relationships with staff. If the parents do not have regular contact with the school, you may need to have help from an interpreter, particularly if there are several families within the school.

How you share the care of pupils with their parents

When you are working in a school, you are taking on the role of pupils' carer in place of their parents. You will need to show that you take parental wishes into account when you are caring for pupils. Parents should feel that they can trust you implicitly and be happy to leave their children in your care. This care should take into account the physical, social and learning needs of pupils.

▷ **Physical needs** – this will encompass the pupil's health and well-being. If pupils are injured, fall ill or need help while they are in school, parents need to know that they will be looked after, or measures that will be taken in the case of an emergency.

▷ **Social development needs** – this part of the pupil's care is their social needs, or interaction with others in the school setting. This will include breaks and lunchtimes. Parents need to feel confident that their child is progressing normally.

▷ **Learning needs** – the school takes on a major responsibility for the learning needs of each pupil. Parents have the right to be informed of each pupil's progress and of any strengths or difficulties they may have.

The role of parents and carers in their children's welfare

Parents and carers are their child's first and most important educators. Although they may not be aware of it, they will be teaching their children from a very early age. Children will learn from their parents' routines and everyday experiences which will form the basis for their habits throughout life. All families will have their own ways of interacting, and children will pick up particular strengths and ways of doing things from the people with whom they spend the majority of their time. In this way, children who are from a family who are gifted in a particular way, such as musically or mathematically, may have the same aptitudes. Similarly, if the parents have bad habits,

▲ Children learn from their parents at home, for example during conversations at mealtimes

such as always being late for school and other appointments, the child will grow up thinking that being late does not matter.

Variations in family practices and cultures

All families are different, and children come to school from a variety of backgrounds. Parents will have their own values, cultures and practices, and they may have different expectations from those of the school. You may find that in your class there are pupils whose parents have values that are different from yours, or those which you are used to. This can be difficult when parents' ideas do not fit in with those of the school.

Case study

You are working alongside a pupil who is from a different cultural background to many of the pupils in your school. Although her needs are such that she has to mix as much as possible with others and develop her social skills, one of the pupils in your group says in front of her that his parents do not want him to mix with her as she is 'different'.

1 Why might there be an issue in this situation?

2 What would you do if a pupil said this to you?

3 Do you think that this could be resolved?

You will need to be aware of any family practices or circumstances which parents have made known to the school, or cultural differences that make some situations sensitive for other pupils. This means that religious festivals which may be important to some of your pupils, such as Diwali or Eid, should be discussed and, if appropriate, celebrated through cooking activities, collages, musical activities, etc. and involving parents if possible. However, you should not expect all families from the same cultural group to have the same ideas and practices and you should be careful to avoid tokenism.

→ Knowledge into action

How are different religious festivals and celebrations from various cultures taught in your school? Can you think of some examples of good practice where parents have been involved in showing children different artefacts or other items?

Different types of family structure

There are many different ways in which people may live together, so it is important not to make assumptions about pupils' home situations. Pupils may live in a variety of circumstances.

Different family circumstances

Nuclear family – this is when children live with their parents and any brothers or sisters. They may be married, or live together.

Single parent family – one parent taking care of a child or children.

Homosexual family – gay or lesbian couples taking care of children.

Adoptive family – foster or adoptive parents looking after children.

Reconstituted family – children are cared for by one natural parent and one step-parent. This may also include half brothers and sisters.

Extended family – grandparents, parents, uncles and aunts sharing the care of children.

Travelling family – parents do not live at a fixed address and travel around with their children.

? Think about it

Think about the different kinds of backgrounds pupils in your school come from. How many variations could there be in the home life which surrounds each individual pupil? Think about the effect this will have on their personality and behaviour.

When families have very sensitive circumstances, for example if a parent has died or is very ill, this will usually be passed on between staff verbally as well as being written down so that everyone is aware.

In your role as a teaching assistant, you will need to be able to establish relationships with all parents and carers. This will mean that you need to be approachable and sympathetic if you have contact with them. There may be times when this is difficult, for example if a parent is unhelpful or does not agree with the school over an issue. If you find that you are faced with a challenging situation, you must not hesitate to involve another member of staff.

Evidence collection

Think about the occasions on which you have had contact with parents. This may have been through a variety of situations, such as formal meetings concerning a particular pupil, or less formal such as helping on school trips. How have you ensured that you:

▶ are consistent with school guidelines and your own role, particularly concerning confidentiality

▶ take account of parents' wishes concerning the care of their children

▶ pass on any information or concerns to the appropriate staff member if necessary?

End of unit test

1 What types of opportunities usually exist for the exchange of verbal information between home and school? What opportunities exist for the exchange of written information?

2 How significant is the role of the parent in their children's welfare?

3 What sort of information will your role allow you to communicate to parents and carers?

4 What difficulties might you or the school have when communicating with parents?

5 How can you reassure parents that you have regard for their own wishes for the care of their children?

6 What difficulties might you have with parents who have different values and practices from those within the school? How might you deal with this?

7 What are the different levels of care that you are expected to have for pupils in your school?

8 What is a 'nuclear family'?

9 How would you react if a parent asked you if they could see the headteacher?

10 What opportunities do you have for meeting with parents? Do you feel that you should have more of these opportunities?

Websites

www.dfes.gov.uk/parents

www.standards.dfes.gov.uk/parentalinvolvement

Appendix

The links between the CACHE Level 3 Certificate for Teaching Assistants (CTA3) and the National Occupational Standards (NVQ)

The CACHE Level 3 Certificate for Teaching Assistants (CTA3) aims to provide an award for candidates who work with pupils individually or in groups under the supervision of a teacher in education and learning support, or wish to work in this field. The award provides the underpinning knowledge and understanding required for the NVQ Level 3 for Teaching Assistants. Each unit has been mapped against the National Occupational Standards and is shown in the learning of each unit.

The following grid shows this mapping in more detail.

CACHE CTA3	National Occupational Standards
Unit 1 The Role of the Teaching Assistant in the School	
1 School structure and job role	3-1, 3-2, 3-3, 3-4, Set A, Set B, Set C, Set D.
2 Relationships and interactions	3-1, 3-2, 3-3, 3-4, 3-9, 3-11, 3-13, 3-15
3 Encouraging positive behaviour	3-1, 3-9, 3-10, 3-11, 3-15
4 The planning process	3-5, 3-6, 3-7, 3-8
5 The learning process	3-9, 3-10, 3-12, 3-13, 3-17, 3-18, 3-19, 3-20
6 Supporting and scaffolding the learning process	3-3, 3-9, 3-14, 3-17, 3-18, 3-19, 3-20
7 Record keeping	3-5, 3-6, 3-7, 3-8, 3-10
8 Policies and procedures	3-10, 3-11
9 Health and safety	3-5, 3-10, 3-11
Unit 2 Supporting Pupils' Particular Learning Needs	
1 The school approaches	3-21, 3-22, 3-23
2 Working with other professionals	3-21, 3-22, 3-23
3 Understanding the terminology and concepts	3-12, 3-13
4 Supporting the pupils	3-9, 3-10, 3-11, 3-12, 2-13, 3-14, 3-15, 3-16

5 Individual differences	3-9, 3-10, 3-11, 3-12, 3-13, 3-14, 3-15, 3-16
6 Factors affecting pupils	3-9, 3-10, 3-11, 3-12, 3-13, 3-14, 3-15, 3-16
7 Different approaches	3-17, 3-18, 3-19, 3-20
Unit 3 Teaching and Learning	
1 Supporting learning	3-9, 3-10, 3-11, 3-12, 3-13, 3-14, 3-15, 3-16, 3-17, 3-18, 3-19, 3-20
2 Supporting the literacy curriculum	3-18
3 Supporting the numeracy curriculum	3-19
4 Support Information Communication and Technology	3-17
5 Working with others	3-21, 3-22, 3-23
6 Working with parents and carers	3-23

Glossary

Anti-social behaviour Behaviour which harms others or destroys the property or feelings of others

Appraisal Process by which staff are required to look at their performance with their line manager and set targets for the coming year

Autism A condition which affects an individual's communication skills

Bilingual/multilingual children Children who are brought up able to speak more than one language

Children Act (1989) Legislation to ensure that children's welfare always comes first: applies to storage of information, health and safety, child protection and the rights of the child

Cognitive development The process by which children learn

Collaborative skills Skills which a team have for working together

Confidentiality Rules within the school to control the spread of information which may be inappropriate for some people to hear

Culture Way of life, beliefs and patterns of behaviour which are particular to social groups

Curriculum plans What the teacher plans for pupils in the long, medium and short term in order to achieve set learning objectives

Data protection Means by which information held on individuals is protected

Differentiation The way in which the teacher plans to teach pupils with different abilities

Disability Discrimination Act (1995) Legislation to prevent discrimination against disabled people, which includes educational settings from September 2002

Educational psychologist Specialist in children's learning and behaviour

Emotional development The development of children's feelings and emotions which enables them to understand and cope with these feelings

Equal opportunities Ensuring that all individuals have the same opportunities and benefits. Some pupils may need to have support for this to happen

Evaluate To consider whether an activity has achieved its objectives

Fine motor skills Skills which require more intricate movements, usually with the hands, e.g. using a mouse, fastening clothes, controlling a pen

Follow-on tasks Tasks which children can be set following completion of initial learning outcomes, which will reinforce what children have just learned

Foundation Stage First stage of education, from age 3 to the end of the Reception year

Gross motor skills Skills which involve the use of larger physical skills, e.g. running, jumping, throwing

Individual Education Plan (IEP) Used to plan targets for children who have special educational needs.

Inclusive education The process by which all children have the right to be educated alongside their peers

Key Stage 1 Children's education from the start of Year 1 to the end of Year 2

Key Stage 2 Children's education from Year 3 to the end of Year 6

Key Stage 3 Children's education from the start of Year 7 to the end of Year 9

Key Stage 4 GCSE coursework in Years 10 and 11

Language acquisition The way in which we learn language

Learning objectives What children are expected to know by the end of the lesson

Literacy Progress Units (LPUs) Catch up sessions for English, taught in small groups

Literacy Strategy National Framework for teaching of literacy skills

Makaton A method of sign language

Maths Challenge Scheme to help improve pupils' achievements in mathematics

Numeracy Strategy National framework for the teaching of mathematics

Observations Watching and making note of pupils' reactions in learning and play situations

Occupational therapist Professional who will assess and work with pupils who have difficulties with fine motor skills

Open-ended questions Questions which require more than a 'Yes' or 'No' answer, e.g. 'How did you work that out?'

Parent A child's birth mother or father, or adult who has been given parental responsibility by a court order

Physiotherapist Professional who will assess and work with pupils who have difficulties with gross motor skills or body function

Positive reinforcement Praise given to pupils to add weight to their achievements

Pupil records Records which are kept in school regarding each pupil. They may include a number of items such as health details, records of achievement, and parents' telephone numbers

Questioning skills The way in which pupils learn to ask questions during their learning

Reading Challenge Scheme to help improve pupils' achievements in reading

Resources Items which are available to support learning in school

Rewards Things to give pupils additional motivation, e.g. merit or house points, certificates

School development plan Document which sets out what the school's priorities will be during the coming year, and how they are to be achieved

School policies Documents outlining the school's agreed principles in different areas, e.g. in curriculum areas such as geography, or non-curricular areas, such as behaviour

Self-esteem The individual's own perception of their worth

Self-reliance The individual's ability to do things independently

SENCo Special Educational Needs Co-ordinator

Sensory impairment An impairment (reduction) of one or more of the senses

Settling-in procedures The way in which a school manages children who are entering a secondary school or transferring to a different class

Social development How a child learns to live and co-operate with others

Special Educational Needs (SEN) Where pupils are not progressing at the same rate as their peers

Speech and language therapist Professional who will assess and work with pupils with speech and language needs

Springboard Non-statutory catch-up programme designed to help Year 7 pupils below Level 4

Statement of Special Educational Needs Given to pupils who may need additional adult support in school for them to have full access to the curriculum

Statutory requirements Requirements which have been set down by law

Stereotyping Generalisation about a group of people which is usually negative, and based on a characteristic of one person in that group

Targets What pupils are expected to achieve over a specified period

Values An individual's moral principles and beliefs which they feel are important

Work teams Group of people working together with a common purpose

Writing Challenge Scheme to help raise pupils' attainment in writing

Index